A TREATISE ON THE PRINCIPAL DISEASES OF THE EYES,

INCLUDING:

DISEASES OF THE EYELIDS, CONJUNCTIVA, CORNEA, SCLEROTICA, CRYSTALLINE LENS, CHOROID, RETINA, AND OPTIC NERVE.

BASED ON

THEODORE J. RUECKERT'S "CLINICAL EXPERIENCE IN HOMŒOPATHY."

By JOHN C. PETERS, M.D.

New-York:

PUBLISHED BY WILLIAM RADDE, 322 BROADWAY.

PHILADELPHIA: RADEMACHER & SHEEK.—BOSTON: OTIS CLAPP.—
LONDON: J. EPPS, 112 GREAT RUSSELL-ST., BLOOMSBURY.—
MANCHESTER: TURNER, 41 PICCADILLY.

1856.

HENRY LUDWIG,
Book & Job Printer, 45 Vesey-st.

TO WALTER STEWART, M.D., (of Natchez,)

Late Physician to the Home for the Friendless. Late Surgeon to the New-York Homœopathic Dispensary. Late Secretary and Treasurer of the New-York Hahnemann Academy of Medicine.

DEAR DOCTOR:

We have been so long, and to me so pleasantly associated together as friends and colleagues; I have so frequently availed myself of your skill as a surgeon, and sought your countenance and counsel as a physician; and finally we have had so much happy experience in the treatment of Diseases of the Eye, both in public and private practice, that common gratitude would compel me to make some public acknowledgment of my manifold obligations to you. But I offer you this little tribute of remembrance as an expression of warm personal attachment, of my high sense of your many kindly and gentlemanly qualities, and of my appreciation of your fine acquirements and great natural abilities in every department of medicine and surgery.

I trust that you will meet with every success in your new field of labor, and that you will forgive my hardihood in forcing this dedication upon you without your knowledge or consent.

Yours very faithfully,

J. C. PETERS.

AMERICAN EDITOR'S PREFACE.

In presenting this more or less complete Treatise on Diseases of the Eyes to the public, I take the opportunity of offering my most cordial thanks for the kind reception which all the books I have edited have met with.

It is also a source of great gratification to me, that my publisher has met with sufficient encouragement to give me a *carte blanche* to compile and edit as many Treatises similar to those already published, as I may find time or inclination to prepare for the press.

Heretofore the Homœopathic literature of this country has been confined principally to periodical publications and to Works on Domestic Medicine, while the Medical profession has not been adequately supplied with Monographs and Treatises especially addressed to them. It is to be hoped that other and more worthy laborers will soon announce themselves. If every capable Homœopathic physician would prepare a monograph upon the disease or speciality in which he takes most interest and has most experience, an invaluable boon would be conferred upon the profession; the labors and responsibilities of the junior practitioner would be very materially lessened; and Homœopathy would acquire a much more secure and scientific basis. We require many more volumes like those of Tessier on Pneumonia, Joslin and Tessier on Cholera, Holcombe on Yellow Fever, Helmuth, Hill and Hunt on Surgery.

J. C. PETERS.

19 *East* 15*th-st., New-York.*

INDEX.

ON

DISEASES OF THE EYE

AND

ITS APPENDAGES.

DISEASES OF THE EXTERNAL SURFACE OF THE EYELIDS.

INJURIES.

1. *Bruises of the Eyelids.*

IN whatever way "black eyes" are produced, every body is generally anxious to get rid of them as soon as possible. Old School writers, such as LAWRENCE and WALTON HAYNES, question whether any of the ordinary allopathic means are of service in hastening the absorption of the effused blood, and the removal of the marks. HAYNES thinks that gentle friction is the only means of hastening the natural process of absorption. He says that there does not appear to be any satisfactory evidence that *cold* applications are useful in promoting absorption—on the contrary, he would rather expect them to retard this process; but they may be useful if the extravasation be increasing in consequence of oozing of blood from some of the injured blood-vessels. The English prize-fighters, according to TYRREL, have much faith in a poultice made with the root of the Black bryony, finely scraped, after the bark is removed, and mixed with crumbs of bread; to be enclosed in a muslin bag and renewed every 6 or 8 hours, until all traces of injury are removed, which will often take place in 48 hours, even when the discoloration is considerable. HAYS has known common tallow, thickly applied, used with apparently the desired result.

The Homœopathic treatment is doubtless far more successful; in all ordinary cases the internal and external use of *Arnica* will probably suffice: 15 to 20 drops of the tincture may be put in a tea-cup half or quite full of water, and cloths wet with this solution frequently applied to the bruised part; a few drops of the tincture may also be taken at a dose internally every 2, 4, or 6 hours, according to the severity of the symptoms. If the skin is broken, Tallow, or simple Cerate, or Glycerine, or Magnesia-ointment may be applied, or *Calendula* used in the same way as above recommended for Arnica.

When the extravasation is considerable, the probability of suppuration is to be borne in mind, and all febrile threatenings attended to. HAYNES says leeches are always worse than useless; *Aconite* should be given if fever, pain, or redness set in; *Rhus*, if much œdematous swelling arise; if the bone, or periosteum about the orbit has been injured, *Symphytum* will prove the best remedy; if the blackness and blueness remain obstinately, *Conium*, internally and externally, is by far the most homœopathic remedy; finally, if a large and firm coagulum of fibrin remain, the solvents of fibrin must be used, such as *Nitrum*, Phosphor., and Hyd. pot.

2. *Burns and Scalds.*

HAYNES says that burns and scalds of the eyelids require the most careful management, as under ordinary treatment they are generally followed by distressing contractions of the lids, owing to the thinness and looseness of the skin, and the mobility of the cartilages of the lids. To prevent or lessen the suppurative stage, of all the applications which he has tried or seen used, none are equal to nicely dressed cotton wool; it is soft, light, and cleanly; when there is merely an abraded surface from loss of the cuticle, it excludes the air and soaks up any superfluous moisture; if suppuration sets in, it absorbs the excess of fluid, and leaves enough for the purpose of sufficient moisture; with it the sore does not grow flabby and indolent, requiring stimulants, as so frequently happens with cold-water dressings, and the granulations are kept in a condition that prevents all necessity for caustic applications.

He has frequently seen sores that have resisted all other applications heal under this, the simplest of all means: the changing of the dressing is readily effected, as any portion adhering to the edges, or to the sound skin, needs only be wetted, while that over the raw surface will always separate readily when surcharged with moisture.

No ordinary mode of treatment will prevent subsequent contraction and deformity of the lids, if much of the true skin, or cutis vera be damaged, or destroyed. But it is all-important to check the period of suppuration. Professor MILLER, of Edinburgh, has used successfully a thick, semi-fluid, watery solution of Gum Tragacanth. He lays it on gently and uniformly over the raw surface, and reäpplies it, if any part becomes imperfect; this material being transparent, permits complete watching and observation of the injured part without removing the dressing; as the sore improves, gold-beater's skin is a useful application. The application of a thick emulsion of white Castile soap, sweet oil and lime-water, &c., sometimes proves too irritating; then a weak magnesia ointment, prepared from the best Henry's magnesia, or an emulsion of gum Arabic and milk, or gum Arabic and almond oil, or sweet oil, may be used. *Rhus*, *Cantharides*, and *Urtica urens* are recommended as the most homœopathic remedies in the first or acute stage, but only about one fourth of the quantities recommended for Arnica should be used.

CASE 1. Dr. DUDGEON says that Aconite is also useful in the inflammation produced by the action of acrid substances in the eye, by wounds, and by burns. A striking instance of ophthalmia from the last-named cause, cured by Aconite, is recorded in the *Allopathic Bulletin Medical*, Belge, (Aug. 1840,) by Dr. BROW. It was a case in which the eye and face had been scalded by hot butter; the lids were red and swollen; the cornea had lost its brilliancy and was covered with a whitish film; the conjunctiva was inflamed, and intolerance of light, excessively violent pains in the eye, and vesicles on several parts of the face were present.

Treatment and Result.—Compresses moistened with a solution of 8 drops of tinct. Aconite in 8 ounces of water were laid over the eye and face, and some of the solution was occasionally dropped into the eye. Alleviation of pain and quiet sleep soon followed, and on the fifth day the cure was complete.

CASE 2. In a case where the eye was burned with a candle, the inflammation yielded speedily to the internal use of *Acon.* 3.—*Brit. Journ. Hom.* Vol. 6, pp. 214. Dr. DUDGEON.

If the edges of the lids have been burned or scalded, especial care must be used to prevent them from uniting; this may always be prevented if the corners have escaped injury. The careful application of gold-beater's skin, or touching the raw surfaces with collodion, after they have been well dried, are thought by HAYES to be superior to all other methods, although a slight depression of the lower lid and elevation of the upper lid, by means of strips of adhesive plaster, so that the edges may always be kept some little distance apart, would doubtless be a valuable adjunct.

3. *Wounds of the Eyelids.*

Of course it is all-important to bring together the edges of a wound of the eyelid or eyebrow very accurately, and to attend to the prevention of inflammation in order to attain that speedy and perfect union which is the best security against subsequent deformity. Accurate union can scarcely be accomplished by means of adhesive plaster; at all events, sutures answer the purpose much better. Small, thin, sharp, almost homœopathic needles should be used with single silk threads, and as many sutures should be placed as may be necessary to unite and keep the divided parts in their proper relation to each other. Soft linen rags, or lint dipped in *Arnica*, or *Calendula-water*, may be applied frequently. Plasters, compresses, and bandages are generally not only useless, but injurious. The threads may be cut out in 12, 18, or 24 hours, for in that space of time the edges of the wound will have become agglutinated either by coagulated blood or coagulable lymph, so as to remain permanently in their proper apposition; by this early removal of the threads we avoid all inflammatory irritation from them, as this does not come on in so short a time.—LAWRENCE.

If no undue inflammation supervene, wounds of the eyebrow and lids generally heal readily; even when lacerated or contused, but little suppuration may take place, and but a slight scar be left, without injury to the eyelid. Still the least neglect may allow the edges of the lids and lashes to be turned in against the eyeball, causing great irritation followed by destructive inflammation of the eyeball, (*entropium;*) or, if the cicatrix be allowed to contract too much, the lids may be turned up, or over from the eye, (*ectropium.*) In wounds of the upper eyelid the levator muscle of the lid may be divided, and falling-down of the lid, or *ptosis,* occasioned. From relying upon strips of adhesive plaster in place of sutures, or from other neglect, fissures of the eyelid, like a button-hole or hare-lip, have been met with, the edges of the wound not having been kept close together, but allowed to cicatrize separately, forming the so-called *coloboma* of the lids. When the eyelid is entirely cut or torn through, the ball of the eye may be injured or irritated, and growing together of the eyelid and eyeball take place, unless the possibility of this is constantly kept in mind, and care taken to prevent it.

It is well known that weakness of sight and blindness have occurred in consequence of wounds of the eyebrows; this will be fully treated of under the head of Amaurosis.

INFLAMMATIONS OF THE EXTERNAL SURFACE OF THE EYELIDS.

BLEPHARITIS.

THESE are most common in children, and in the upper lid; when the cellular tissue is involved and suppuration occurs, which it is very apt to do, the only point which it is very important to attend to, is to limit the extent of suppuration as much as possible; if medical treatment does not do this, it is all-important to open the abscess as early as possible, because if the skin of the lids be allowed to become detached from the subjacent parts by a large collection of matter, the consolidation of the abscess will produce such contraction of the lid that it will no longer be able to cover the eyeball, and *Lagophthalmus*, or a constant open state of the eyelids will be produced, exposing the eye to the frequent entrance of foreign particles and other causes of irritation; in more favorable cases a turning over of the lid, or so-called eversion, or *Ectropium*, will ensue. LAWRENCE has seen at least half a dozen instances in which distressing deformity has resulted from this cause. In scrofulous inflammation of the cellular tissue of the lids the physician should be particularly on his guard, because the matter extends laterally, and has but little disposition to approach the surface. The opening should be made parallel to the natural folds or wrinkles in the skin of the lids, as the scar will then be hardly perceptible, appearing like one of the ordinary transverse folds of the skin. HAYES relates a case in which an inflammatory abscess of the upper lid was mistaken for severe purulent ophthalmia with excessive secondary swelling of the lid, that part being of a dark red color, greatly swollen, hot and painful; the edges of the lids being encrusted with matter, and the patient unable to separate them to the smallest extent; the whole presenting a sufficient resemblance to purulent ophthalmia to mislead an ignorant, or careless practitioner.

In the lower lid, it is not uncommon to meet with a small circumscribed abscess immediately over the lachrymal sac, which might readily be mistaken for disease of the sac itself; for the swelling, either by its pressure on the sac, or by displacing the inferior punctum lachrymale and interrupting the course of the secretions of the eye from the nose, occasions a watery condition of the eye, (*epiphora*,) and a dryness of the nostril of the same side.

Chronic abscess of the upper lid is also very apt to be overlooked; the pain is trifling, the lid is tumefied and œdematous, but the skin does not appear tense and shining, and in fact, as TYRRELL says, the whole feels like a dropsical swelling when the cellular membrane is not fully distended.

Treatment.—In the early stages of acute abscess, *Aconite* and *Belladonna* will be required in alternation, aided by an occasional dose of *Mercurius;* when matter has formed it should be let out at once, and *Hepar. sulph.* and *Silex* given in alternation; if there be much inflammatory suppuration, *Tartar emetic* is the best remedy; in chronic abscess, *Hepar. sulphur* may be relied upon in alternation with *China,* if there be a feeble state of the system. In erysipelatous inflammation of the lids, *Aconite* and *Rhus*, or *Cantharides*, *Mezereum*, or *Euphorbium* will be required. *Crocus* has been recommended homœopathically after surgical operations upon the eyes and lids, especially when throbbing and itching pains are present; it has also been used in traumatic ophthalmia with good effect.

ATTOMYR recommends quite a number of remedies in *Blepharitis*, or in inflammation of the outside of eyelids, viz: Aconite, Bryon, Calc., Euphorbium, Graphit., Hepar. s., Kali., Lycopod., Magnesia, Mercurius, Natrum, Phosphor, Rhus, Senega, Sepia, and Sulphur.—Aconite, Bryon., Euphorbium, Kali, Mercurius, Phosphor, Rhus and Senega doubtless being most homœopathic to quite acute attacks; Graphite, Hepar s., Sepia and Sulphur being most suited to the intractable sub-acute and irritable varieties; while Calcarea, Lycopod., Magnesia, and Natrum are best suited to slight and sluggish attacks. *Aconite* is thought to be most useful in acute inflammation of the right *upper* lid, with red, hard swelling; *Hepar* in sub-acute inflammation of the *upper* lids, with redness and swelling; *Kali*, when there is great swelling of the right *upper* lid, especially toward the nose; *Natrum*, when there is swelling of the *upper* lids without much pain, or redness; *Bryonia*, when there is redness, swelling, and acute inflammation of the *lower* lids; *Calcarea*, when there is sub-acute inflammation and swelling, especially of the *left lower* lid; *Graphite*, when there is redness and painful sub-acute inflammation of the *lower* lids and internal angles of the eyes; *Magnesia*, when there is a torpid and chronic inflammation and swelling of the *lower* lids, with redness of the angles of the eyes; *Mercurius*, when there is acute disease, with great swelling and burning pains, especially in the *left lower* lid; *Phosphor*, when there is acute inflammation and swelling of the *lower* lids; *Euphorbium*, when there is severe inflammation of *both* lids, with violent itching and irritation, but with a rather pale swelling, and profuse secretion of pus from the edges; *Lycopodium*, when there is chronic inflammation of *both* lids, with swelling, pain, and much secretion; *Mercurius*, when there is violent inflammation of the upper and lower lids, with burning pains, profuse secretion of tears, and matter; *Rhus*, when there is the most violent inflammation of *both* upper and lower lids; *Senega*, when there is swelling, burning and aching of the eyelids, without very great redness, especially when the upper and lower lids of the *right* eye are principally affected; *Sepia*, when there is sub-acute inflammation, with much swelling and some redness of both upper and lower lids; *Sulphur*, when there is a sub-acute, but painful and irritable inflammation of both lids.—(*See Primordien eine Naturgeschichte der Krankheiten. Vol.* 2. *pp.* 90 *to* 105.

Secondary Inflammations of the Lids.

LAWRENCE says that the eyelids are often involved in external inflammation of the ball of the eye; that is, in common, catarrhal, purulent, and scrofulous ophthalmia. We do not see a severe case of these affections, particularly of the first three, without more or less inflammation of the lids; hence, from the condition of the lids we may derive considerable information respecting the state of the eye, when we cannot actually see the latter. This influence, LAWRENCE says, is not reciprocal; the more important organ, the eye itself, reäcts upon the subordinate parts, viz., the lids; but the latter do not act upon it. The conjunctiva is only a little reddened in erysipelatous inflammation of the lids, although they are often enormously swollen and bright red, with the cellular tissue in a state of purulent infiltration, and mortification. The same observation holds good in most cases of variolous and traumatic inflammations of the lids. But in internal ophthalmia, the lids do not often become secondarily involved, that is, if the disease is confined to the internal tunics.—LAWRENCE.

Too much confidence must not be placed in these assertions; in a case of true erysipelas—still under treatment—about the right forehead, temple, and right lids, attended with vesication, rapid formation of almost gangrenous sloughs upon the temple, forehead, and upper eyelid; also with excessive œdematous swelling of both upper and lower right lids, with entire closure of the right eye and partial closure of the left from the excessive swelling, I found the conjunctiva not only greatly swollen and œdematous, but the cornea became dim, the pupil contracted and irregular, with a hazy or smoky appearance of the eye, and discoloration of the iris, evidently proving that the external inflammation had extended as far as the iris, causing erysipelatous inflammation of the conjunctiva, cornea, and iris.

Dropsical Swelling of the Lids. (*Œdema.*)

The lids are swollen and dropsical in Bright's disease of the kidneys, and in general dropsy, and in anasarca of the face.

Treatment.—Arsenicum, Marsh marigold, and Merc. corrosiv. If the swelling be so great as to close the lids, the watery fluid should be let out by puncture.

Inflammatory œdema of the lids occurs sometimes from trivial causes, such as the irritation of styes, bites or stings of insects, or leeches; the lids are often enormously swollen in inflammation of the lachrymal sac; the eyes are often closed in erysipelas. But these inflammatory œdemata of course generally subside without much harm when the disease which caused it is subdued.

Treatment.—If the ball of the eye become at all involved, punctures and scarifications of the outside of the lids are extremely important, in order to reduce the swelling which is pressing upon the eye, as rapidly as possible. Rhus, Cantharides, Apis mell., Mezereum, Urtica urens, all deserve attention.

CASE 4. A child, aged 2½ years, had suffered for 2 days with redness of both eyes, lachrymation, and nocturnal agglutination; he rubbed his eyes very much, was restless and sleepless; finally, the whole neighborhood of the right eye became œdematous, involving the orbit, cheek-bones, and wing of the nose.

Treatment.—Rhus 30, removed the whole affection in 2 days. —*Annals.* Vol. 1. p. 203. BUSCHK.

CASE 5. A man who worked much by artificial light, and who had long been troubled with styes, first on one lid, then on another, was suddenly attacked with burning pains in both eyes, and dimness of sight, followed by an œdematous swelling of the lids of the left eye, extending over the neighboring parts, and preventing the opening of the eyes. The glands about the neck and ear of the same side were swollen, red and painful.

Treatment.—One dose, each, of Rhus 12 and 18, and of Pulsat 12, removed the whole disorder in 10 days.—*Genl. Hom. Jour.* Vol. 12, p. 22. Dr. HARTMANN.

Emphysema of the Lids.

This may arise from injury of the lachrymal sac, or from fracture of the bones of the nose, or nasal sinuses near the orbit. It is generally not extensive, and soon disappears.

INFLAMMATION OF THE EDGES OF THE LIDS.

THIS disorder has received many long names, such as *Ophthalmia Tarsi*, *Psor-opthalmia*, *Lippitudo*, *Tinea Ciliaris*, *Blear Eyes*, *&c:*

According to LAWRENCE, in acute and simple *Ophthalmia Tarsi*, the margin of the lids, the tarsal cartilage and glands, and the adjoining mucous membrane of the internal surface of the lids are involved. The edge and neighboring part of the lid are swelled, bright red, and painful; the mucous membrane under the lid is of a scarlet color and villous; motion of the lids causes an acute pricking pain, with feeling as if there was sand in the eye and grit on the edges of the lids; there is a watery condition of the eye, intolerance of light, and more or less feverishness. The roots of the eyelashes are dry and stiff at first, then become moistened by increased secretion, and finally become more or less stuck together every night. The Meibomian glands soon participate in the affection, which originally begins on the margin of the eyelids, in the thin and delicate skin in which the eyelashes are placed, and upon which the duct of the Meibomian glands open; these glands are situated so near the primitive seat of the disorder, that they soon become involved by contiguous sympathy; they no longer pour out the mild unctuous matter which is destined to lubricate and soften the edges of the lids, but their secretion is suspended, so that in the morning the edges of the lids are stuck together by the increased conjunctival discharge, which has become incrusted by the evaporation of its watery parts during the night. In this way the lids are often so firmly agglutinated together every morning as to require a tedious process of softening and bathing with warm liquid applications before they can be parted. Finally, when the secretion from the Meibomian glands is renewed, it is altered in quality, being thick and viscid, and very apt to accumulate in hard lumps or masses at the roots of the eyelashes. Some of these morbid secretions of course get into the eye itself, spread over the cornea and irritate its surface, rendering it dull and turbid, impairing the vision, and causing various ocular delusions, such as rings or haloes around the candle, or its flame seems split into stars.

So many tissues are involved in this disorder, viz., the root of the eyelashes, the edges of the lids, the Meibomian glands, and the conjunctiva of the lids, that the disorder is apt to prove obstinate, as the cure depends very much upon an accurate selection of the few remedies which act upon all these parts, or upon an adroit alternation of those which act specifically upon the Meibomian glands, with those which act more particularly upon the edges and conjunctiva of the lids. When the patient is scrofulous, or cachectic, or careless, of course the disorder becomes still more intractable.

The name of *Tinea ciliaris* is given when pustules like those of *Tinea capitis* form on the edges of the lids, especially about the roots of the lashes; these break and pour out a yellowish matter, concreting with more or less firm, yellowish, or yellowish-brown scabs, which mat the eyelashes together, and sometimes adhere very closely to the surface of the lids. As this affection is seated along the roots of the eyelashes, it affects their growth, altering their form and direction; the ulcerations may finally extend deeper and deeper, and at last destroy the roots or bulbs of the eyelashes, which come away with the scabs.—LAWRENCE.

A still more obstinate and intractable variety of the disease has received the name of *Psorophthalmia*, on account of the severe irritation and itching which attends it, and from the supposition that the vesicles or pustules are true itch-pustules.

Blear-eye and Lippitudo are other names given to some stages or peculiarities of chronic inflammation of the edges of the lids, especially when the free margin of the lid becomes thickened and the regularity of the eyelashes disturbed; for instead of having a uniform direction, some of the lashes become directed upwards, others downwards, or in various irregular positions. The collection of coagulated secretion about the roots of the lashes becomes more abundant, and when taken away, extensive ulceration around the hairs will often be found. These ulcers gradually spread, and at length communicate together, so that the margin of the lid presents a continuous raw surface; at the same time the ulceration extends in depth so as to destroy the follicles from which the lashes grow; then the lashes fall out, and are not again reproduced. The destruction of all the lashes subjects the patient to constant attacks of inflammation, excited by the lodgment of particles of dust, &c., upon the globe of the eye, which else had been warded off by the lashes in the process of involuntary winking. The edges of the lids finally exhibit a thickened, florid and excoriated condition, constituting true *Lippitudo.*—TYRREL.

Treatment.—A very large portion of the treatment falls to the share of the patient, or his attendants. The lids if possible, should always be prevented from becoming agglutinated at night; or, if this cannot be accomplished, they never should be separated in the morning until the matter by which they are glued together has been completely softened. By forcing the lids roughly open the irritation is kept up, and the discharge daily aggravated; tepid milk and water should be used, or the agglutinated eyelashes should be smeared for some five minutes with warm milk, in which a bit of fresh butter, i. e., without salt, has been melted; then, a soft sponge wrung out in warm water should be held to the lids, and finally the softened crusts carefully removed. At night, the edges of the lids should be touched with Glycerine, or perfectly fresh Simple Cerate.

The edges of the lids should be examined carefully by the physician, every few days, with a magnifying-glass, and all the inverted lashes carefully pulled out, for these hairs are a source of great irritation to the eye, and will speedily induce inflammation and opacity of the cornea. This process also enables the oculist to get at the excoriations and small ulcerations, and apply the specific remedies directly to them.

From Dr. HEMPELL's New Repertory to Jahr's Manual, page 241, we learn that *Borax* is homœopathic when the eyes become closed at night with a hard, dry gum, which irritates the eyes like sand; *Alumina*, when there is a profuse secretion of mucus, especially at night, with dry eye-gum in the morning; *Argentum nitricum*, when the eyes are filled with mucus, and closed with crust of dry gum, which has to be soaked before it can be removed, or the eyes opened; Muriate of Ammonia, Nitrate of potash, and Carbo animalis also deserve attention. On page 271, we find that *Kreosote* is indicated against chronic swelling of the margins of the lids; *Eupatorium*, when there is redness of the margin of the lids, with glutinous secretion from the Meibomian glands; *Spigelia*, when there is inflammation of the margins of the lids, with ulceration and smarting soreness; *Mercurius*, when there is swelling and redness of the edges of the lids, with scurf and ulcerations; *Clematis*, when there is inflammation of the margin of the lids, with ulceration; *Euphrasia*, when the same state is present, with much headache.

Calcarea and *Sulphur* are homœopathic to the more obstinate and chronic cases, and we find that HAYES, of Philadelphia, recommends equal parts of rhubarb and prepared oyster-shells, every night, in sufficient doses to produce two stools daily; or equal parts of Cream of Tartar and Milk of Sulphur; and asserts, under this treatment, he has cured cases in a few weeks, which had run on for years, and in one case for 19 years.

In the Dominant School, a variety of more or less stimulating and hence homœopathic remedies are generally applied to the edges of the lids: of these, the preparations of Mercury and Silver are the most common, and, it is said, the most successful. I have seen a solution of Merc. corrosiv., 1 grain to the ounce of water, or an ointment of 1 or 2 grains to the ounce of simple Cerate, used with very great, and radically curative benefit.

Syphilitic Affections of the Eyelids.

Syphilitic ulcerations sometimes affect the eyelids, generally at their edges, but sometimes on their external or internal surface; in the one case, going on to destroy the whole thickness of the lid; in the other, producing a deep and foul ulceration. It is of course of great importance to distinguish their true nature, in order that, by the timely employment of the general treatment for Syphilis, the progress of the ulceration may be arrested. This of course will be easy for any one at all conversant with the disease or its treatment.

TURNING IN OF THE EYELASHES.

TRICHIASIS.

THIS is a growing-in of some or more of the eyelashes against the eyeball; the border of the lid remains in its proper position, which constitutes the distinction between Trichiasis and Entropium.

Distichiasis, again, is merely a variety of Trichiasis, in which the misdirected eyelashes are disposed, though not very regularly, in a row distinct from the others which remain properly directed. The faulty eyelashes in these two disorders are generally the natural hairs which have been made to take a wrong direction, in consequence of disease of the edge of the lids, cicatrices, &c. Sometimes, however, the hairs are supernumerary, and of new formation. Sometimes the misdirected eyelashes are confined to a part only of the border of the eyelid, in other cases the whole border of the eyelid is involved along its whole extent. It is not uncommon to find both Trichiasis and Distichiasis affecting the lids of both eyes. The offending eyelashes are sometimes very few in number, and so pale and fine that they very frequently escape even somewhat careful notice, and the inflammation of the eye which they occasion will be attributed to some other cause, unless a careful exploration of the state of the edges of the lids be made with a good magnifying-glass. (WHARTON JONES.) It is one of the most common affections of the eye, and although it does not rapidly destroy this organ, yet, if allowed to proceed unchecked, or if merely partially relieved, it becomes, from the constant irritation and inflammation of the eyeball which it causes, one of the most destructive diseases. It is scarcely necessary to say that Trichiasis and Distichiasis are merely varieties of the same affection; the supposed independent, or new row of lashes which has been assumed to exist in the latter, is a mere deception, arising partly from the irregular though natural manner in which the eyelashes are placed on the edges of the lids, owing to the different planes in which their follicles lie; a fact which seems to be frequently overlooked, although familiar to the earlier anatomists. In fact this so-styled Distichiasis may be artificially produced, and the permanent misdirection accurately imitated in a perfectly healthy lid, by separating the inner row of eyelashes, and bending them toward the globe of the eye.—HAYNES WALTON.

It is far more important, however, to trace out the mode of origin of the disease. It may arise from the matting together of the lashes in long-continued purulent discharges from the eyes; but by far the largest number of cases arise from certain diseased changes in the lid itself, nearly all of which arise from scrofulous inflammation. The misdirection of otherwise healthy eyelashes is supposed by HAYNES nearly always to arise from unhealthy changes in the fibro-cellular tissue in which the cilia-follicles lie; thickening or other apparent disease of the lids is not a necessary accompaniment, although it may be and often is superadded. When the eyelashes, instead of having their natural shape and size, are also imperfectly developed, then more or less disease of the hair-follicles has been added, arising from unhealthy states of the edge of the lid.

The disorder, as before said, requires very careful examination of the edges of the lids; the eyelashes that fret the eye may be so minute as to escape even careful observation of those unaccustomed to search for them, and unfortunately, minuteness does not diminish their power of mischief. Sometimes only one or two hairs are inverted without any apparent cause, the lid and the rest of the lashes being quite natural, and in this case, the misdirected hair is almost always so slender and light-colored as to render close examination necessary to detect it. But the sensations of the patient are very accurate; the feeling of a foreign body rubbing the eye is almost always expressed; it causes, at times, merely uneasiness without inflammation; or inflammation may be caused with ulceration and opacity of the cornea, severe pain, with intolerance of light and the greatest irritability; finally, sight may be destroyed by the effects of repeated attacks of acute inflammation of the cornea, but even then the patient's sufferings are not at an end, for pain will be excited as often as he moves his eye, until all the offending lashes have been extracted.

Treatment. When the irritation is caused by well-formed but inverted eyelashes proceeding from a healthy lid, they may be pulled out with advantage, because although the lashes soon grow again there may not be a return of the inversion, and even if the hairs so pulled out show a tendency to become distorted to a like degree, their injurious effect can be anticipated, and the process of extraction repeated, again and again, with advantage. But when the pulling out of the offending lashes is followed, as it often is, by an increase of inverted or abortive lashes, then the use of the Cilia forceps has reached its limit and should be discontinued. The length of time, or the frequency with which this will become necessary, depends very much upon the manner in which the lashes have been extracted, and the general care which the patient takes of his eyes, diet and general health, and the judicious use of specific remedies against the disease of the lids, hair-follicles, &c. The majority of the finest eyelashes are not pulled out, but are merely broken off, because they are generally carelessly pulled at with a jerk, and the short portion left irritates like a short bristle. The patient should present himself weekly; a magnifying-glass should be used, and if the hairs be very fine and pale, some black extract like Belladonna may be applied to the edge of the lid which if rightly used will blacken even the finest lashes so as to render them quite visible; then forceps without teeth should be employed, the holding part being merely rough-polished, so as not to cut or break off the hairs, and they should be held close up to their points. When the eyelashes are exquisitely fine and slip through even the best-made forceps, HAYS has found it an infallible plan to damp their points with a saturated solution of Shellac in alcohol, and to grasp the hairs for a moment or two before pulling them. Finally, the eyelash should be grasped near its root and slowly drawn out in a straight line, by which means it will generally be drawn out by its root. Unless all these precautions are used, there cannot be a doubt that the frequent pulling out of the lashes is very hurtful to the hair-follicles, renders the direction of them more perverse, tends to irritate the lids and involve the contiguous follicles, and so to multiply the trichiasis.

In some obstinate cases the careful application of some depilatory to each offending follicle may be resorted to.

But, besides these palliative means, the judicious use of remedies which act specifically upon the edges of the lids must be carefully followed up. (See page 12.)

Thickening and induration of the edges of the lids. (TYLOSIS.)

The edges of the lids, after long-continued slow inflammation, become thickened, indurated and knotty, especially in scrofulous subjects; they ulcerate irregularly, and incrustations form about the lashes; this swollen and knotty state of the lids, in which their margin often loses altogether its natural figure and appearance, has been technically called *tylosis.*—LAWRENCE.

All the lashes should be extracted, the crusts removed, and specific remedies applied locally and internally; especially Argent nitric, Mercurius, Kreosote, Clematis, and Euphrasia.

Loss of the Eyelashes. (PTILOSIS, MADAROSIS.)

Destruction of the hair-bulbs either by ulceration or injury causes a permanent loss of the eyelashes, which may be either partial or general. The loss is irremediable, but the effect on the personal appearance is much less than would have been expected, especially in those with light hair. In some cases the local application of Cantharides, and dilute Ung. Hydrarg. Nitrat. have ultimately restored the lashes of natural size, number and color. The homœopathic remedies for *Alopecia* may be tried, viz., *Plumbum acet.*, *Paris quad.*, *Hepar*, *Alumina*, and *Phosphor.*

INFLAMMATION OF THE ANGLES OF THE EYELIDS.

THE most important of these are the diseases of the internal angle of the lower lid, either seated in the lachrymal sac and passages, or external to these.

According to ATTOMYR, a swelling often appears at the internal angle of the eye, near the lachrymal sac; it is red, yellowish-red, or bluish-red, shining, tense, and painful; it is apt to be bean-shaped, and extend downwards and outwards over the neighboring parts of the lids and cheek. The eyelids and part of the face are apt to swell and become œdematous: very frequently the inflammatory swelling extends to the adjacent lachrymal organs, to the meibomian glands, and the white of the eye. The lids are apt to stick together at night, the tears to run over the eyelids, and the corresponding nostril to become sensitive and dry, while sneezing is easily provoked.

As long as suppuration and ulceration do not set in, the disorder is technically called by the old-fashioned name, *Anchlyops;* when these latter do occur, it receives the equally absurd name of *Ægilops.* The disorder seems more closely allied to phlegmonous erysipelas, or to boils, or styes in its nature; at least, it usually is as obstinate and intractable in its course, and rarely ends short of suppuration. The abscess, when formed, either opens outwardly upon the cheek, or else bursts into the lachrymal sac, or progresses in both directions simultaneously.

It may be distinguished from acute inflammation of the lachrymal sac, by the much slighter degree of pain and fever with which it is accompanied. In acute *Dacryo-cystisis,* or inflammation of the sac, the local suffering and the constitutional disturbance are much more considerable than might have been expected from the small extent of the disorder; but not more than can be accounted for by the great vascularity of the tissues of the sac, and from its being surrounded by an unyielding bony receptacle.—LAWRENCE.

Treatment. According to ATTOMYR, *Belladonna*, *Mercurius*, *Natrum*, and *Petroleum* are the principal remedies. The indications for *Belladonna* are: throbbing pain in the lower eyelid, near the internal angle, with great inflammatory swelling at this point, and profuse flow of tears. Inflammation and suppuration of the left punctum-lachrymale, with burning and aching pains. Great painfulness of the internal angle of the left eye, with itching, sticking together of the lids, involuntary lachrymation, frequent sneezing, and redness of the whites of the eyes.

Mercurius is indicated when there is an inflammatory swelling near the lachrymal bone; great swelling, redness and agglutination of the lids, which are very sore to the touch; many red vessels on the white of the eye; heat and lachrymation of the eyes; watering and weeping of the eyes, frequent sneezing.

Natrum is indicated when there is violent inflammation and purulent swelling of the lachrymal sac, which bursts in about four days; inflammatory swelling of the right upper eyelid, without redness of the white of the eye, with aching, dimness of the vision, and some hard mucus in angles of the eye; lachrymation; sticking together of the lids; unusually violent, frequent and long-continued sneezing.

Petroleum is the most homœopathic remedy when there is an inflammatory swelling in the internal angle of the eye, almost as large as a small pigeon-egg, with burning and aching pains, and lachrymation; when much water can be pressed out of the corners of the eye; and there is frequent sneezing, with drowsiness.

Among other remedies, *Argentum nitricum*, *Bryonia*, *Calcarea*, *Cinnabaris*, *Graphit*, *Sepia*, *Silex*, *Stannum*, and *Zinc* deserve attention.

Polypi and Fungi of the Angles of the Lids.

CASE 6. A child aged 1 year, had a Polypus with a neck, growing from the external angle of the right eye; it had attained the size of a sugar-plum.

Treatment. In 8 days after taking Lycop. 200, the swelling was smaller; in 14 days it had disappeared entirely.—Dr. GROSS.

CASE 7. Field-Marshal Radetzky, when 70 years of age, was attacked with inflammation of the eye, followed by a swelling in the internal angle of the eye, about the size of a bean, and which soon took on the appearance of a spongy fungus.

Treatment. After the use of various homœopathic remedies this dangerous disorder gave way before the use of Thuya 30, 1 drop in 8 ounces of distilled water, a table-spoonful per dose 3 times a day, aided by the external use of Tinct. Thuya, 6 drops in 4 ounces of water, to be applied warm every 2 hours. Every 8 days the above treatment was alternated with Carb. animalis 30, in daily doses, aided by the external use of a solution of Carb. an. 12, applied to the fungus with a camel's hair pencil. The cure was rapid. *Genl. Hom. Jour.* Vol. 20, p. 165. Dr. HARTUNG.

HORDEOLUM, OR STYE.

STYE, as is well known, is a small inflammatory tumor at the edge of the eyelid, attended with more or less heat and pain, and going on to suppuration. It is closely allied in its nature to boils and felons, differing perhaps only in its location. It has been supposed by some, but erroneously, to be an abscess of the meibomian glands; others suppose that like a boil it is merely seated in the cellular tissue near the edge of the lid; while Dr. ZEIS has suggested that styes have their seat in the capsules, and glands of the roots of the eyelashes. In accordance with the latter supposition, Dr. ZEIS asserts that styes may be arrested at once by plucking out the eyelashes at the part affected, and WHARTON JONES says, as the lashes fall out at any rate, there can be no objection on the score of saving them; besides, they almost always grow again.

Treatment. According to LAWRENCE a stye generally goes through its regular course, under the old treatment; he thinks premature lancing is injurious, and in general it is best to leave the disorder to its natural course, probably because no specific remedies are known in his school against this trifling but annoying disorder, while leeches, purgatives, poultices, and low diet are altogether too severe for such a lilliputian disease. According to ATTOMYR, *Ferrum aceticum*, *Phosphor*, *Pulsatilla*, *Rhus*, *Sepia*, and *Staphysagria* are the principal homœopathic remedies. *Ferrum* is indicated when there is redness and swelling of the upper and lower lids, with a kind of stye filled with pus, on the upper one, while the lower is covered with purulent mucus; when the eyes are red and burning, and the eyelids stick together.

Phosphor.—When the styes are most frequent on the *lower* lid, the eyes being sensitive to light; when the whites are red, with itching, soreness, and much burning; when acrid water flows from the eyes; when the lids stick together, are hot and sore, and the internal angles are ulcerated; all attended with dimness of sight.

Pulsatilla has been recommended by KNORRE against styes, from personal experience. GROSS thinks that it will disperse them in two or three days, although *Sulphur* will have to be given afterwards, if there is a chronic disposition to relapses. LOBETHAL also speaks highly of it. It is most indicated when the styes are attended with inflammation of the whites of the eyes, with sores of the corners of the lids, and of the nostrils; when the eyes water, and stick together.

Rhus is recommended when there are large, red swellings, like styes, on the left lower lid, near the angle of the eye, with aching pains, and lasting for six days; when the eyes are red, and stuck together with matter in the morning, and there is much purulent mucus about the lids.

Sepia is one of the best remedies when the styes are extremely slow in suppurating, and have an obstinate and chronic predisposition to return again and again. VEHSEMEYER cured a boy, aged twelve, who had been troubled with a hard tumor, of the size of a small pea, on the lower lid, remaining after a stye, which he had had two years before; it was attached to the tarsus, and obstructed the motion of the lids. He received *Sepia* 30, one dose every eight days; after the second dose, pain, inflammation, and suppuration set in, in the indurated spot, which broke after the third dose, and he remained perfectly cured.

Sulphur is also almost indispensable in chronic cases, especially when there is much swelling of the lid, with redness, burning pain, and hard matter between the lashes; when the eyes are sensitive to light, and the lids are apt to stick together.

Staphysagria has been recommended by HERING when styes recur frequently on the lids, or leave indurated spots behind them, or when they do not gather and break, but become indurated, especially when the lids are apt to glue together, with biting and burning pains in the corners, and much dry matter collects between the lashes.

CASE 8.—TIETZE cured a man, aged 44, who had frequently suffered with inflammations of the eye, and who had been for nine weeks in the following state:

Symptoms.—Both eyelids of the right eye were somewhat swollen, and bluish-red; the whites of the eye were red and injected, especially at the internal angle; both eyelids were covered with styes in their first stage; at night the lids were stuck together by hard, yellow scabs; he complained of aching pains when the eye was uncovered, and often had burning in the lids. His pulse was hard and frequent, and he was costive.

Treatment.—*Staphysagria* 15, 3 doses, one drop per dose, cured him entirely.—*Archiv.* Vol. 19, part 3, p. 170.

In ordinary homœopathic treatment, *Pulsatilla* is recommended as the first remedy to be used; while *Merc.* and *Hepar* are to be relied upon when suppuration has set in. HARTLAUB has recommended *Alumina* when there is predisposition to the frequent recurrence of styes on the upper lid; *Colocynth* proved homœopathic to a stye on the left eye; *Mercurius* to styes on the upper eyelid, when this was thick, swollen, and red; *Natrum mur.* to a large stye on the internal angle of the right eye; *Senega* to styes on the edge of the right lower lid. *Thuya* cured a chronic case, in a woman who had suffered so long and frequently, and had received so little benefit from allopathic treatment, that extirpation of the edge of the lids was thought of; it was used both internally and externally.

Inflammation and Abscess of the Meibomian Glands.

The appearance of this disease on the external surface of the lid resembles that of stye very decidedly; but it is of much rarer occurrence, and its nature will at once be recognized on everting the lid, when the affected gland, or glands, will be seen distended with yellow matter, extending on the under surface of the lids, from their edges some little distance towards the attachments of the lids to the orbits.

Treatment.—When ripe, the turgid gland may be opened, and the matter be evacuated by a touch of the lancet. According to ATTOMYR, *Colchicum* has been found homœopathic to inflammation and ulceration of the Meibomian glands of the lower lid of the left eye, with swelling of the lids, and great irritation of the nerves of the eye; *Digitalis*, in simple inflammation of these glands; *Indigo*, when the inflammation of the Meibomian glands of the lower lids was attended with slight headache, toothache, noises in the ears, and beating in the forehead; *Nickel*, when there is burning pain in both eyes, much watering of the eyes, and decided swelling of these glands.

Enlargement of the Meibomian Glands.

According to TYRREL, we sometimes meet with an irritation of the eye, as if some foreign substance were in it, between the lid and the ball of the eye; on everting the lid, a small tumor may be found of a deep red color, and having a close resemblance to a small cluster of healthy granulations, only being more firm to the touch; the white of the eye is usually a little inflamed, and sometimes a considerable degree of ophthalmia will be present. This disease differs from stye, in being seated on the inner surface of the lid, and more frequently on the lower lid, while styes are most common on the upper lid, and always on the outside of any of the lids.

Treatment.—*Thuya*, *Colchicum*, *Nickel*, and other remedies are suited to this disorder.

Tumors of the Eyelid.

They are generally small, and consist of Styes, Horns, Warts, Glandiform-, Steatomatous-, Vesicular-, and Tarsal-tumors.

Styes have already been fully treated of.

Horns on the lids are said by HAYNES WALTON to consist of inspissated sebaceous matter, and owe their existence to the drying and hardening, as fast as it escapes, of the contents of encysted tumors, or of the sebaceous follicles which supply the soft material.

Treatment.—When medical treatment fails, a single stroke of the knife will be sufficient to remove a horn from the lid; the excrescence should first be pulled forwards, and the separation should be made through the skin, in order that the cyst from which it grows, may be entirely taken away, or else a return of the disease will almost surely take place. HARTMANN says he has cured them with *Antim. crud.*

Warts should, as a rule, not be excised, on account of the injury which will be inflicted upon the cartilage of the lids. *Thuya*, *Soot*, *Sabina*, *Causticum* and *Calcarea* are the principal homœopathic remedies.

Glandiform tumor is common in children, and was so named by TYRREL, from its resemblance to a salivary gland; it is frequently present on the lids and face simultaneously, and

HAYNES says it is, he believes, never solitary. When fully formed, its appearance is characteristic, being mottled, and the gland-like structure is at once recognizable. In a very recent state it resembles a sebaceous tumor. As several are almost always seen in the different stages of development, some of them may have softened in the centre and suppurated, and having burst their cyst, protrude and become surrounded with an incrustation which makes them look like warty growths. MACKENZIE thinks that it is an albuminous tumor; while LAWRENCE supposes that it commences as a small, smooth prominence, with a flattened surface and a small pin-like hole in the centre.

Treatment.—*Thuya*, *Merc.-corrosiv.*, and *Calcarea*, are the most homœopathic remedies. The surgical treatment consists in cutting the tumor across with a free incision, and squeezing out its contents with the thumb-nail; if the cyst does not separate at the same time, it must be pulled out gently with the forceps. WALTON HAYNES.

Steatomatous-tumor, or *Milium*, is a superficial deposit of Steatoma, generally called *milium*, from its resemblance to a *millet-seed;* it is not confined to the eyelids, but frequently appears on the cheeks in great numbers; it seldom exceeds a pin's head in size, except when it grows at the edge of the eyelid, or between the eye and nose.

Treatment.—Whether large or small, they may be cut across, and their contents squeezed out. DR. GUEYRARD has cured even large steatomatous tumors with *Thuya*, 15th dilut., a dose every night and morning, in about one month.

Vesicular Tumor.—TYRREL says that he has frequently seen the cuticle elevated near the free margin of the lids into a small vesicular tumor containing water, or serum. They are not attended with any pain or marked symptom, unless they project inwards toward the eye, which they rarely do. These vesicles, from the thinness of their contents, are semi-transparent; seldom larger than a swan-shot; and several are often present at the same time upon the lids. They are sometimes very slow in growing, lasting from five to twenty-five years, when, instead of serum, they are apt to contain a glairy fluid.

Treatment.—When small, a simple puncture will effect a

cure; or *Rhus*, or Cantharides, Mezereum, Euphorbium, or Marsh-Marigold may be required internally and externally. When of a large size, the cyst may be required to be removed, or cauterized.

Tarsal Tumor.—The situation of this differs from that of stye in being above the edge of the tarsus, or cartilage of the lid, and some distance away from the eyelashes. When small, the tumor is scarcely visible on the outer side of the lid, and can only be felt beneath the skin of the eyelid like a small shot under the finger; but if the lid be everted, or turned over, a discolored spot on the under surface will indicate the point of attachment between the tumor and the cartilage of the lid. It slowly increases in size, so that many weeks or months may elapse before it has acquired sufficient size to attract much attention on the outside of the lid. The spot before alluded to on the under or inner side of the lid is at first red, then becomes yellow in its centre, and finally acquires a bluish tinge. When it is very visible externally, it has been termed *Grando;* while the barbarous name of *Chalazior* is applied to the internal tumor. It is supposed to have its seat in the structure of the tarsal cartilage, and to have a more decided disposition to point on the inner side of the lid than the outer. TYRREL truly says that the diagnosis of this little disease is important, as it is very readily cured, when recognized, by simply everting or turning over the lid, and puncturing its cyst through conjunctiva of the lid and tarsus. On the other hand, if an attempt be made to excise it from the outer side of the lid, the cartilage will be injured, and much deformity of the lid will follow, occasioning the patient subsequent and permanent inconvenience. If the tumor be allowed to increase and burst of itself, a small fungus-like substance will rise up through the opening. The tumor itself is said to consist of gelatiniform fibrinous matter, not inclosed in a cyst, but simply contained in the cavity which it has formed for itself in the substance of the tarsal cartilage.

Treatment.—*Bryonia* is said to have proved homœopathic to a tumor as large as a pea upon the lower lid of the left eye; *Calcarea* cured an inflamed tumor upon the right lower eyelid, as large as a big pea, in the person of a child aged 1½ years;

two doses caused resolution, without the occurrence of suppuration. When the digestive organs are deranged, *Colocynth* may prove curative to both disorders; *Mercurius* and *Natrum* deserve attention, although *Staphysagria* or *Silex* may be required.

Encysted Tumors of the Lids, not connected with the Tarsal Cartilage.—These are most frequent in children; they rarely originate in the adult, although they occasionally exist at that period of life, having been allowed to remain untouched from infancy. They are more common in the neighborhood of the lids and the orbit than in any other part of the body; they are generally not discolored; arise without pain or inflammation; and have a rounded, firm and elastic feel; they are generally movable, but occasionally are attached firmly to the periosteum; they vary in size from that of a small pea to that of a pigeon's egg, or larger.

It is thought that nothing but excision will remove these tumors. If this be decided upon, the cyst should be dissected out entire. The contents are usually sebaceous, but occasionally glairy. Frequently, a number of small and fine hairs are mixed with these matters, and then the interior of the cyst presents a decidedly cuticular appearance, from the surface of which numbers of these fine hairs are often found growing.—LAWRENCE.

When the cyst is firmly attached to the periosteum or bone, it is thought advisable not to operate upon them, as very extensive mischief sometimes results; inflammation and sloughing may ensue, by which the bone may become exposed, and finally exfoliate very decidedly. *Baryta, Sepia, and Silex* are the most homœopathic remedies.

Naevus Maternus.—The eyelids, as well as other parts of the body, are occasionally the seat of the so-called *mother-marks* and moles. I have cured several cases by the local application of Muriate Tincture of Iron; while my friend, DR. BOLLES, has cured several cases by internal remedies alone.

Scirrhoid Induration of the Eyelids.—This is not cancerous, although it resembles cancer. It consists of a hard, tuberculated warty-like degeneration of the whole thickness of the edge of the lid, commonly of the lower, traversed by varicose vessels, and ending in ulceration. It is most common in old people.

Treatment.—*Thuya*, *Baryta muriat.*, *Iod. pot.*, *Iod. hydrarg.*, and other remedies, deserve attention.

INFLAMMATIONS OF THE INTERNAL SURFACE OF THE EYELIDS.

A. Simple Inflammation.

(CONJUNCTIVITIS PALPEBRARUM.)

THIS differs from the catarrhal, or muco-purulent variety, principally by the lesser quantity of mucus, or muco-pus which is secreted; by the minor degree of swelling of the lids, and by the smaller size and more vivid color of the blood-vessels which form the inflammatory redness of the affected part. According to TYRREL, it commences with a slight degree of pricking pain, a feeling of heat and stiffness in the lids, either with a sense of dryness of the surface, from the want of moisture, or with a scalding sensation, from an increase of acrid tears which flow over the lower eyelid to the cheek. Frequently, there is a feeling as if some foreign substance were lodged upon the inner and under surface of one or the other lids. Great intolerance of light is not often present, although exposure to bright light augments the suffering. Unless the attack be speedily relieved, pain of a sharp and severe character is apt to set in, and it, as well as the sense of heat about the eye, is aggravated by lying down.

The blood-vessels of the white of the eye, (conjunctiva of the eyeball,) are remarkable for pursuing a slightly *tortuous* course from the circumference of the orbit towards the margin of the cornea. The largest vessels may be seen passing from near the attachments of the recti muscles, and gradually diminishing in size as they proceed towards the cornea, but at the same time sending off numerous minute branches, which freely connect with others from neighboring vessels; so that a beautiful web-like aspect results. These *crooked* and *tortuous* blood-vessels are also remarkable for the ease with which they may be pushed for a short distance from side to side, by means of slight pressure of the lid against them.

The principal causes are: sudden changes of temperature, exposure to cold winds and damp, especially when influenza prevails; lodgment of foreign bodies under the lids, especially the upper, such as dust, sand, metallic particles, etc. The lodgment of particles of dust, fine sand, mortar, or cinders, is so frequent a cause of simple inflammation of the internal surface of the lids, and of the conjunctiva of the ball, that careful inquiry and search should generally be made for them, especially if the patient has been exposed to injury from any of these exciting causes, or the disease has set in very suddenly without other evident exposure, and the suffering is instantaneously acute, and remains obstinately persistent. Foreign substances are easily detected on the inner surface of the lower lid, or upon the conjunctiva over the cornea or sclerotica; but when they have lodged under the upper lid, unless the physician is familiar with the manner of everting or turning this over, he will find much difficulty in detecting them, or his rough and clumsy attempts will soon oblige the patient to refuse to submit to further bungling. Some of the lashes and part of the lower edge of the upper lid should be grasped by the surgeon; the patient be directed to look downwards, so as to turn the ball of the eye as far down as possible, while the upper lid is gently drawn away, or out and down from the eyeball; a fine probe should be laid upon the lid, just above the upper edge of the tarsal cartilage; and then, if the lid be lifted up against the probe, it will readily turn over, so as to expose the greater part of the under surface of the upper lid. The offending particle may easily be wiped off; and if the patient be directed to turn the ball of the eye upwards, the surgeon still retaining his hold of the lid, it will promptly return to its natural position, and the whole operation will have been performed with great celerity, and very little suffering to the patient.

Treatment.—Simple inflammation of the internal surface of the eyelids is almost always a very manageable disease, rarely withstanding judicious treatment longer than three or four days. Aconite and Antimony, or Aconite and Pulsat., or Acon. and Euphrasia, internally; gentle bathing of the eye, and a weak solution of Aconite or Pulsatilla, followed by a small quantity of Alumina or Zincun, applied three or four times a day to the internal surface of the lower lid, will generally suffice to effect a cure in the above-mentioned space of time.

B. Catarrhal Inflammation of the Lids.

This is distinguished from simple inflammation by the greater profuseness of the serous and mucous discharges from the lids; and from purulent-, Egyptian-, and gonorrhœal-ophthalmia, by the lesser severity of the local symptoms, lesser malignity of the inflammation, and the more mucous than purulent nature of the discharges. In catarrhal ophthalmia there frequently is little or no accompanying constitutional disturbance, but sometimes all the symptoms of catarrhal fever are present, such as lassitude, chilliness, with fever at night, quick pulse, hot and dry skin, and restlessness. There is at first a watering of the eye, from increased flow of tears, combined with serous exudation from the congested vessels of the conjunctiva; but a muco-purulent discharge soon sets in, formed of a profuse mucous flow from the conjunctiva, and increased secretion from the Meibomian glands. The conjunctiva of the lids, the semi-lunar fold and caruncle, are first attacked, and become red, thickened, and villous. Soon afterwards, the disorder extends to the conjunctiva of the ball of the eye. This disorder will of course be treated of more fully under the head of general catarrhal inflammation of the eye.

Treatment.—Aconite and Antimony, or Aconite and Pulsatilla, or Aconite and Baryta muriatica, or Kali hydriodicum, are excellent remedies.

C. Granular Lids and Vascular Cornea.

This is one of the most formidable consequences of purulent ophthalmia, or of the catarrhal, in its severer forms. The disease may either be formed during the acute attack, and remain after it has subsided; for catarrhal and purulent ophthalmia commence in the conjunctiva of the lids, and spread from thence to that of the ball; but they disappear in the contrary order, leaving, first, the ocular portion of the membrane, or that in which they appear last, and linger along in the palpebral portion, or that in which they first appeared. The disease may linger in the conjunctiva of the lids in so trifling a degree as to escape the observation of the careless practitioner, who may be satisfied with a general marked improvement of the white of the eye; but in order to prevent the insidious formation of granular disease, the under surface of the upper and lower lids should be carefully examined, even after all acute disease seems to have been completely subdued; and if the mucous membrane of the eyelid has not perfectly recovered its natural aspect, the remedies should be continued until all appearance of disease has subsided.—TYRREL.

According to the same author, after acute catarrhal, or purulent inflammation of the eye has subsided, so that the sight becomes almost perfect, the patient may retain some so-called "weakness" or "irritation" of his eyes, attended with a watery condition of them on exposure to bright light, or cold air. The increased secretion from the eye is as thin and watery as the tears at first, and it is apt to flow over the cheek; the eye feels irritated, as if fine dust or grit had got under the lids; and finally, a more sticky and colored secretion is formed, which collects about the angles of the eye, and among the roots of the eyelashes. Soon vision becomes impaired; the sensation of the presence of a foreign body between the eyelids and ball of the eye is felt whenever these parts are moved suddenly; there is a sense of weight and stiffness in the upper eyelid; vessels carrying red blood will be seen passing from the upper part of the eye towards the upper part of the cornea, and the cornea itself soon becomes opaque and dim, especially at its upper part.

If the under surfaces of the lids be examined in the way already pointed out, the conjunctiva will be found more red than natural, and roughened from the enlargement of its villi. Besides the florid appearance and the small elevations upon the mucous membrane of the lids, this becomes thickened, and by degrees the red color assumes a deeper tint; the enlarged villi become more numerous and prominent, so that when the under surface is exposed by everting the lid, it resembles very much the surface of a healthy ulcer, and this resemblance is heightened in some cases by the adherence of quantities of the opaque, viscid, and puriform secretion. In consequence of this resemblance, the disease has been termed *Granular conjunctiva*, or *granulated lids;* and from the accompanying redness, dimness and vascularity of the cornea, the collective disorder has received the name of *Granular lids and vascular cornea.* But, in fact, the small red projections are not real granulations, like those formed during the healing of a healthy ulcer, but merely the natural villi of the mucous membrane greatly enlarged.—TYRREL.

When the disorder is fully formed and established, it is a most troublesome affection, and extremely obstinate; subject to sudden and violent exacerbations from the slightest causes, and often aggravated in the course of a few days by the very treatment which seemed most beneficial a short time before. This great tendency to *relapse* is a marked feature of the disorder; it might with great justice be termed *relapsing ophthalmia.* It must also be regarded as the local manifestation of a constitutional disorder, as no one who has seen several hundred cases of the disease, or who has repeatedly seen from twelve to twenty afflicted with it, in the same room with dozens of other patients with diseases of the eye, will have the slightest difficulty in recognizing these cases, from the pallid and suffering expression of their countenances, even at a distance at which it would be perfectly impossible for him to detect the vascularity of the cornea. TYRREL says that he has observed that granular lids and vascular cornea arises most frequently in those persons who have been treated very actively and allopathically, and much reduced in strength; and that it generally proves obstinate in proportion to the feeble condition of the patient. The *Sycotic* diathesis may have much more to do with it than the scrofulous, gonorrhœal, or syphilitic, upon which so much stress has been laid.

HAYS admits four varieties or stages:

1st. The conjunctiva is simply reddened and villous.

2d. It resembles an ulcerated surface, the granulations exhibiting most of the phases presented by such a sore; sometimes being small and pale, at others large and flabby, and bleeding on the slightest touch.

3d. The granulations may have a warty appearance, being firm and pale, cutting like cartilage, and bleeding but little.

4th. The mucous membrane is thickened and fissured like the surface of a mulberry.

The granulations are most frequent and abundant on the whole under surface of the upper lid, and on that small portion of the lower where it passes from the lid to the ball of the eye, especially towards the outer angle. The vascularity of the cornea is frequently confined to the upper half of this body, viz., to that portion over which the rough surface of the upper lid moves; consequently, the lower half of the cornea generally remains transparent. In some cases, however, the vascularity may cover the whole surface of the cornea like a net-work, and its mucous covering, or the conjunctiva of the cornea, may become so loosened and thickened as to exhibit that state which has been technically called *Pannus*, in which the boundary of the cornea can hardly be seen.—LAWRENCE.

Treatment.—SAUNDERS has the credit of being the first who discovered the true character of this chronic disorder, and explained the mode in which it destroys sight; but, unfortunately, he always endeavored to correct it by operative means, and frequently employed either the knife or scissors to remove the prominent villi, and to render the surface smooth. TYRREL supposes that he considered the projecting parts to be really granulations, and did not dream of their being enlarged mucous villi. Of course, great injury was often done by removing them. The surface rendered smooth by operation with the knife or scissors, often presented greater irregularity a few days subsequent to the operation, but of a somewhat different character; the projections, which in the first instance had been uniform in size and elevation, afterwards became much more irregular, both in shape and projection; in fact, real and irregular, spongy granulations sprang up from the wounded surface, and took the place of many of the uniformly-enlarged villi of the mucous membrane. Finally, more or less hard scars or cicatrices formed, and incurable disease of the lids and cornea was the consequence.

But the most common allopathic treatment is by means of escharotics, of which Sulphate of Copper, Nitrate of Silver, Acetate of Lead, and Alum, are the most common. These remedies are, of course, more or less homœopathic to the disease, and, if used at all, should be used carefully and gently.

We have seen that the disease generally arises from preceding purulent, muco-purulent, or severe catarrhal ophthalmia; yet HAYES says, if Nitrate of Silver or dilute Nitric Acid be applied, the first effect of the application is to produce a puffiness of the lids with increased lachrymation, with some burning, which subside in a few hours, and a *purulent* discharge takes place. In some cases, the effects just mentioned become excessive, and persist for several days, arising either from the remedy having been too severely or frequently applied, or the wrong one being selected; and a change must consequently be made, either in the remedy, or the freedom of applying it. A very common error is the too frequent repetition of local applications.—HAYS. I have succeeded best with rather weak applications, applied not more than once a week, and then merely as adjuncts to proper internal treatment. If they be applied every two or three days, it will soon be found that a remedy, which at first seemed to have a most happy effect, will soon exert a most injurious one, and the patients will go on for weeks and months together, sometimes improving, sometimes relapsing, and altogether making a very unsatisfactory progress, until they become completely tired out, and cease to attend. The local application should not produce more than a slight smarting, when employed. If it causes pain of more than one minute's duration, it is too strong. It is rarely that an application which causes continued suffering effects any good. In the dominant school, these applications are generally used so much too strong, that TYRREL even thinks that in obstinate cases, the cure will be promoted by a frequent change of the local remedy; and he rarely allowed a patient to use one kind of local application more than four or five days continuously. He would have been much more successful, if he had only allowed them to be used once in four or five, or more days.

But, as the constitution sympathizes so largely with this local disorder, local treatment alone will not suffice. LAWRENCE says that he cannot adduce much personal experience in favor of escharotic treatment. WALTHER, from abundant experience, says that the benefit derived from them is, on the whole, inconsiderable, even when methodically and cautiously employed; they either do not effect a complete cure, or else bring it about very slowly. He is, indeed, often astounded when he sees one of the most delicate organs attacked with a series of applications so powerful and destructive as nitric acid, corrosive sublimate, and arsenic.

The methodical internal use of Aconite, Arsenicum, Baryta, Thuya, Sabina, &c., aided by the local application of a weak solution of the same remedies, and occasional resort to Argentum nitricum, Plumbum aceticum, Zincum sulph., &c., will generally suffice to effect a cure.

CHANGES OF THE SHAPE AND POSITION OF THE EYELIDS.

EVERSION, OR TURNING OVER OF THE LIDS.

(*Ectropium.*)

By the turning over, or outwards of the lids, they are necessarily drawn away from the eyeball, their conjunctival surface turned out, the edges of the lids and the lashes are displaced upwards or downwards, according as the upper or lower lid is the seat of *Ectropium.* The eyeball, being thus deprived of the protection of the eyelid, is exposed to constant irritation, by which a chronic conjunctivitis is kept up, weakening the eye, and leading to specks, ulcerations, and vascularity of the cornea. In some bad cases, repeated attacks of inflammation lead at last to destruction of the eyeball.—Wharton Jones. Still Ectropium is not only more rare, but generally much less severe in its effects than its opposite affection, *Entropium*, or turning in of the lids. In the former, the eyeball may suffer from want of necessary moisture, and from a distressing sensation of cold in the eye; the patient is annoyed with the flowing of the tears over the cheek, especially when the lower lid is affected, and is perpetually exposed to injury of the eye from inability of the lids to wipe off, and brush away flying particles of dust. The exposed surfaces of the mucous membrane of the lids are always irritated and congested, or inflamed, and this irritation always extends more or less to the ball of the eye; yet it is surprising how seldom such influences prove absolutely destructive to vision.—Haynes Walton.

Although it is generally supposed in the dominant school, that these affections of the lids can only be remedied by a more or less severe operation, still it would seem that a very large proportion of cases may be prevented or removed by appropriate medical treatment.

1. According to WHARTON JONES, the simplest and most common form of Ectropium is usually the result of some chronic inflammation of the conjunctiva, or of Ophthalmia tarsi; and it is almost always the *lower* lid which is the seat of this form of the disease. The skin of the eyelid and cheek becomes excoriated by the discharge constantly dropping from the eye, and finally becomes contracted, drawing the eyelid downwards and outwards. This displacement is also favored by a general relaxed state of the tarsus, and protrusion of the thickened and sarcomatous conjunctiva, the whole forming *Ectropium from excoriation and contraction of the skin of the eyelid, together with a thickened and sarcomatous state of the conjunctiva.* In old people, the thickened and sarcomatous state of the conjunctiva seem in W. JONES's opinion to operate more frequently in producing eversion of the lid, than does any appreciable amount of contraction of the skin.

Treatment.—W. JONES advises the occasional application of Nitrate of Silver; but the internal remedies for chronic catarrhal inflammation, especially of the angles of the lids, for relaxation of the tarsus, and for a thickened and sarcomatous state of the lids, should also be perseveringly used. Thuya deserves particular attention.

HAYNES WALTON, however, gives a rather different view of these cases; he says certain changes of thickness of the conjunctiva may alone evert the tarsus, while the edge of the lids, the lashes, and the glands all remain intact. In all such cases, which had come under his observation, irritating substances had been used for the conjunctival affections, and had, he believes, been the cause of the eversion of the lids. He refers to the case of a soldier, who had been discharged for some inflammatory affection of the eye, and who assured him, that when he left the army the lid had not turned out, but that the Ectropium had come on a few months after the regular application of Sulphate of Copper, three times a week for nine months, when he would no longer submit to it.

2. As has already been mentioned, one of the effects of cicatrization of abscesses in the substance of the eyelids, is also one of the most common causes of Ectropium. (See p. 5.)

According to Walton Haynes, the most frequent seat of this suppuration is the lower and outer point of the edge of the orbit; and it is most important in the treatment of these abscesses to manage them rightly, and open them early, so that as little of the cellular tissue of the lid may be lost by suppuration as possible; for the actual loss of skin from the presence of the abscess may be very slight, yet if much of the cellular tissue be destroyed, it will contract so much in healing, as to pull aside the skin and bind it down.

Treatment.—The operative proceedings are best given by Haynes Walton. (See Operative Ophthalmic Surgery, pp. 182–202.) Arsenicum, Thuya, and other remedies, will be required internally. The excoriation and consequent contraction of the skin may be palliated by the use of Glycerine, Sweet-oil and Lime-water, &c.

3. Acute Ectropium is apt to take place in *purulent ophthalmia,* in consequence of the great tumefaction of the conjunctiva of the lids. When the inflammatory œdema of the lids, which was for a time excessive, begins to subside, no proportionate diminution of the swelling of the mucous membrane may take place, and the swollen and granulated conjunctiva loses that counterpoise which the external swelling of the lid afforded it; finally, it is forced outwards by the action of the muscles of the lids. If the protrusion be not immediately returned, the upper point of the eyelid and retroverted cartilage will act like a ligature upon the parts protruded, and thus lead to still greater swelling; and as the swelling increases, the stricture will become still greater by the involuntary and spasmodic effort of the orbicularis muscle to bring the tarsus into its proper position.—Wharton Jones. The same author also says, that in the ophthalmia of new-born infants, eversion of the lids readily takes place when the child cries, or when the eyes are being washed and cleansed. The lids may be easily returned to their proper position, if the attempt be made at once; but, if they be left everted for any considerable time, the spasmodic efforts of the muscles, and the increased accumulation of blood

in the protruded mucous membrane, will render the return of the lids painful and difficult.

Treatment.—The remedies for inflammation and swelling of the mucous membrane of lids must be relied upon, viz., *Bellad.*, *Pulsat.*, *Euphrasia*, *Baryta muriatica*, *&c.*

According to HAYNES WALTON, another class of cases of *Ectropium* is the consequence or termination of disease of the lid itself, and occurs principally in the under lid, owing generally to inflammation of the eye, and almost always of a scrofulous kind. The white of the eye is first inflamed, and lachrymation follows with more or less intolerance of light; afterwards, the Meibomian glands are involved, and the entire edge of the lid becoming implicated, the eyelashes drop out, or become stunted, followed by that state generally called Lippitudo; and finally, eversion of the lid occurs. In this form, HAYNES says, there seems to be not only actual loss of substance of the lid in the rounding of the edge, but the cartilage and tarsal ligament shrink. This seems to him to receive corroboration in the circumstance, that in the Lippitudo which generally precedes the Ectropium, it is not uncommon to observe inability to close the lids, except with great effort. He thinks that one may venture to surmise that the inflammation which lingers so long about the lid may so far alter that portion of the orbicularis muscle on the edge of the lid, as to impair its supporting or binding influence. Again, it is generally supposed that the eversion of the lid is owing principally to the contraction of the skin, from the excoriating influence of the tears; but he regards roughness, and even excoriation of the skin, as a frequent consequence, not the cause of eversion; because both are common in lippitudo, where eversion is absent. The direction of the tarsus, too, somewhat indicates that it is not entirely influenced by the tension and contraction of the skin; for it is not so much pulled down or away from the eyeball as turned outwards. The bright, villous, puffy, and swollen condition of the conjunctiva of the lids he also regards as generally the result of its constant exposure, and cannot be the cause of the eversion, when, as is frequently the case, only a small portion of this membrane, and merely that which is permanently exposed, is so altered.

Ulcerations of the skin, however, namely, such as penetrate

the skin and sub-cutaneous cellular tissue sufficiently to produce a scar and great contraction of the cellular tissue, will doubtless be followed by eversion of the lid; but simple ulceration, which does not involve the whole depth of the true skin and some of the cellular tissue beneath, is not usually associated with Ectropium.

Treatment.—The debility of the orbicular muscle, caused by long-continued neighboring inflammation, may be removed by the patient internal and external use of Nux vomica, Ignatia, or Angustura; the disease and contraction of the cartilage, by Mezereum, Merc. corrosiv., or Staphysagria.

INVERSION, OR TURNING IN OF THE LIDS.

(ENTROPIUM.)

THIS is more injurious to the eye than *Ectropium*, as it is generally accompanied with great mechanical irritation, from the rubbing of the inverted lashes against the ball of the eye, which often produces severe inflammation, with ulceration and opacity of the cornea. The distress occasioned by the friction of the margin of the lid and the eyelashes against the ball, when an attempt is made to use the eye, together with the intolerance of light, which is usually present in a greater or less degree, forces the patient to keep the eye always closed or half-closed, and as much as possible at rest.

According to LAWRENCE, a temporary inversion, particularly of the lower lid, will sometimes occur in chronic, and some cases of acute ophthalmia; the edges of the lids are then drawn inwards by a spasmodic action of the orbicularis muscle, occasioning constant winking, particularly when attempts are made to use the eye; and while the contraction of this muscle forces the eyelid inwards, and retains it in its unnatural position, the swelling of the inflamed conjunctiva, between the ball and the lid, pushes the opposite margin of the tarsus outwards. If we draw the skin gently downwards, the lid will return to its natural position; but the patient will soon wink, and the orbicularis muscle will turn the lid in again.

Another variety occurs in aged persons. In them there is a relaxation of the integuments; the skin of the lids loses its elasticity, and falls into wrinkles; the fat is absorbed from the surrounding parts, and thus loose folds are formed in the lids; the balance between the external surface and the mucous lining of the lids is lost, and inversion is the consequence. (*Entropium Senile.*) The entire lid forms a round roll, with the eyelashes lying in its interior; but as the lashes and edge of the lid do not rub against the eye, there may be little or no irritation, and inversion may be present without the patient being aware of its existence.—LAWRENCE.

WHARTON JONES places great stress upon the combined influence of relaxation of the integuments of the eyelid, and spasmodic contraction of the orbicularis palpebrarum muscle, in the production of turning in of the eyelids. But as the relaxed and superabundant state of the skin of the lids is not insisted upon as the essential cause of the Entropium, while spasmodic contraction of the orbicularis muscle has been known to cause it, the principal part of the medical treatment should be directed to allaying the spasm. It might be possible to do good by applying to the lid some preparation of Plumbum, sufficiently strong to cause contraction of the integuments and paralysis of the muscle.

A *contracted* and deformed state of the tarsal cartilage is also put down as an efficient cause of Entropium, when it occurs in long-continued ophthalmia tarsi, or catarrhal-, or scrofulous conjunctivitis. The cartilage then often becomes indurated and contracted on its inner surface, whilst it is shortened transversely, or from angle to angle; the effect of which is, that the margin of the eyelid is turned in directly against the eyeball, and cannot be brought back to its proper position by any traction upon the skin of the lids, as in Entropium from relaxation. The edge of the eyelid remains curved inwards; the margin is often thickened and irregular; while the eyelashes are few and dwarfish, and also inverted; the whole forming a combination of Entropium with Trichiasis.—W. JONES.

HAYNES WALTON almost entirely denies the influence of any other causes, except excessive development and spasmodic contraction of the orbicularis and tensor tarsi muscles.

Treatment.—DR. DUDGEON has the credit of being the first to suggest a homœopathic remedy for the curable cases of Entropium. He suggests Borax, as applicable to some form of catarrhal and senile ophthalmia, particularly when accompanied by Entropium. It is homœopathic to itching of the inner canthus, so that the patient must rub it; itching of the eyes, with feeling as if sand were in them; rawness of the outer angle of the eye; burning in the eye; the lashes incline to *turn in* towards the eye, and inflame it, especially at the outer angle, where the edges of the lid are quite raw; inflammation of the outer angle of the right eye, with derangement of the lashes, and agglutination of the lids at night; inflammation of the edges and inner angle of the lids, with nocturnal agglutination, so that the eyes are glued up with hard gum, which irritates the eye like sand; sticking together of the lids; irritation of the eyes, and lachrymation.

The spasm of the orbicularis and tensor tarsi muscles may be allayed by the use of Nux, Ignatia, or Angustura; or, if these fail, by the external and internal use of Bellad., Stramon. or Conium.

CONSTANT OPEN STATE OF THE LIDS.

(LAGOPHTHALMOS.)

This barbarous name is given to a constant *open* state of the eyelids; the consequence of which is, that the eye is exposed to the entrance of foreign particles, and other causes of irritation, as in eversion of the lids. WHARTON JONES admits three principal forms:

1st. From paralysis of the orbicularis muscle, allowing unrestrained and excessive contraction of the levator musle of the lids.

2d. From shortening of the upper lid to such an extent as not to cover the ball of the eye properly; the consequence of cicatrization of wounds, ulcerations, and other causes.

3d. Congenital imperfect development of the lids.

In the first variety, the paralysis of the orbicularis is merely one of the symptoms of paralysis of the portio dura of the seventh pair of nerves. It may be so complete, that the upper eyelid is immovably drawn upwards; but generally it is not so complete, the eyelids being capable of closing somewhat, although not perfectly. While the upper eyelid is drawn upwards, the border of the lower lid falls down and somewhat out from the eyeball, and allows the tears to fall down upon the cheek. The most common removable causes of this paralysis is the pressure on the nerve by an enlarged lymphatic gland, or other tumor; or the paralysis may be rheumatic.

Treatment.—When an enlarged lymphatic gland is the cause of the disorder, Calcarea, Silex, Baryta, Kali hydriod., Conium, &c., may be used. When there is paralysis of the orbicularis muscle, Arsenicum, Plumbum, or Conium, and Bellad., or Stramon., are the most homœopathic remedies; although the internal and external use of Nux vom., Ignatia, or Angustura may be required.

FALLING DOWN OF THE UPPER EYELID.

(PTOSIS.)

This is the opposite of *Lagophthalmos*, as the upper lid, instead of being retracted upwards, falls down over the eye, and cannot be raised sufficiently to admit of free vision; the levator muscle is paralyzed, and allows the unrestrained and excessive contraction of the orbicularis. The patient can only open his eye by raising the lid with his finger. The third pair of nerves is involved, in the simple paralytic variety.

In other cases, ptosis may arise from injury of the levator muscle, in wounds of the upper eyelid. When but little of the substance of the muscle is destroyed or torn, the ptosis may disappear after the healing of the wound, from reünion of the muscle; but if the muscle be much torn, this will not be the case.—W. JONES.

It is also asserted, that extension and relaxation of the skin of the eyelid will allow the lid to fall down permanently, especially when the muscles have long been macerated in chronic œdema about the eye.

Treatment.—Arsenicum, Plumbum, Nux, Ignatia, and Angustura are the principal remedies.

ADHESION OF THE EYELIDS TO THE EYEBALL.

(SYMBLEPHARON.)

The most common accidental cause is the action of quick-lime or mortar upon the eye. H. WALTON says, he has twice watched the effects of quick-lime from the commencement, and, like every one else who has attempted it, totally failed in stopping the accustomed after-effects, viz., adhesion of the lids to the ball.

WALTON also suspects that in other cases, the prevalent treatment of ophthalmia in the dominant school by escharotics may sometimes play no unimportant part in producing these adhesions, knowing, as he does, that nitrate of silver is often used in substance, and in very strong solutions and ointments, in a most lavish manner; a practice which he has known to produce sloughing. He quotes DESMARRES, (who is fully alive to this abuse of caustic,) who says, he has been informed by DR. FURNARI, that during his stay in Africa, he had seen and operated on so large a number of symblepharons from that cause, that he was quite tired of them.

Severe purulent ophthalmia, or burns or scalds of the conjunctiva, may also be followed by loss of substance, sloughing, or ulceration, followed by adhesion.

Treatment.—This can only be preventive, or operative.

ADHESION OF THE EDGES OF THE LIDS.

(ANCHYLOBLEPHARON.)

This does not require particular description.

Treatment.—Principally preventive.

ENCROACHMENT OF THE SKIN OF THE NOSE UPON THE INTERNAL ANGLE OF THE EYE.

(EPICANTHUS.)

This can only be remedied by operation.

DISEASES OF THE EYEBALL.

A. DISEASES OF THE EXTERNAL COAT OF THE EYEBALL.

1. INJURIES.

a. Bruises of the conjunctiva, cornea, and sclerotica.

THE majority of slight injuries of the conjunctiva require the simplest treatment only.

Ecchymosis, or effusion of blood into the sub-mucous cellular tissue, may come on spontaneously, or be produced by violent efforts, such as coughing, especially in hooping-cough, or be the result of mechanical injuries to the part. The darkness of the color is so great that the patient is generally frightened when he sees it, and the appearance may puzzle any surgeon who is not familiar with it. The color of the effused blood is at first bright red, but gradually becomes of a deep brownish red; when it is deep-seated and abundant, it has a dark, liver color. It is well to know that the blood is often very slow in being absorbed, although it sometimes disappears in a week or two.

Treatment.—Millefolium, Hammemelis, and Chamomilla are the most important remedies.

b. Burns and Scalds.

These have been sufficiently alluded to under the head of Symblepharon, p. 42.

c. Wounds.

Of the conjunctiva.—These are generally not serious, unless very extensive, or in persons whose state of body is favorable to inflammation.

Of the cornea.—The effects of wounds or irritations of this organ are far more serious. LAWRENCE has seen considerable uneasiness follow a small and scarcely perceptible scratch from the finger-nail of an infant.

According to WHARTON JONES, when chips of fine metal, splinters of glass, stone, or hard wood, penetrate only so far into the cornea that a portion of the foreign body remains projecting, very great irritation ensues; but if the offending body has sunk fairly into the substance of the cornea, it may produce very little reäction; or it may become enveloped in a capsule of lymph, and cease to be a cause of irritation, although the affected part of the cornea will remain permanently opaque. More frequently, however, ulceration of the cornea takes place around the foreign body, which thus becomes loose at the bottom of the ulcer, and requires but a touch of some instrument to effect its detachment. The use of a cataract-needle, or -knife, is often required to remove particles of steel and the like, which are firmly lodged in the cornea; but the attempt at extraction should not be continued too long, for by-and-by they will become looser, and be more readily removed.

Injuries, or even slight scratches of the cornea, by means of the spurs of wheat or rye, such as often happen to reapers, or from chestnut-burrs, may lead to an abscess of the cornea, which may break into the anterior chamber of the eye, causing *hypopion*, or deposit of pus behind the cornea. This latter accident is particularly apt to occur if the injured person continues to work in the heat of the sun, and to eat and drink heartily. When such inflammation begins, a pink zone is first seen in the sclerotica, around the cornea; this redness becomes deeper and more extensive; the cornea loses its transparency, often becoming dull and turbid, and finally ulcerates around the foreign particle; the ulcer may break externally and the foreign particle drop out, or it may penetrate internally, and both matter and the foreign body may fall into the anterior chamber of the eye.

Injuries from wounds received from fire-arms and percussion-caps, whether exploded by means of a hammer, or by children's cannons and pistols, are a most frequent cause of blindness. In 939 cases of blindness, in children from 6 to 15 years of age, no less than 341 were caused by these dangerous playthings; while only 37 cases arose from accidents while playing ball, or with bows and arrows, &c.; and only 201 cases arose from inflammation of the eye, not excited by mechanical causes. It is well to know, that in some cases the fragment of a percussion-cap has been driven into the posterior chamber of the eye, while the wound in the cornea has healed so rapidly and perfectly, that the entrance of a foreign body into the depths of the eye has remained entirely unknown; but in the course of a few days or a month, violent inflammation may come on, and the cornea will become dim, especially at the previously-injured part.

Penetrating wounds of the cornea, are peculiarly mischievous from their allowing the aqueous humor to escape, and the iris to prolapse into the wound, and adhere there.—LAWRENCE.

Of the Sclerotica.—Wounds of this membrane are said not to be of much consequence in themselves, but they become important from the accompanying injury of the conjunctiva, but especially of the adjoining internal tunics of the eye. Still LAWRENCE has seen complete blindness caused by a single small shot which struck the sclerotica obliquely, and did not enter the eye; the state of the health of the patient at the time of the injury is, in the majority of such cases, a matter of more consequence than the extent, or manner of the injury.

It is peculiar to the sclerotica, that cutting wounds of this membrane do not unite; the opening remains permanent, and this is the case even in the punctured opening made in the operation for cataract. The sclerotica is also so much harder and more brittle than the conjunctiva, that a violent blow on the eye will sometimes burst it, without dividing the mucous membrane outside of it.

B. INFLAMMATION OF THE WHITE OF THE EYE.

Simple-, and Catarrhal-conjunctivitis.

This disorder is generally produced by exposure to cold, and although it is frequently a simple inflammation, still its seat in a mucous membrane impresses upon it all the peculiarities of a mucous, or so-called catarrhal-inflammation, which many suppose to be specific in its character. It certainly requires for its cure the remedies which act specifically upon the mucous membranes, yet it is difficult to conceive of a simple inflammation of a mucous membrane, which does not bear all the signs of a catarrhal inflammation.

According to DUDGEON, it is the most common of all the ophthalmiæ; is usually accompanied by catarrh of other parts, more especially of the nose; and it seldom penetrates deeper than the conjunctiva; therefore it is not generally dangerous. There are three stages:

1st. The *dry* stage, in which there is itching and stiffness of the lids, burning and heat in the ball of the eye, and sensation as if sand or dust had got into it; this proceeds from the dryness of the eye, owing to a deficient secretion of mucus. The white of the eye loses its usual bright and clear white appearance, and seems dim; the lids are somewhat red externally, slightly swollen, heavy and stiff; the white of the eye is more or less red.

In the 2d, or *sero-mucous* stage, there is a watering of the eye from increased secretion of tears, and excessive exudation of a thin sero-mucous discharge from the vessels of the conjunctiva; these secretions often possess a peculiar acridity, so as to produce scalding, and to corrode and inflame the cheek. In this stage, the peculiar redness of the eye, which is distinctive of conjunctival inflammation, becomes very violent; the redness is superficial, and of a bright scarlet color, forming a striking contrast to the rose or pink tint, which belongs to inflammation seated in the sclerotica. The enlarged and reddened bloodvessels in conjunctivitis also present characteristic peculiarities; they are quite superficial, and by pressing the lid against the ball of the eye, they will be found to be movable, or may be pushed in every direction, showing that they belong to the conjunctiva, and not to any deeper seated membrane; they also pursue a peculiarly tortuous course, subdividing and inosculating as they approach the cornea, presenting a marked contrast to the small, straight, pink, and rectilinear vessels of an inflamed sclerotica. The redness is generally irregular, or in patches, as some bundles of vessels are commonly more filled with red blood than others; numerous minute branches also shoot off from the main bundles, and freely join or anastomose with neighboring vessels, so that a beautiful web-like appearance is formed, through which parts of the sclerotica may be seen of its natural color, especially in the neighborhood of the cornea. But in the severer attack of the disease the whole white of the eye becomes uniformly red and swollen; and spots of extravasated blood may even be noticed here and there. Sometimes little vesicles or pustules are formed by the effusion of serous, or sero-mucous, or muco-purulent fluid under the conjunctiva, especially in the neighborhood of the cornea.

Catarrhal inflammation seldom produces much swelling of the conjunctiva, at least nothing like the state of chemosis, which occurs in erysipelatous inflammation, or purulent ophthalmia.

The pain is generally not great; the intolerance of light is often slight, so that the patient may be able to open his eye to the light, even when there is considerable redness. But when the neighboring mucous membranes are also involved, there may be pain and sense of weight about the frontal sinus and antrum, more or less catarrhal fever, chills, heat, headache, disordered stomach, foul tongue, and impaired appetite.

In the 3d, or *puro-mucous* stage, there is increased mucous secretion from the conjunctiva, often of a purulent appearance, so that the whole disorder may in some cases be scarcely distinguishable from mild purulent ophthalmia. Still, this increased mucous discharge is one of the principal characteristics of catarrhal ophthalmia, although the quantity may be just sufficient to collect in small masses at the corners of the eye, or form a whitish streak at the bottom of the fold of the conjunctiva of the lower lid; or there may be enough to form copious incrustations about the root of the lashes, to agglutinate the edges of the lids at night, and to form a more or less thick layer over the cornea, giving rise to so many imperfections and delusions of vision.

It may be complicated with scrofulous ophthalmia, or with rheumatic disease of the sclerotica.

Treatment.—Simple inflammation of the conjunctiva is generally very amenable to treatment, although ATTOMYR gives a long list of no less than twenty-nine different remedies, as useful against it. Of these, Aconite, Ammonium, Argenti nitras, Arsenicum, Belladonna, Borax, Bromine, Clematis, Mercurius, Phosphor, Pulsatilla, Staphysagria, Stramonium, Thuya, and Zinc, may be selected as most homœopathic to the *acute* varieties; while Alumina, Calcarea, Graphite, Hepar, Kali, Lycopod, Nux, Sepia, Silex, and Sulphur may be more appropriate against the *sub-acute*, chronic, and obstinate cases.

DUDGEON says, when the affection is recent, in the first stage, and the chief symptoms are: dryness, itching or smarting sensation in the eyes and lids, feeling as if something had got into the eye, frequent winking and occasional discharge of tears, the white of the eye being uniformly or partially reddened, little or no mucus secreted, and the conjunctiva of the lids is comparatively redder than the ball, then a dose or two of *Sulphur* in almost any dilution, usually suffices to effect a rapid cure.

When there is an excessively annoying, dry, and burning feeling in the eye, with frontal headache, and more or less congestion to the head, *Belladonna* will be useful, although it may have to be preceded, or alternated with Aconite.

If the flow of tears is considerable, and of an acrid character, with a corresponding watery discharge from the nose, attended with sneezing and other indications of the first stage of catarrh of the nose, *Euphrasia* will be the best remedy.

If along with a copious flow of tears, there is much smarting and burning pain, the tears being peculiarly acrid and corrosive, or if there is much swelling of the conjunctiva of the ball, (*chemosis*,) or an œdematous condition of the lids, then *Arsenicum* will be found useful.

If there be much mucous discharge, or extravasation of blood (*ecchymosis*) into the substance, or from the surface of the white of the eye, *Chamomilla* should be borne in mind.

When the inflammation is intense, the mucous secretion excessive, the redness of the eye considerable, and the caruncula particularly inflamed and enlarged, the internal and external use of *Argentum nitricum* will prove specific.

When the Meibomian glands are much affected, and the edges of the lids are red and swollen, the secretion forming deep yellow crusts upon the eyelashes at night, *Mercurius* and *Hepar s.* may be given with advantage.

When the evening exacerbations, which are usually present, are well marked, *Pulsatilla* will be found useful.

In slight catarrhal ophthalmias from exposure to cold and wet, *Dulcamara* is regarded as specific.

These, DUDGEON says, are the chief remedies for simple acute catarrhal ophthalmia, and will generally be found sufficient to meet all its varieties. Still KNORRE found Digitalis useful when the eye-disease occurred after the sudden suppression of coryza; and Kali bichrom. should not be forgotten.

In the CHRONIC forms, when the secreting apparatus of the lids is much involved, Mercurius, Hepar, Euphrasia, Arsenicum, Pulsat. and Sulphur, are chiefly to be trusted to. Where the caruncula and general conjunctiva are the seat of the chronic mucous affection, Argent. nitric., Lycopod., Zinc., Rhus, and Bryonia may be called in play. When there is a tendency to the formation of pustules, vesicles, or indolent ulceration, Euphrasia, Arsenicum, Sulph., Colc., Mercurius, and Silex may be indicated. The sensitiveness to light (*photophobia*) accompanying pure catarrhal ophthalmia, is seldom important, but when it exists to any degree, and fails to yield to the other remedies, Conium and Belladonna will almost certainly bring relief.—DUDGEON.

To those who are practically familiar with the above mode of treatment, especially if associated with the local application of a weak solution of Sulphate of Zinc, or Nitrate of Silver, it will be a matter of surprise, that the blood-letting, cupping, leeching, purging, low diet, blisters, recommended by LAWRENCE and all the writers of the dominant school, should ever have been considered necessary, even in the dark ages, much less at the present time. Still it may be, that many homœopathic physicians overlook the attendant functional derangements of the liver, stomach, skin, or uterus, upon which TYRREL places so much stress; or neglect to remove those peculiar conditions of irritability or debility, which render so many cases intractable.—PETERS.

INFLAMMATION OF THE SCLEROTICA.

SCLEROTITIS.

Rheumatic Ophthalmia.

THE sclerotic coat of the eye is that which is immediately under the mucous, or outer coat, or the so-called white of the eye; inflammation of the sclerotica is generally a much more painful and troublesome affection than inflammation of the white of the eye, or conjunctivitis; it also extends much more readily and frequently to the cornea and iris, and sometimes from thence to the internal structure of the eye.

According to LAWRENCE, the symptoms of sclerotitis are redness of the eye, pain, intolerance of light, increased flow of tears, and more or less fever. The redness of the eye in sclerotitis is quite peculiar:

1st. There is a red, or pink zone, or circle immediately around the cornea.

2d. The red and distended blood-vessels pursue an almost straight course from the edge of the cornea outwards in all directions towards the circumference of the eye, while, in conjunctivitis, the redness commences in the circumference of the eye, and diminishes the nearer it approaches to the cornea; while the enlarged blood-vessels pursue a remarkably tortuous course.

3d. The character of the red tint differs remarkably in the two cases, being of a rose-red, or pink, or almost violet hue, forming a striking contrast to the bright scarlet-color which is peculiar to conjunctival inflammation.

In severe cases, however, the conjunctiva soon participates in the affection; the cornea quickly assumes a dull appearance, and loses its transparency and polish; the iris is also apt to become involved in the attack.

The pain is often very severe, and extends to the back of the orbit of the eye, to the neighboring parts, and more or less to the corresponding side of the head. Not unfrequently the eye itself is comparatively easy, and the patient complains of pain in the brow, temples, cheek, or side of the nose. Often the suffering increases towards night, and becomes so much aggravated as to prevent sleep, and only abates considerably towards morning. The pains are also worse in cold, windy, and wet weather, and relieved by a mild and warm temperature of the air, although warm applications to the eye increase them. Intolerance of light is also a marked symptom from the commencement; the pupil contracts to exclude the light, and the patient avoids exposure to it; this also forms another striking contrast between sclerotitis and conjunctivitis; for, in the latter the patient generally opens the eye freely, and experiences no pain from exposure to light.

Sclerotitis may arise indirectly from unhealthy states of the system, but most frequently it is rheumatic in its nature, and is caused by exposure to cold.—LAWRENCE.

Treatment.—According to HARTMANN, in the commencement of the disease, if the inflammation be slight, *Pulsatilla* will remove the pain, and the accompanying inflammation of the conjunctiva, while Bryona will remove the inflammation. In severe cases, *Mercurius* will be required; while *Clematis erecta* is pronounced the most suitable remedy when there is pressure in the eyes, intolerance of light, profuse flow of tears, sticking together of the eyelids in the morning, and a decided tendency to inflammation of the Iris. *Euphrasia* is thought to be the most useful remedy, when the pains in the eye have become intolerable, and the inflammation has extended to the cornea, with severe hemicrania.

INFLAMMATION OF THE CORNEA.

CORNEITIS.

ACCORDING to LAWRENCE, inflammation of the cornea may be either acute, or chronic; but its course and character are most frequently of the latter description; in general, the appearances commence gradually and proceed slowly, and hence the uneasiness is greater than the mere degree of visible change would lead us to expect; for the same reason, the recovery is tedious.

The complaint begins with dullness of vision, the cornea being at the same time hazy; it loses its transparency and exhibits a general cloudiness, with increasing imperfection of sight, objects appearing as if seen through a cloud or mist. This nebulous condition of the cornea may be general, or partial; in the latter case, it is continued insensibly into the healthy structure. The cornea may be generally of a dull gray color, or like ground-glass; it may exhibit the various degrees of haziness, or opacity so dense as to conceal the iris and pupil.

Frequently, small vesicles or pustules form on the surface of the cornea; occasionally pus or matter is deposited into the substance, or between the layers of the cornea, and may break into the anterior chamber of the eye, forming *hypopion*, or may accumulate at the lower edge of the cornea, producing an appearance which has been called *onyx*, or *unguis*, from its resemblance to the white mark at the root of the nails. Sloughing of the cornea rarely occurs except in the purulent ophthalmia of new-born infants, and in gonorrhœal ophthalmia, or when the inflammation is very acute and excessive, or happens in persons with great general debility, and reduced local action.

Considerable pain and sense of tightness in the eye, and pain in the brow, or forehead, often accompany the affection, especially in its early stages, in which we also find the tongue coated, and the system feverish. There is increased sensibility to light, which is the more remarkable, as the dimness of the cornea must diminish the quantity admitted into the eye; but it must be remembered that the sclerotica is generally involved in the inflammation, and that intolerance of light usually occurs when that membrane suffers. Inflammation of the cornea is often of long duration, continuing for many months; or, after going through an acute stage with pain and feverishness, it assumes a more indolent character, and is protracted indefinitely; the disease lasts, but the patient does not suffer. It may be produced by cold and wet, but especially by external injuries, although it is common enough as a spontaneous affection in persons of unhealthy constitution, especially the scrofulous.—LAWRENCE.

The Iris is generally involved to a greater or less degree, and is often followed by contraction of the pupil, effusion of lymph, and consequent permanent adhesion of its margin to the capsule of the lens.

Treatment.—Euphrasia, Hepar sulph., Iodine, Baryta, Mercurius, and Spigelia have been recommended.

Having thus made some general and cursory remarks upon the various diseases of the external parts of the eye, I now proceed in accordance with RUCKERT'S plan, to treat more particularly of the action of the different remedies for some of these states.

1. ACONITE.

General Remarks.—IT is regarded in the dominant school as an arterial sedative, and anæsthetic remedy, yet FLEMING found 10 drops of the tincture of the root to cause general trembling, violent headache, pain in the eyeballs, constant lachrymation, and intense photophobia, although the white of the eye was not at all reddened. He also says that slight giddiness and dimness of vision are very common effects of Aconite, and that it may cause dull, heavy pains in the eyeballs, dimness of vision, profuse secretion of tears, pain and watering of the eyes without redness of them, black specks floating in the field of vision, dazzling, and dimness of vision.

Claudius Richard had a case, in which it proved homœopathic to such a frightful and painful inflammation of the eyes, with lachrymation, that the patient wished himself dead rather than to be obliged to endure such agony long.

Dudgeon supposes that the above case resembled an attack of purulent ophthalmia, but I can find no proof to that effect; besides, Aconite acts far more specifically upon the serous and fibrous tissues than upon the mucous, and is much more homœopathic to rheumatic inflammation than to purulent, or suppurative. This is a very important point, as Dudgeon has been led to recommend it as homœopathic to purulent, Egyptian, and gonorrhœal ophthalmia. It probably exerts a more specific action on the Sclerotica, Cornea, and Iris, than upon other parts of the eye, except perhaps the Retina; the severe pains, intolerance of light and lachrymation, with but slight redness of the eye, point rather to irritation or inflammation of the sclerotica and cornea, than of the conjunctiva.

Its action upon the *Iris* is equally decided and peculiar. Flemming says, when the conjunctiva is slightly painted with Aconitine, *contraction* of the pupil speedily takes place, and continues for several hours. Pereira has observed it to cause *contraction* of the pupil in some amaurotic cases of several years standing, and in which the iris was insensible to, and underwent no change on exposure to strong light. Flemming also applied *Aconitine* to the eyeball of a rabbit; the pupil commenced to *contract* in three minutes; in five minutes it was scarcely one sixth the size of that of the other eye; when the contraction was at its extreme, the pupil was insensible to light; at other times it retained some of its mobility; this contraction of the pupil persisted for nine hours. It will be seen, that its action upon the iris is opposite to that of Bellad. and Stram.; it may prove homœopathic and curative to the contraction of the pupil which attends Iritis; to headaches, congestions, inflammations, and dropsy of the brain, and apoplexy when attended with contraction of the pupil.

FLEMING says, that its sympathetic action on the *retina* is remarkable; for, when applied to one of the temples, or one side of the forehead, more or less blindness of the same side will be produced; it is apt to cause giddiness with confusion of sight; headache, with vertigo and dimness of vision; in four cases FLEMING found it homœopathic to almost total blindness from paralysis of the Retina, or Iris. In one of MATTHIOLUS' cases it proved homœopathic to intermitting amaurosis; three times the patient became perfectly blind, and recovered his sight.—PETERS.

b. NOACK advises it in catarrhal ophthalmias only when they also bear a rheumatic character, especially when chemosis,—that is, great redness and swelling around the cornea—has taken place; when there is heat and burning in the eye, especially in the left, great photophobia, inflammation and lachrymation of the eyes, with excessively severe pain; swelling and inflammation of the eyes, with redness of the conjunctiva and sclerotica; in inflammations excited by the presence of a foreign body in the eye, attended with redness, stinging pain and aching in every part of the eye, intolerance of light, and lachrymation; dryness of the eyes and heaviness of the upper lids; painful, tense, red, and hard swelling of the lids, especially in the morning; sensation as if the whole eyeball were pushed into the orbit; prickling and smarting of the eyelids, as if a cold were about to set in; soreness and itching of the eyelids; yellowness of the whites of the eyes; sparks and mist before the eyes, with flashes and scintillations; luminous vibrations, and tremulousness of light.—PETERS.

c. According to HAFF, Aconite is a useful remedy against inflammation of the eyes, excited by mechanical injuries; it is most beneficial in the early stages, although it may be used at a later period, especially if severe pain and intolerance of light are present.—Archiv., vol. viii., part 8, p. 185.

d. HERING recommends it when the eyelids are red, inflamed, swollen, and hard, attended with burning, heat, and dryness of the eyes; it may then be given in repeated doses; and also when the lids are yellowish-red, swollen, or of a shining red, and almost transparent, attended with burning and tension, and with secretion of much mucus from the eyes and nose.

e. GROSS says, that Aconite, 30, if used early, will frequently break up attacks of Ophth. neant.—Archiv., vol. x., part 2, p. 63.

CASE 9.—A coachman, aged 45, addicted to brandy-drinking, had had severe catarrhal ophthalmia for 7 days; the lids, especially the upper ones of both eyes, were much swollen, red, hot, and painful; profuse secretion and discharge of purulent mucus from the eyes, with lachrymation. The white of the eye was much swollen, reddened, and formed a soft wall round the cornea—chemosis; the cornea of the right eye was clear and sound, while that of the left eye was dull and gray, with a small, flat, roundish ulcer. There was great intolerance of light, constant flow of tears, continual tearing and shooting pains in and about the eye, so much aggravated at night as to render sleep impossible. There was the sensation as if the eyeball was swollen and enlarged, and would come out of the socket. The sight of the left eye was imperfect and dim; there was constant confusion in the head, and fever in the evening.

Treatment and Result.—Aconite 12, every two hours for two days, and then the 15th dilution was used; after the second night the patient could sleep comfortably; in five days he could open his eyes himself, as the swelling of the lids, inflammation of the white of the eye, the purulent secretion, and intolerance of light were much lessened; on the tenth day, he was comparatively well, although the ulcer still required the use of Tinct. Sulph.—*Gen. Hom. Journal.* Vol. 19. DR. KNORRE.

CASE 10.—A woman, aged 28, suffered with a similar, but still more severe attack of inflammation of the eye.

Treatment.—Aconite 3, was given in two-drop doses, every two hours, and two drops of Tinct. Sulph. every evening; the cure was perfected in 7 days.—*Ibid.* DR. KNORRE.

2. ALUMINA.

General Remarks.—Dr. DUDGEON has recommended this remedy in *Ophthalmia senilis*, which is a chronic inflammation of the conjunctiva of the eyes and lids, in which the angles and edges are also much involved. It is most indicated when there is a burning, prickling, smarting pain, as if from an acrid substance in the angles of the lids; violent itching in the eyes, canthi, (angles,) and lids; smarting as if from soap in the eyes, and burning, with increased mucous secretion and itching, redness of the eyes, with rawness in the angles, and weakness of sight; in the evening he sees a halo around the candle, and must often wipe his eyes, which become glued together at night; redness of the right eye, with raw feeling and lachrymation; inflammation of the white of the right eye, without much pain; falling out of the eyelashes; weakness of the lids; they are disposed to droop, without the patient being sleepy; partial paralysis of the upper lid, (ptosis;) it hangs down and half covers the eye; lachrymation and increased secretion of mucous fluid; nocturnal agglutination of the lids, persisting for several weeks, and attended with diurnal conjunctivitis, and increased mucous secretion.—*Brit. Journ. Hom.* Vol. 6, p. 217.

b. I have often used a weak solution of Sulphate of Alumina in chronic catarrhal affections of the lids, with very great benefit; the local, combined with the internal application of specific remedies, often proves far more efficacious than the internal use alone.—PETERS.

3. AMMONIUM.

General Remarks.—ATTOMYR recommends this remedy in inflammations of the conjunctiva, especially when the conjunctiva of the *cornea* is particularly involved, and vascularity of the cornea is present; if the irritation of the eye be very great, it may be assisted with Tabacum, used internally, in small doses.—PETERS.

4. ANTIMONIUM TARTARICUM.

General Remarks.—DUDGEON says that it has been recommended in rheumatic ophthalmia, while the known anti-rheumatic virtues of this drug are a further confirmation of the propriety of using it in such cases. I have always regarded Antimony as a remedy peculiarly apt to excite suppuration and purulent inflammation, and have used it with much success, both internally and externally, in the several forms of catarrhal, muco-purulent, and purulent inflammations of the eyes. DUDGEON also hints that it may prove homœopathic to gouty ophthalmia, as it causes burning and smarting of the eyes, with redness of the conjunctiva, especially in the evening; redness and inflammation of the eyes, with swelling of them, and distention of the *ciliary* vessels. It ought to prove homœopathic and specific against *Pustular* ophthalmia.—PETERS.

5. ARGENTUM NITRICUM.

General Remarks.—Dr. DUDGEON, after quoting the effects of Nitrate of Silver upon the eye, observed by Dr. MÜLLER, of Vienna, from small doses taken internally, remarks: "The symptoms of Nitrate of Silver, which we owe to the industry of Dr. MÜLLER, are the more valuable, as they were not produced by the *local* action of the drug upon the eye, but by its action when taken internally in small doses, (from the 2d to the 30th dilution;) they afford a remarkable corroboration of the long credited specific action of *Silver* upon the eye, and, he believes, prove the employment of eye-washes containing lunar caustic to be efficacious in virtue of their homœopathic action. They teach us, moreover, that in Nitrate of Silver we possess a remedy of remarkable powers in some very important and dangerous inflammations of the eye; a remedy, which, to judge *à priori*, is second to none in affections of the mucous membrane of the eye, especially in those of a hœmorrhagic character; *à posteriori*, we have ample proof of its efficacy from the records and experience of the old school. It may be objected that the Allopathic cures were effected by the local application of solutions of lunar caustic to the eye, and that they were owing to the general stimulant, astringent or corrosive properties of the drug, and that the quantity used was such as to be quite opposed to the notion of a homœopathic specific action. To this DUDGEON says, he may reply that the stimulant or astringent properties of a solution of lunar caustic dropped into the eye, are insignificant with those of many other substances that have little effect in inflammatory diseases of the eye; one obvious reason of this being, that the instant the solution comes in contact with the secretions of the eye, it is decomposed, and an inert chloride of silver is formed, which is speedily washed away by the gush of tears which ensues; thus the action of the caustic is but momentary, and *the quantity infinitesimal.* DUDGEON also says that he must be allowed to say a few words respecting the use and utility of local applications in eye-diseases: "Many eye-diseases are of a strictly *local* character, attended by no constitutional symptoms whatever; whilst others again are eminently dependent on the constitution of the patient. It is obvious, then, that though it would be vain to attempt the cure of constitutional eye-diseases by local remedies, there is no absurdity in treating a purely local disease by *local* means." He would have no hesitation in employing the appropriate remedy locally; experience has shown the advantage of using a solution of Arnica in cases of wounds and bruises of the eye; and he doubts not, that other remedies may be applied *locally* with advantage. For his own part, his experience of the *local* employment of Nitrate of Silver, especially in Ophth. neonatorum, and the severer kinds of catarrhal ophthalmia, has been so striking, that he would be very sorry to dispense with this remedial means in these and other diseases. The solution which he has been in the habit of employing contained from 2 to 4 grains of the nitrate to an ounce of distilled water, and should be carefully introduced beneath the eyelids with a camel's hair pencil, once every two, three, or four days, according to the severity of the symptoms.—*Brit. Journ. Hom.* Vol. 6, p. 218.

b. LAWRENCE gives the credit to MR. MELIN for being the first to use nitrate of silver, locally, in diseases of the eye; he was led to adopt this mode of treatment in ordinary conjunctival inflammation, because he was unwilling to treat the disease as actively as was the common practice in the dominant school, and because he could not believe that a mere local disorder could require such extensive depletion and depression, as was usually practiced and recommended. He used 4 grains to the ounce, applied twice a day; it excited pain and a sensation of roughness, with an increased flow of tears, for about 20 minutes, after which the eyes felt much relieved, and in a few days the cure was effected. Since that period, up to 1840, he had treated nearly 300 cases of acute ophthalmia, some of them of a severe nature, in a similar manner, without either local or general bleeding, and thus has had ample opportunities of proving its efficacy.

CASE 11.—A male infant, aged 14 days, had suffered since its birth with severe inflammation and swelling of the eyes, with profuse muco-purulent discharge, (oph. neonatorum.)

Treatment.—Argent. nit. 6 was given internally, and a solution of one grain to the ounce of distilled water was applied twice a day; a cure was effected in 7 days. Similar happy results were witnessed in many other cases.—*Brit. Journ. Hom.* DR. DUDGEON.

CASE 12.—A girl, aged 7, had measles, 3 weeks before, and inflammation of the white of the left eye for 2 days, with profuse flow of tears, great intolerance of light, discharge from the nose, and constipation.

Treatment.—Bellad. 3 was given twice a day, and on the 6th day, the eye was much worse, there was great pain, with fever; Acon. 3 was given 3 times a day, and soon removed the pain and fever, but the inflammation of the eye persisted with more or less intensity, for 7 weeks, notwithstanding the use of Puls. Euphrasia, Arsenicum, Sulphur, Nux., Acon., and Calcarea, and even attacked the other eye; the pain was often violent and the intolerance of light was often excessive during the day, although it lessened towards night. DUDGEON now resolved to try the *Silver*, but as he had no dilutions of the Nitrate, he administered Argent. met. 6, in solution, a spoonful every night for a week; this completely and permanently removed a very troublesome inflammation, without the necessity for any local application.—*Brit. Jour. Hom.* Vol. 6, p. 220. DR. DUDGEON.

6. ARNICA.

General Remarks.—This remedy has long been supposed to possess the power of promoting the absorption of extravasated blood, such as occurs from injuries, bruises, or rupture of blood-vessels. SOBERNHEIM asserts that it facilitates the circulation of the lymph, and increases the absorbent powers of the whole lymphatic and venous systems, and thinks that this conjecture will account for its well-known efficacy in extravasations of blood induced by mechanical injuries, such as falls, blows, concussions, and rupture of blood-vessels. But there is another side to this picture; the same author says, that in consequence of its acrid properties, it may cause congestion of blood towards internal parts, such as the heart, chest, and head, causing palpitation, headache, pain in the chest, and difficulty of breathing; its acrid action upon the skin and kidneys may even go so far as to produce extravasations of blood from both these parts. RICHTER says that one of its most marked actions is upon the activities of the skin, whose functions it may arouse from the deepest torpor; and the breaking out of perspiration, which, at times, is of a *reddish* color, on the chest, is one of its most common and constant effects.—PETERS.

b. DUDGEON says, besides the obvious use of Arnica in wounds, bruises, and traumatic inflammations of the eye, some of its effects would indicate that it might prove useful in rheumatic inflammation of the eye. He also adds, that we are more indebted to experience and analogy for its use in traumatic affections of the eye, than we are to any aid which we receive from the record of its pathogenetic effects upon this part. He also says that the local application of a weak solution of Arnica is advisable in some cases of recent traumatic ophthalmia, but care must be taken that it be not too strong; five or six drops of the tincture, in an ounce of distilled water, will suffice.—*Brit. Jour. Hom.* Vol. 3, p. 220.

CASE 13.—A man injured his eye, 15 days before, with the spur of an ear of grain; there was an ulcer, of the size of lentil, on the cornea, and the white of the eye was much inflamed and reddened.

Treatment.—Arnica water was applied externally; and 1 drop of the tinct. was given, internally, twice a day. A cure was effected in 7 days.—*Gen. Hom. Jour.* Vol. 3, p. 78. TURREL.

CASE 14.—A man aged 30, received a violent blow on the right eye thirteen days ago; the eye was violently inflamed; the cornea was dim, and marked by a small whitish-gray spot; the sclerotica was covered with a net of red vessels; there was lachrymation and intolerance of light.

Treatment.—10 drops of Tinct. Arnica in water, was applied externally from time to time, and effected a complete cure.—*Archiv.* Vol. 19, pp. 3, 163. Dr. TIETZE.

CASE 15.—A lad, aged 18, received a violent kick from a horse upon the right eye, followed by considerable inflammation and swelling of the lids, inflammation of the white of the eye, lachrymation, and violent pains.

Treatment.—Arnica 6. In the course of six days all the symptoms were improved, except the profuse flow of tears and the pains in the eyes, which were relieved by Euphrasia.—*Archiv.* Vol. 5. pp. 3, 24. Dr. BAUDIS.

CASE 16.—The following case from allopathic practice, DUD-

GEON thinks will prove the efficacy of Arnica in rheumatic inflammation of the eye. A robust man, aged 50, caught cold, and on the following day there was considerable lachrymation, shooting and tearing pains in both eyes, and in the surrounding parts, increased in bed and by warmth. The next day the white of the eye was much reddened; there was intolerance of light, and all the symptoms of a violent rheumatic fever.

Treatment. The patient was kept in a dark room, was bled, leeched, purged, and sweated, all in vain; the disease increased, the pains, lachrymation, and intolerance of light grew worse, and finally the eye-ball resembled a piece of red flesh. For a fortnight more, anti-rheumatic and derivative remedies were used, and even Corrosive Sublimate was used internally and externally without effect; finally an infusion of Arnica-flowers was given (from 1 to 1½ drachms in 6 ounces of water, one half to be taken night and morning for three days, then omitted for two days, and resumed again;) in seven days the inflammation and intolerance of light were much diminished, and soon entirely removed.—*Brit. Jour. Hom.* Vol. 6, p. 221. Dr. RHUMMEL.

7. ARSENICUM.

General Remarks.—CHRISTISON says that in persons under the influence of this drug, the conjunctiva is often so injected as to seem inflamed; the eyes are apt to be red and sparkling; giddiness and intolerance of light may occur; and the eyes become bloodshot, attended with burning pains. WOOD and BACHE say that it is homœopathic to œdema, especially of the face and eyelids, attended with a feeling of stiffness of these parts, and a livid circle about the eyes. HUNT says if the use of Arsenicum be continued in small doses for a few days, or possibly weeks, a pricking sensation will be felt in the tarsi, and the white of the eye will become slightly inflamed, and that a slight degree of conjunctivitis in forty-nine cases out of fifty, takes precedence of the more grave affections which indicate an over-dose. In one case, HUNT gave five-drop doses of Fowler's solution, three times a day, for thirty-five days, when a conjunctivitis set in, which lasted for seven weeks. In a second case, the same doses caused tenderness of the tarsi, but no redness, in the course of five days; in fifteen days, the conjunctiva of both eyes was slightly and partially inflamed; in five days more, the eyelids became stiff and itchy, with increased stiffness and pricking every evening. In a third case, the white of the eye became inflamed, and the eyelids puffy, in a fortnight. In a fourth case, the eyes became exceedingly weak in fourteen days; the lower lids were puffed and swollen, the conjunctiva reddened, and the eyes watery, so that the tears were always ready to flow. In a fifth case, the conjunctiva became inflamed in twenty-six days; the lower eyelids swollen and puffy, the eyes itched and were weak; the conjunctiva was much inflamed, with severe pain in the orbit. In a sixth case, the whites became slightly inflamed and the eyes weak, at the end of eighteen days. In a seventh case, from five drops, three times a day, the patient complained at the end of three days, of excessive weakness of the eyes, sensations of smarting, itching, and pricking in the eyelids, and of a copious secretion of tears; in seven days more, from two and a half drops, three times a day, decided conjunctivitis ensued; from one drop, three times a day, for five days more, the conjunctivitis did not improve, but rather grew worse; even from half-drop doses, the conjunctivitis remained very troublesome; dimness of sight set in, and the left eye became so singularly affected, that the patient could only see half of an object with it. In an eighth case, five drops, three times a day, for three weeks, rendered the conjunctiva very red, sore, and injected; at the end of six weeks, the conjunctiva still remained inflamed, and the lids tumefied. Judging from a few other facts, and from those afforded by the ninth case, it would seem that Arsenicum acts more decidedly and injuriously upon the left eye; after taking it for some weeks, both eyes became inflamed; then the right eye became better, but the *left* one remained considerably inflamed; in two weeks more, the medicine being continued, both eyes again became inflamed and painful; but the right eye, though somewhat inflamed, looked more natural than the left; finally, both eyes became inflamed, attended with a copious fluid discharge from the nose.—*Hunt on Diseases of Skin.*

b. DUDGEON says that Arsenicum exerts a most extensive action upon the eyes; the conjunctiva is not alone the seat of its action, but the sclerotica and choroid membranes also. It is homœopathic to some stages or varieties of catarrhal, scrofulous, rheumatic, arthritic, and scorbutic ophthalmia; also in some stages of Egyptian and gonorrhœal, and more especially when the pains are extremely violent and burning, and the secretions of an acrid, serous nature. An intermittent character of the symptoms is another indication for its use. He has also found it very useful in exanthematic ophthalmia, in that following measles, especially when the lachrymation is excessive, and the tears produce corrosion of the cheek, and doubts not that it will be found equally serviceable in some cases occurring during, or after scarlet fever, or varioloid. It seems to him to be the only remedy from which we may expect any advantage in the ophthalmia from uterine phlebitis. From its producing swelling of the eyes and a beating like that of a pulse in the eyes, each throb being attended with a stitch; and from its well-known specific influence upon the hœmorrhoidal vessels, and the typical character of some of its effects, it would seem that it must prove homœopathic and useful against hœmorrhoidal- and menstrual-ophthalmia.—*Brit. Journ. Hom.* Vol. 6, p. 318.

c. According to GROSS, it is almost the only reliable remedy in obstinate inflammations of the eye, occurring in connection with influenza, and attended with ulcerations of the cornea, and very annoying intolerance of light.—*Archiv.* Vol. 13. part 2. p. 96.

d. HERING recommends it when the lids are only inflamed on their internal side; are red, painful, burning; and the eyes can scarcely be opened.

CASE 17.—A maiden, aged 14, of delicate constitution, and who had suffered for 48 hours with a violent inflammation of the conjunctiva, was cured by Arsen. 24, in 12 hours.—*Archiv.* Vol. 8, p. 2, p. 75. AG.

CASE 18.—A man of athletic frame, and bilious, sanguine temperament, had suffered, for 6 days, with a violent and painful inflammation of the white of the eye, with simultaneous internal ophthalmia; he had already been bled and leeched without benefit; then received Puls. 6 with some relief; but Arsen. 12, 2 drops in water, taken in the course of 7 hours, improved the case decidedly; the cure was then perfected by Puls. and Euphrasia.—*Gen. Hom. Jour.* Vol. 34, p. 76. BECHET.

CASE 19.—A maiden, aged 22, who had frequently suffered

with erysipelas, had had inflammation of the conjunctiva, with swelling of the lids for 8 days.

Treatment.—Arsen. 800, in solution, every 2 hours, cured her in 48 hours.—*Gen. Hom. Jour.* Vol. 36, p. 148. DR. SCHELLING.

CASE 20.—A servant-girl was attacked with inflammation of the eyes, after taking cold, and had suffered for several weeks with inflammation of the conjunctiva and sclerotica, attended with great intolerance of light.

Treatment.—Allopathic treatment had been tried without avail; and Bellad. did not afford any relief; but Arsen. 30 effected a cure in a few days.—*Archiv.* Vol. 12, part 3, p. 11. DR. HERMANN.

CASE 21.—A man, aged 28, of delicate, weakly, and cachectic habit, had suffered for 14 days with a typically recurring inflammation of the eye.

Treatment.—Acon. and Bell. were given without effect; Arsen. 30 effected a cure within three days.—*Archiv.* Vol. 18, part 2, p. 43. DR. STAPF.

CASE 22.—A delicate and slender woman, aged 32, had suffered for some time with an inflammation of the white of the eye, which recurred, regularly, every afternoon at 4 o'clock.

Treatment.—Arsenicum 30, a dose every night and morning, soon effected a cure.—*Quarterly Jour.* Vol. 1, part 2, p. 257. DR. LORBACHER.

CASE 23.—A violent inflammation of the eye, with effusion of pus in the anterior chamber, was considerably relieved by Rhus; but a relapse occurred from imprudence in diet, attended with aggravation of all the symptoms, and the addition of congestion to the head, bleeding of the nose, constipation, anxiety, restlessness, and despondency.

Treatment.—Arsenicum 4 was given every 3 hours, and the whole disorder was gradually removed in 14 days, the gradual absorption of the pus going on all that time. Euphrasia was applied externally.

CASE 24.—A woman, aged 54, had suffered with catarrh of the head for 5 weeks, and with inflammation of the eye for 8 days, attended with swelling of the lids, redness of the, sclerotica and pain in the eye-balls.

Treatment.—Arsen. 6, 1 drop every night and morning,

effected a cure in 5 days.—*Gen. Hom. Jour.* Vol. 39, p. 36. DR. HAUSTEIN.

According to RÜCKERT, the above 8 cases furnish the following clinical indications for the use of Arsenicum in inflammation of the eye.

Swelling and spasmodic closure of the eyelids, which cannot be opened on account of the inexpressible pains; adhesion of the eyelashes; injection of the conjunctiva, which is covered with red blood-vessels and forms a wall around the cornea, (chemosis;) redness and granular appearance near the cornea; bluish redness of some of the blood-vessels. Violent pains from opening the eye, especially at night, when the sufferings are most severe; violent *burning* in the eye, which prevents the patient from eating or sleeping; *burning* and piercing pains in the eye; profuse discharge of corrosive tears on opening the eye; hot tears; small ulcers upon the cornea; dimness of sight; contraction of the pupils. *Excessive intolerance of light;* feeling as if the eyes had not room enough in the orbit, and were being pushed or pulled out; redness of the white of the eye, and dimness of the cornea; *intermittent* inflammation of the eye, commencing in the morning or afternoon, and diminishing by 10 o'clock at night. Aching and throbbing pains; annoying pulsation in the ball of the eye and its neighborhood. Dimness of vision; cannot see small objects, even when quite near; and large objects only at the distance of 10 feet.

Review.

Arsenicum is most suitable against congestion and inflammation of the conjunctiva, with swelling, inflammation, and spasmodic closure of the lids, and ulceration of the cornea.

It is most beneficial against *burning* and *intermittent* pains, when all the sufferings are increased at night.

Doses.—Arsenicum 4, 12, 16, and 24, were each given in 1 case; the 30th dilution in 3 instances; the 800th in 1 case. The 12th, 30th, and 800th potencies were given in solution, and in repeated doses; the 4th dilution was administered every three hours.

It was given both in acute and chronic cases, and the cures were effected in a few days, in every instance.

8. AURUM.

General Remarks.—DUDGEON supposes that gold acts not only on the superficial, but also on the deeper-seated structures of the eyes; that it will be found useful in some cases of rheumatic and syphilitic ophthalmia; while its efficacy in scrofulous affections should lead us to think of it in strumous ophthalmia; indeed it was employed successfully by Dr. LOBETHAL in such a case.

CASE 25.—A girl, aged 7, affected with scrofulous ophthalmia and great photophobia, was rapidly cured by the internal use of aurum 3, and the external application of an eye-wash made with 3 grains of aurum 1, in water.—*Brit. Journ. Hom.* Vol. 6, p. 321.

Baryta.

This remedy exerts a very specific action upon the eyes; according to PEREIRA, it has caused dimness of sight, double vision, ringing in the ears, pain in the head, and throbbing in the temples; also catarrhal discharges from the eyes, nose, and ears. Still, PEREIRA says that HUFELAND has used it with very great benefit in scrofulous affections of delicate and sensitive parts, such as the lungs and eyes.

DUDGEON says that it is homœopathic when the eyeballs are painful; when there are violent pains in the left eye, and thence over the temple to the ear; itching, burning, pressure, raw and dry feeling in the eyes, with sensations as if dust or grains of sand were in them; dry heat, burning and pressure in the eyes with lachrymation; redness of the white of the eye, with a white vesicle or pustule near the cornea; collection of matter on the lids in the morning; sticking together of the lids at night; inflammatory redness of the internal surface of the lids; swelling of the lids, especially in the morning.

DUDGEON has found it useful against ulceration of the cornea; SCHRETER used it with benefit in glandular swellings, eruptions behind the ears, and well-marked scrofulous ophthalmia.

Belladonna.

General Remarks.—At present we will confine our attention as far as possible to the effects of Bell. upon the external parts of the eye; in two cases the conjunctiva was highly injected, the whole eye prominent and preternaturally brilliant; in another, the eyes were prominent, *dry*, and exceedingly brilliant, the conjunctival vessels fully injected, there was *a total absence of lachrymation*, and motion of the eye was attended with a sense of dryness and stiffness; the face was red and turgid. H. M. GRAY. CHRISTISON says that it sometimes renders the eye-ball red and prominent, with flushing of the face and glistening of the eyes. PEREIRA says it may cause suffusion of the eyes, injection of the conjunctiva with *bluish* blood, protrusion of the eye, with dull appearance in some, or ardent and furious expression in others. DUBREYNE says that in some cases the eyes are dull and haggard, in others red, and the pupils exceedingly dilated.—PETERS.

b. DUDGEON says: In the pathogenesis of Bellad., we find indications for its use in almost every kind of ophthalmia; but it is not so homœopathic to the blenorrhagic forms as some other remedies, and consequently is less to be trusted to as a sole remedy in Egyptian and gonorrhœal, and the purulent ophthalmias of young children, than for the removal of casual symptoms, such as violent pains, congestion, and excessive intolerance of light. It is highly serviceable in catarrhal, scrofulous, arthritic, rheumatic, syphilitic and erysipelatous inflammations of the eye; and for excessive intolerance of light, when it occurs in the course of other ophthalmia. The experience of most homœopathists will furnish them with examples of the power of belladonna over the slighter forms of catarrhal and scrofulous ophthalmia. As a sole remedy, DUDGEON has seldom found it sufficient in these affections, but eminently useful in subduing the attendant photophobia and the congestion of the head so often accompanying the various inflammations of the eye.—*Brit. Journ. Hom.* Vol. 6, p. 324.

c. HERING recommends it when there is burning and itching in the red and swollen lids, which stick together and bleed when they are pulled apart, or even become everted, or are at least heavy, and as if paralyzed.

d. GROSS recommends Bellad. 3, in repeated doses every night and morning, against frequently-recurring inflammatory redness of the internal surface of the eyelids.

CASE 26.—A man, aged 38, of scrofulous constitution, and

subject to sick-headaches, was attacked with inflammation of the *right* eye, after taking cold; the white of the eye was much reddened and swollen; the eyelids itched and burned; the pupils were contracted; there was great intolerance of light; piercing, burning, and aching pains in the eye, and finally the left eye began to be involved; the attack was preceded by rending and drawing pains in the bones on the right side of the forehead.

Treatment.—Bellad. 30, in one-drop doses, removed the whole disorder in four days.—*Annals*, Vol. 2, p. 198. Dr. TRINKS.

CASE 27.—A young man, aged 23, of scrofulous constitution, who had been subject to inflammations of the eyes since his 14th year, was attacked with inflammation of the *right* eye, after taking cold; there was profuse lachrymation, with drawing and piercing pains, increased by use of the eye, and attended with intolerance of light.

Treatment.—Bellad. 30, three doses effected a cure in ten days.—*Gen. Hom. Journ.*, Vol. 12. p. 10. Dr. HARTMANN.

CASE 28.—A young, blooming maiden was the subject of a perfectly intermitting inflammation of the *right* eye, which commenced regularly every morning at 8 o'clock; it was attended with violent throbbing pains in the right temple, piercing pains in the eye, swelling and redness of the lids, great redness of the conjunctiva, profuse flow of tears, and intolerance of light. The whole attack passed off in a few hours to return again next day.

Treatment.—Bellad. 24, and Arsenicum 3, were given without effect; Aconite 20, in solution, produced relief. A relapse which occurred several months afterwards was not relieved by Aconite, but was promptly cured by Bellad. 12, two drops in water, three doses per day.—*Hygea.*, Vol. 4, p. 130. Dr. GRIESSELICH.

CASE 29.—A man, aged 25, had suffered for three weeks with a violent inflammation of the *right* eye; the eye looked like a raw piece of flesh; the conjunctiva was dark red; there was an ulcer upon the cornea; the lids were much inflamed, and the lower one everted; there was a profuse discharge of an acrid, corrosive matter; intense piercing and digging pains, with excessive intolerance of light.

Treatment.—Bellad. 400, removed the inflammation and pains in nine days; the cure of the ulcer and the corrosion of the lid was effected by sulphur and euphrasia.—*New Archiv.* Vol. 5, part 1, p. 85, Dr. STAPF.

CASE 30.—A girl, aged 20, was exposed to a draught of air after being over-heated; there was aching and watering of the *left* eye; inflammation of the conjunctiva; the cornea became dim and turbid (corneitis;) the sight was almost extinguished, and objects were only seen as if through a thick, black mist; black stripes seemed to move to and fro before the eyes.

Treatment.—Bellad. 400, caused improvement at the end of four days, and on the tenth day, the patient was comparatively well, except that objects seemed dim and indistinct, and as if seen through a fog. Cannabis effected a perfect cure.—*New Archiv.*, Vol. 3, part 2, p. 117. Dr. H., in F.

Review.

Of these five cases, three occurred in males; two in females all between 20 and 38 years of age.

In two cases, the patients were scrofulous; in three cases, the attacks was brought on by cold.

In all five cases, the inflammation attacked one eye only; the *right* eye in four instances, the left in one.

In four cases, the conjunctiva was much reddened and swollen; in two cases the cornea was affected, or even ulcerated. Great intolerance of light and lachrymation were present in every case. In three cases, the lids were much inflamed and reddened; and in one, they were everted.

The attending pains were throbbing, piercing, aching, and drawing, and extended to the neighborhood of the eyes.

Chamomilla and Belladonna have proved useful when there was hæmorrhage from the eyes.

The symptoms were aggravated by use of the eyes, by bright light, by external pressure, and in the evening.

DOSE.—Bellad. 12, 2 drops, in solution, proved useful, after
" 24, had failed;
" 30, was given in two cases;
" 400, do do do

The attacks were generally acute, but chronic in one case, and intermitting in another.

The cures were effected in from four to nine days.

BERBERILS VUGARIS.

DUDGEON suggests that this remedy will be found useful against arthritic ophthalmia, especially when there is a fine, frothy or gritty deposit on the edges of the lids; also against rheumatic inflammations of the eyes, when there is constant burning and dryness, with feeling as if sand were in them, with great redness of the inner surface of the lids, inflammation of the caruncula, stiffness of the lids, pressing out and throbbing in the eyes, pains darting into the eyes from the temples or forehead, or from the eye to the forehead, &c.—*Brit. Journ. Hom.* Vol. 6, p. 325.

BORAX

Is recommended in affections of the edges of the lids, especially when accompanied by entropium; when there is itching, burning, and rawness of the eyes, as if sand were in them; when the lashes turn in towards the eye and inflame it, especially at the outer angle, where the edges of the lids are quite raw; inflammation of the corners of the eye, with displacement of the lashes, and sticking together of the lids; glueing up of the lids at night, with a hard, dry gum, which irritates the eye like sand.—*Ibid*, p. 325.

BOVISTA

Is recommended by DUDGEON in affections of the eyes, consequent upon, or attended by eruptive cutaneous diseases, especially when there is burning in the eyes, with extraordinary heat in the cheeks; inflammation of the eyes and angles of the lids, sticking together of the lids.

BRYONIA.

DUDGEON thinks that it will prove useful not only in rheumatic ophthalmia, but also where the sclerotic coat and aqueous humor are principally affected; when the inflammation is attended with an unusually copious secretion of purulent mucus; when there is sudden swelling of the eye, with pain, discharge of matter, and redness and swelling of the conjunctiva.

CALCAREA CARBONICA

Is recommended by HAHNEMANN when there is burning and excoriation of the lids; burning and cutting in the eyes when reading by artificial light; cutting pains in the eyelids; piercing, and itching in the eyelids, with sticking together.—*Chronic Diseases*, Vol. 2, p. 209.

HERING recommends it when there are burning and cutting pains in the lids, especially while reading; it is often useful after Sulphur.

DUDGEON thinks that it is one of our most important ophthalmic remedies, especially in scrofulous cases; also in affections of the eyes, attendant upon or subsequent to cutaneous eruptions, especially when there is excessive itching; it has proved useful in a few cases of rheumatic and traumatic ophthalmia; also in arthritic cases, and in most chronic cases of inflammation of the eyes, consequent upon measles, scarlet fever, small-pox, or dentition.

CASE 31.—It proved useful in a chronic case of inflammation of the eyelids, in which the lashes were much disturbed and destroyed, the lids swollen, sore, ulcerated, and secreting a sticky, purulent fluid, attended with violent piercing and burning pains.

Treatment.—Calc. 30, in 8 ounces of water, 1 tablespoonful, per day.—*Archiv.* Vol. 14, part 1, p. 6. Dr. GROSS.

CASES 32 to 39.—Dr. B., of D., has published seven cases, cured by Calcarea, but his detail of symptoms is scanty, and he generally used sulphur previously.

The instances in which Calcarea alone effected a cure, or produced marked beneficial effects, collectively present the following "*group of symptoms:*"

Both eyes were much inflamed, with violent piercing pains; profuse secretion of matter, and sticking together of the lids.

Burning of the eyes in the evening; feeling of sand in the eyes; stitches of pain in the eyes; watering of the eyes in the open air.

Whitish opacity of the cornea (corneitis,) so that the patient only saw a faint glimmer of light; great opacity of the right cornea, so that the patient could no longer see with that eye; *ulceration* of the cornea, and flocculent opacity of it.

Red and green haloes around the candle in the evening; intolerance of candle-light.

Among *the accompanying affections*, were: drawing and rending pains in the forehead and right shoulder-blade; frequent dry cough; sensitiveness to every shock or emotion; profuse and long-continued menstruation.

Dullness of hearing.—The author remarks that he has cured numerous cases of inflammations of the eyes with Calcarea, especially when caused by the suppression of itch with some mercurial ointment; but that the results with Calc. were invariably most favorable when *deafness* was simultaneously present with the eye-affection.

Review.

Of the above seven cases, four were males and three females, from the ages of 4 to 25 years. In two cases the patients were of a spongy, scrofulous constitution; in one case, the ophthalmia remained after measles; in one, from itch suppressed by mercury; in another from the suppression of scald-head.

The inflammations were chronic, attended with profuse secretion of matter, considerable disease and ulceration of the cornea, and with destruction of the eye-lashes.

DOSE.—Generally Calcarea 30, frequently preceded by Sulphur. (Also see page 13.)

CALENDULA,

According to DUDGEON, deserves attention in lacerated and incised wounds of the eye; it is supposed to be as useful as Arnica is known to be in bruises, and, like it, may be applied externally, in the form of a wash or lotion. It may also be of use when the white of the eye is inflamed, attended with headache.

CAUSTICUM,

According to DUDGEON, is deserving of attention in the treatment of most cases of chronic inflammation of the eyes, and has been found of especial service where opacities of the cornea have resulted from inflammatory affections of the eye. He also thinks that it will prove as useful in some rheumatic, arthritic, and scrofulous affections of the eyes, as it is known to be in rheumatic, gouty, and scrofulous affections in general.

CASE 40.—A woman, aged 40, had inflammation of the left eye, with corrosive lachrymation and shooting pains; the candle seemed surrounded with a green halo; shooting pains extended from the eye into the head; there was an exacerbation of all the symptoms in the evening and at night.

Treatment.—Sepia 30, produced some amelioration, which remained stationary at the end of a month, when an eruption broke out over the whole body; two doses of Sulphur 60 and 30, allowed the disease of the eye to regain all its former intensity. Then Causticum 30, was given, and the affection rapidly declined, no further medicine being required.—*Archiv.* Vol. 17, part 27. Dr. B. in D.

CASE 41.—A peasant woman, aged 40, had suffered with her eyes for 14 years; they were always reddened, had violent shooting pains, and her sight was so dim that she only saw as if through a mist; there were continual beatings and noises in the head, flowing catarrh of the head, and an eruption about the neck.

Treatment.—Sulphur 30, was given without effect; three weeks after, Causticum 30, was administered, and removed all the symptoms in six or seven weeks; no other medicine was required.—*Ibid.* p. 30.

CASE 42.—A robust man, aged 30, had had bad eyes for several years; he felt, especially in the evening, burning and shooting pains, with a feeling as if he had sand in them; he had continual noises in the head, putrid taste in the mouth, and dull pain in the stomach after eating.

Treatment.—Pulsat. 30, produced marked benefit at first, but at the end of three hours, all the symptoms reäppeared; then a single dose of Causticum 30, effected a complete and radical cure.

CASE 43.—A girl, aged 18, had had itch during the previous summer, and was treated with sulphur and mercury, internally and externally; soon afterwards she was attacked with a violent ophthalmia, with purulent discharge and great swelling of the lids. She was giddy in the evening, and had never menstruated.

Treatment.—Pulsat. 4, removed the giddiness, but left the other symptoms as before; a fortnight afterwards, a single dose of Causticum 30, sufficed to cure her, and to cause the appearance of the menses.

It is supposed to be most homœopathic when there is excessive itching of the eyes, with smarting, as if from the application of salt, with burning and dryness, stiffness, intolerance of light, and constant winking.

CHAMOMILLA,

According to DUDGEON, is best suited to catarrhal ophthalmia with much mucous secretion, and to the ophthalmias of new-born infants, when the white of the eye only is affected; it would be unsafe to rely upon it alone when there is ulceration of the cornea, or inflammation of the more deeply-seated structures of the eye. It is particularly indicated when the attack is recent, and when there is a tendency to bleeding from the congested mucous membrane. If a remedy be requisite for the ophthalmia accompanying dentition, chamomilla will generally suffice, particularly if the infant is not decidedly scrofulous.

CASE 44.—A child, aged 3 weeks, had had constant diarrhœa for a fortnight, at first greenish, then like clear soup, and finally watery and fetid, attended with violent screaming and squirming. The eyes were closed by great swelling of the lids, and on opening them forcibly, the white was found much reddened; blood flowed from the eyes every time the infant cried; its whole body was covered with a miliary eruption, and the face was excoriated, probably from the acridity of the secretions from the eyes. There was extreme restlessness, entire loss of sleep, heat of head and body, without perspiration, and coldness of the extremities. The child refused all nourishment, even from its mother's breast, and was excessively emaciated.

Treatment and Result.—Chamomilla 12, one drop; in an hour it fell asleep for three hours, then awoke quietly and took some drink; in two days its diarrhœa lessened, it had ceased crying, the eyelids were less swelled, but it could not open its eyes; the whites and edges of the lids were less red, but the bleeding had not diminished; the heat of the body was moderate, the eruption less red, and desquamation had commenced. The *Chamomilla* was allowed to act for two days more, when Bellad. 30, removed the remainder of the symptoms; for in two days after, the bloody tears and swelling of the lids had disappeared, and the eyes had resumed their natural appearance. Three weeks after, the emaciation had much diminished.—*Archiv.*, Vol. 6, part 2, p. 38. Dr. HARTMANN.

CASE 45.—An infant, aged 6 weeks, had, from its birth, a considerable swelling of the lids, with redness and profuse purulent discharge; the disease went on increasing, especially that of the left eye, which could not be opened at all, whereas the right still opened, but only when the light was dim. On separating the lids forcibly, the eyes were perceived highly reddened, especially the left. The mouth was covered with small canker-sores; the child cried very much, and had liquid, yellow, and chopped stools.

Treatment.—Chamomilla 12, was given, and in two days the child was quieter, the lids less swollen and red, and the eyes opened spontaneously; in two days more there was no more swelling or redness of the lids, the eyes opened without difficulty, the intolerance of light and the inflammation had entirely disappeared; the aphthæ had much diminished, but there were still several glairy stools per day. A small dose of Mer. sol. 12, removed the remainder of the complaint.—*Annals*, Vol. 2, p. 200. Dr. SEIDEL.

CASE 46.—A lad, aged 14, of robust constitution, was suddenly seized with severe inflammation of the eyes, from change of weather. His physician immediately ordered a large number of leeches, a blister, and some internal remedies; but his parents objected, and a homœopathic physician was called.

Symptoms.—Severe tearing headache, painful pressure on the orbits, throbbing in the temples; eyelids so swollen as completely to close the eyes; the white of the eye was all inflamed and red, and so much swollen as to form a projection around the iris, (*chemosis*;) the cornea was somewhat opaque, especially that of the right eye, in which the inflammation was most intense; objects could not be distinctly seen; they seemed as if covered by a thick mist; candle- and day-light were intolerable, so that he was obliged to remain in darkness; the least change in the air of the room, the slightest examination by the physician, or the approach of night, caused great suffering. There was want of sleep; great restlessness; fever, increased at night; feeling as if the right eye would burst out of its orbit; sensation as if grains of sand were in both eyes.

Treatment.—Chamomilla 6, to be repeated in two hours; on the next day the inflammation was much diminished, the swelling of the conjunctiva around the cornea was less, but the pain in the head and eyes still persisted. *Phosphoric acid* 30, caused a quiet night and peaceful sleep, and the improvement was so rapid that a cure was perfected on the fourth day.—Dr. SCUDERY.

CHINA.

Dr. DUDGEON says: "The great benefit that has been found to result, in allopathic practice, from the employment of bark and its preparations in certain affections of the eye, more especially in scrofulous and rheumatic ophthalmia, would naturally induce us to bear them in mind in our homœopathic practice; in fact, until future provings shall have furnished us with more accurate indications for its employment, we must be content to be guided, in a great measure, by the experience of our allopathic brethren. It is most useful in chronic scrofulous ophthalmia, when the redness of the eyes is slight, but the intolerance of light, and other symptoms, severe; in certain stages of rheumatic and other chronic ophthalmiæ; and in those inflammatory affections of the eye, consequent upon onanism.

CASE 47.—A girl, aged 17, scrofulous, and subject to frequent attacks of ophthalmia from her infancy, was attacked with a recurrence of the disease. The white of the left eye was slightly reddened; motion of both eyes was difficult, as if sand were beneath the lids. There was a *periodical* aggravation every evening, about 11 o'clock, when the following additional symptoms occurred: great lachrymation of the left eye, sensitiveness to light; pressing pain on the orbit, which pain sometimes descended from the eyebrow into the lid, and caused this to close spasmodically; remission of the pains for several minutes; frontal headache.

Treatment.—Three hours before the next attack, one drop of China 12, was given, but the paroxysm occurred at the usual hour with increased violence; still, it did not recur on the third day, and there was no relapse.—*Archiv.*, Vol. 3, part 3, p. 77. Dr. CASPARI.

CASE 48.—A lad, aged 8 years, was attacked last autumn, after a slight cold, by a *periodical* ophthalmia of a peculiar character. Every morning at 10 o'clock, he experienced a painful pressure and drawing in of the forehead and temples, which increased every day in violence; soon afterwards his eyes became red, and commenced to weep; there was contraction of the pupils and great sensitiveness to light. Touch and motion gave him great pain. The paroxysms lasted severely for three hours, after which the pains gradually diminished; then there was a remission until evening, during which the skin was covered with perspiration. During the attack the pulse was quick, and face red; after the paroxysm, the face was pale and the debility great.

Treatment.—The catarrhal origin, and morning paroxysms led to the use of Nux vom. 30, but without effect; Euphrasia lessened the pains, but the attacks came on at the usual hour. Then *China* 12, was given, and on the following day the attack came on an hour later, and was less severe; two doses more of China, within forty-eight hours, effected a perfect cure.—RAU.

CASE 49.—A young lady had suffered for some days with the following remarkable symptoms: a pain in the eye, which included not only the eyeball and all the part contained in the orbit, but also the superciliary sinus, and extended along the eyebrow to the temporal bone; it was of an excessively violent character, as if a knife were thrust betwixt the orbit and ball, and moved around in the orbital cavity, in order to scoop out the eye; while it lasted the eye wept, but was neither inflamed, nor particularly red. This pain commenced every morning about 8 o'clock, with the same violence, and the last trace of it disappeared about two or three o'clock, P.M.

Treatment.—After using some general means, *China* was administered, and with such rapid effects that a cure was effected. —DR. ST. MARTIN.

CASE 50.—A man, aged 40, healthy and robust, felt much weakened immediately after bathing in the river in June; the next day he had heaviness of the head, disagreeable taste, eructations, and furred tongue; the day after, notwithstanding the use of full doses of Senna, he could not open his eyelids, which were glued together; the conjunctiva was reddened, the pupils contracted, the lids red and swollen, there was epiphora, extreme intolerance of light, heat, tearing in the orbit, disagreeable taste, violent headache, and thirst, moderate fever, with full and hard pulse, and dryness of the skin.

Treatment and Result.—Leeches, cold compresses, tartar emetic, and calomel were given without effect, but on the following day not a trace of the ophthalmia was observable; but the day after it returned with all its former intensity, and its *intermittent* character was fully recognized. Another intermission and subsequent fit were allowed to elapse, after which a few doses of *Sulphate quinine* were given; no trace of the ophthalmia returned, although the patient was obliged to write a great deal.

CONIUM,

This remedy will be more fully treated of under the head of scrofulous ophthalmia. It has been found useful in some cases of traumatic ophthalmia.

CASE 51.—A man, aged 60, was attacked with inflammation of the eye, after an injury with a splinter of wood.

Symptoms.—Enlarged blood-vessels ran from the inner corner of the eye to the edge of the cornea, which was opaque and depressed in the centre; there was aching pain in the eye-ball, increased by looking at a bright light; a sensation of swelling of the eyeball, swelling of the lids and cheek of the same side; itching, lachrymation, and adhesion of the lids, with dimness of sight; rending pains in the right side of the head; and aggravations every evening.

Treatment.—Conium 2, ten drops in a teacupful of water, one teaspoonful every morning and evening; a cure was effected in six days.—*Genl. Hom. Journ.*, Vol. 39, p. 34. HAUSTEIN.

CROCUS,

According to DUDGEON, has long enjoyed a reputation in allopathic practice, as an external remedy against various ophthalmic affections; it enters into the composition of many eye-washes. It has been recommended homœopathically after surgical operations on the eye, when there are throbbing and itching pains. It has been used in traumatic and scrofulous ophthalmia with good effect.

It is very useful against pain in the eyes, produced by looking through spectacles of too great magnifying power. Also against the consequences of exposure of the eyes to smoke; and inflammation of the eye, produced by weeping; as it produces a sensation in the eyes as if the patient had wept too much, the eyes being all swollen and tense, and looking as if one had wept violently.

DULCAMARA

Is supposed to be the most homœopathic remedy against inflammation of the conjunctiva, with chemosis.

CASE 52.—A soldier, aged 24, of robust constitution, had inflammation of the eyes with chemosis; the disease had lasted a week.

Treatment.—He took Tinct. Dulcamara in drop doses, and was much better at the end of 7 days; the chemosis having ceased, he then took Tinct. Coccul. for redness of the conjunctiva. DR. HORATÜS.

EUPHRASIA.

DUDGEON says, it is immaterial now to inquire whether it first obtained a reputation as a medicine for the eyes from its signature, that is, from some fancied resemblance between its form and the human eye; or, as is more probable, from the experience of peasants relative to its beneficial influence on the eye. Certain it is, that its ophthalmic virtues have been pretty generally believed in, as is still farther corroborated by the passage in Milton:

> "Then purged with Euphrasy and Rue;
> The visual nerve, for he had much to see."

Many treatises have been written by allopathic authors, commending it as a true polychrest medicine in eye-diseases; but the most modern panegyrist of Euphrasia is DR. KRANICHFELD, of Berlin, who has given a detailed account of all that has been said about it by ancient authors, and lauds its efficacy not only in inflammation of the eye, but in cough, hoarseness, earache, headache, and vertigo, and brings forward cases illustrative of its power. Still, DUDGEON says, that its pathogenesis gives only obscure indications for its employment in catarrhal, rheumatic, and scrofulous ophthalmia, while experience has taught that it is peculiarly useful when there is a constant flow of tears, and intolerance of light, with disease of the cornea.

b. According to RUMMEL, Euphrasia, when used both internally and externally, not only accomplishes much against specks of the cornea, but also cures inflammation of the cornea, and blenorrhœa of the conjunctiva.

c. My practice, says DR. LOBETHAL, compels me sincerely to recommend to my colleagues Euphrasia, whose curative virtues have often been tested with success in ophthalmia. It has appeared to me most useful in rheumatic, catarrhal, and scrofulous cases, and where there was considerable mucous secretion from the inflamed eye; also in blenorrhœas of the eye; in all of which cases I employ Euphrasia at once, internally and externally; in the former case, in drop-doses of the tincture; in the latter, from 2 to 5 drops in 4 ounces of water.

CASE 53.—A powerful young lad, aged 14, had suffered for 4 months with considerable intolerance of light in both eyes, worst in the evening; there was a rosy redness of the sclerotica with great vascularity of the conjunctiva; his whole state was farther aggravated by accidental injury to the left eye, by a bit of straw.

Treatment.—Euphrasia 4th dilut., 10 drops in 3 ounces of water, in table-spoonful doses; and application of a wash made with 10 drops of Tinct. Euphrasia; a cure was effected in 10 days.—*Hygea.* Vol. 18, p. 42. DR. SEGIN.

CASE 54.—A man, aged 50, had suffered for 6 weeks with ulceration of the cornea, against which he had already used several external remedies without avail.

The left eye was most involved, and seemed swollen and smaller; the meibornian glands were greatly inflamed and enlarged; red vessels passed from the conjunctiva on to the cornea, and emptied themselves upon a deep ulcer there; the whole cornea was dim, and conical in shape. The iris was discolored, and the pupils contracted.

Treatment.—Euphrasia, 3d dilut., was given twice daily; and a wash of Euphrasia 3d, in 100 drops of alcohol, was applied externally. A cure was effected in 3 weeks.—*Practical Observations.* Vol. 3, p. 17. DR. THORER.

CASE 55.—An infant, aged 6 months, had had inflammation and swelling of the lid of the right eye for 8 days, and of the left for 1 day; the eyes themselves were also inflamed; there was a flow of mucous matter from them, mixed with blood; the lids stuck together at night; there was a fluent coryza by day, and stoppage of the nose at night.

Treatment.—One dose of Euphrasia produced marked amendment in 2 days, and a cure by the 6th day.—*Annals of Klinical Homœopathy.* Vol. 1, p. 167.

CASE 56.—A robust woman, aged 22, had suffered for 10

days with ophthalmia, from taking cold; the conjunctiva of the lids and eye-balls was red; large red vessels were seen running from the outer and inner angles of the eye to the cornea; there was a continual itching and feeling as if sand were in the eyes; lachrymation and intolerance of light; the right eye was more painful than the left, and the accompanying catarrh of the nose was more troublesome in the right nostril than in the left.

Treatment and result.—Euphrasia, 3d dilut.; in 2 days she was improved in every respect, and the amendment went on, with a few interruptions, until the 5th day, when the cure was completed, without any other remedy having been used.

CASE 57.—A gentleman was attacked with inflammation of the eyes, without assignable cause. The symptoms were: headache in the forehead, with pressure in the temples; inflammation of the internal surface of the lids, with intolerable pains; intolerance of light; abundant flow of irritating mucus from the eyes; constant flow of tears; burning itching in the eyes; sticking together of the lids; black spots and mist before the eyes; habitual constipation, and depressed, restless disposition.

Treatment.—Aconite afforded only temporary relief; Cham. and Nux produced no good effect; Euphrasia, on the contrary, followed by Calc. on the 3d day, effected a cure by the 10th day.—*Archives.* Vol. 5, p. 375. DR. SCUDERY.

CASE 58.—An old woman had dimness of the cornea, following inflammation of the right eye, after an attack of gout; there was complete obscuration of the cornea.

Treatment.—After the subsidence of the acute inflammation, the prolonged use of Euphrasia removed the dimness of the cornea completely.—*Gen. Hom. Jour.* Vol. 5, p. 163.—DR. KNORRE.

It has also been used successfully in one case against profuse flow of tears, and piercing pains in the eyes; in another, against the dimness or opacity of the cornea, remaining after ulceration; in a third case, to cure ulceration of the cornea; and a fourth, to remove an acrid discharge of tears.

Dose.—The Tincture was given in drop doses in 1 case; and applied externally in 2 cases. The 1st dilution was given in solution, in 1 case. The 3d was administered internally and externally in 3 cases; the 4th, in 1 case, and the 200th in 1 case.

GRAPHITE

Is indicated when there is a paralytic pain in the lids; itching, smarting, and heat in the eyes; burning in the eyes, with collection of matter in the angles; lachrymation, redness, and intolerance of light; redness and painful inflammation of the lower lid and internal corner, with acrid tears; suppuration of the eyes; weakness and redness; frequent lachrymation and much mucus; dry mucus on the lashes; sticking together of the lids; great sensitiveness to light, with redness of the white of the eye; greater sensitiveness to sunlight than candlelight.

DUDGEON says, in the above symptoms we have well marked indications for the employment of Graphite in scrofulous, and catarrho-scrofulous ophthalmia. KNORRE found it useful in scrofulous ophthalmia, with ulceration of the cornea and great intolerance of light. It may be used in herpetic affections of the eyes and lids; and HARTLAUB says it opens the gummed-up eyes of scrofulous children, when there is a simultaneous eruption upon the face. WEBER recommends it in gouty ophthalmia, in the contraction and irregularity of the pupils. It may also be thought of against chronic or tedious erysipelatous inflammation of the eyes.

CASE 59.—A man aged 40, formerly syphilitic, had inflammation of the conjunctiva extending over the margin of the cornea; constant secretion of purulent matter; sticking together of the lids; intolerance of day and candlelight; burning pain about the eyes; pains in the throat, as if ulcerated; constipation and dejection of spirits.

Treatment.—Sulphur and Nux were given without benefit; Graphite 30, was then given, one dose per day, and in 4 days improvement commenced, while a cure was perfected in one month.

HEPAR. SULPHUR. CALC.

Against pain and pressure in the eyes; burning pains in the bones above the orbit; rawness of the external angles, with accumulation of mucus; inflammation and swelling of the eye, with redness of the white; soreness of the eyes, which gum up at night; mucus is secreted and the eyes become dim, so that he can not see well in the evening; eruption of pimples on the upper lids, and under the eyes; intolerance of light.

DUDGEON says, it is homœopathic to scrofulous, catarrhal, and exanthematic inflammations of the eyes; there are also some indications for its use against rheumatic eye-affections. It is more particularly suited when the meibomian glands are much involved, with copious secretion from them, intolerance of light and vesicles on the conjunctiva. SCHROEN says, he has frequently used it with success in inflammation of the eyes attended with burning pains at the edges of the lids, redness of internal surface of lids, intolerance of light, lachrymation, enormous secretion from the meibomian glands, and consequent agglutination of the lids, pustules on the sclerotic, and even on the cornea, with vascularity of the cornea. Still he could not discontinue its use for some time, or else the same symptoms would return; when the intolerance of light was excessive, Belladonna was required. HARTMANN regarded it as indispensably necessary in the cure of scrofulous blepharo-ophthalmia, given in alternation with Digitalis and Mercurius.

HERING advises it when inflammations of the eye do not yield to Aconite, when there are aching and pressing pains, with rawness of the lids.

The Tinct. Hepar. Sulph. is useful against inflammations of the lids, when the meibomian glands are involved, when styes and much pus is present.

CASE 60.—A lady had been treated allopathically for 27 weeks, without benefit; there was an ulcer upon the cornea, and several vesicles or pustules upon its edges; pus was effused into the anterior chamber of the eye, (*hypopion;*) the globe of the eye was inflamed; there was excessive intolerance of light; burning, piercing, and aching pains, increased by moving the eye; and piercing, bursting headache.

Treatment.—Hepar. s. 9, 1 dose every other evening, for 8 days; then Euphrasia 3, in the same way. In 14 days, the ulcer of the cornea was healed, and the pus had disappeared. Pulsat. 3, in 1-drop doses, daily, was given against the remaining vesicles or pustules.—DR. ELWERT.

CASE 61.—A piece of steel flew into a young man's eye and remained adherent there, followed by violent inflammation of the conjunctiva, lachrymation, intolerance of light, acute pain, and difficult motion of the eyes.

Treatment.—Hepar. 2, soon produced relief, and the foreign body was easily removed.—CASPARI.

CASE 62.—A lad, aged 16, robust, blonde, and frequently exposed to cold, had been sick for 14 days; the lids were swollen; the conjunctiva of the lids inflamed; the angles were raw and ulcerated; increased secretion from the glands; sticking together of the lids; intolerance of light and use.

Treatment.—After several doses of Tinct. Hepar. Sulph., both eyes were cured in a few days.—*Hygea.* Vol. 6, p. 397. GRIESSELICH.

CASE 63.—A woman of plethoric constitution had been plagued often and much with catarrhal inflammation and blennorrhœa of the eyes for many years. The lids of both eyes were inflamed, excoriated, running as if corroded, especially at the internal angle; the inner surface, especially of the lower lids, were red and inflamed; heat, pain as if from a burn, smarting and itching of the lids; lids and angles stuck together with purulent mucus; large red vessels on the conjunctiva; intolerance of light; colored and dim halos around the candle; pressing pains in the eyes, forcing her to shut them.

Treatment.—The cure was effected by repeated doses of Hepar. s. 3.—KNORRE.

CASE 64.—A little boy, aged 2 years, had tinea capitis which had extended to his face; inflammation of the eyes, and a small ulcer on the left cornea; his hair had fallen off profusely, leaving bald places on his scalp; he had crusts and scabs on his head, face, and neck; his eyes were closed by the swelling of the lids, and there was a profuse discharge of purulent mucus; frequent calls to stool, difficult evacuations; some perspiration at night; peevish, fretful humor.

Treatment.—One dose of Hepar. s. 3, was allowed to act for 5 weeks; the improvement then still continuing, no further medicine was given, and he was quite well in 5 weeks more.—DR. SCHRETA.

Review.

These few cases are sufficient to prove the powerful curative influence of Hepar. s. in diseases of the conjunctiva and cornea, especially when the meibomian glands are also involved. The instance of Hypopion (case 60) is of great practical value.

IGNATIA.

Dudgeon says we can infer from the pathogenesis of this remedy, its utility in catarrhal, and catarrho-strumous ophthalmia. Hartlaub says it is best suited against an irritated state rather than in fully developed inflammations. Wurzler recommends it after operations on the eye, where there are violent shooting pains in the temples and eyes. Hartmann considers it to be specific in the ophthalmia of new-born infants, especially if preceded by a dose of Aconite. Dessaix has cured traumatic ophthalmia with it. The well-known efficacy of Ignatia against the effects of great grief induced Watzke to give it in a case of injury of the eye, which seemed to be much aggravated by that state of mind, and which had resisted all the antiphlogistic treatment of the old school.

IODINE.

Against pressure in the eyes, as if from sand; tearing pain around and under the right eye; tension, shooting and cutting stitches in the eyes, with some inflammation. *Watery, white swelling of the lids;* dirty yellowness of the whites of the eyes, with some red vessels traversing them; lachrymation.

It is supposed to be useful against syphilitic, mercurial, and scrofulous eye affections.

KALI BICHROMICUM.

Dudgeon thinks that this will prove one of our most important ophthalmic medicines; Dr. Drysdale and he have found it useful in catarrhal, and catarrho-scrofulous ophthalmia, and used it occasionally as a collyrium with advantage; its action seems nearly confined to the conjunctiva, the deeper-seated strictures being scarcely affected by it; it may be thought of in strumous ophthalmia and in the Egyptian.

It is indicated when there is excessive itching and smarting; soreness of the caruncula; great burning and smarting; heaviness, soreness, and swelling of the eyes in the morning; pain as if sand were in the eyes, lachrymation, intolerance of light; constant winking of the eyes on account of excessive photophobia, with lachrymation and burning pain; tolerance of candlelight; redness of the edges of the lids of the conjunctiva and of the lids; agglutination of the lids; redness of the whole conjunctiva, with aching, heat, uneasiness, and lachrymation; sticking together of the lids; yellowness of the sclerotica with some congestion; swelling and inflammation of the eyelids, with eruption upon them and on the face; tenderness of the eyes, redness of the conjunctiva, with *tendency to granulation;* violent inflammation of the eyes, with intolerance of light and dimness of vision; pustules on the cornea, with surrounding indolent inflammation; specks and leucoma of the cornea; dirty yellowness, discoloration and swelling of the conjunctiva; brown spots on the white of the eye, heat and redness of the eyes, with thickening and roughness of the inner surface of the lids, (*granulation.*)

KALI HYDRIODICUM

Is indicated when there is cutting, smarting, and burning in the eyes, with secretion of muco-purulent matter; violent burning in the eyes; intolerable burning in the lids, with intolerance of light; burning of the eyes, redness of the lids, and lachrymation; considerable swelling of the conjunctiva around the cornea, (*chemosis;*) great swelling of the lids, with increased mucous secretion; purulent mucus in the angles of the eyes; constant watering of the eyes; inclination to shield the eyes from the light.

It seems most homœopathic to catarrhal and catarrho-scrofulous affections; but it has proved useful in the dominant school against rheumatic iritis and scrofulous ophthalmia.

KREOSOTUM.

Dr. Wahle, to whom we owe our knowledge of the physiological action of this drug, considers it indicated in a variety of diseases of the eye. Dudgeon supposes it to be most homœopathic to catarrhal and catarrho-strumous ophthalmia, with great epiphora and excessive acridity of the tears.

It is indicated when there is continual great heat in the eyes, with lachrymation; pressure, burning and scalding, with heat and watering as if something had got into the eyes; sticking together of the lids; itching, smarting, and inflammation of the sclerotica; watering of the eyes; constant watering of the eyes, which swim in tears; hot acrid tears, like salt water, causing smarting and burning of the cheeks; the eyes look as if one had been weeping.

LACHESIS.

DUDGEON thinks that the rather lengthy list of symptoms attributed to Lachesis does not afford many distinct indications for its use in ophthalmia; it is perhaps most homœopathic to catarrhal and rheumatic imflammation.

CASE 65.—A government official was forced to discontinue his functions on account of a violent inflammation of the left eye; the conjunctiva of the eye and lids was red and swollen; the cornea was depressed, there was a small ulcer and abscess upon it; the eye burned, and felt as if sand was in it; there was great dryness of the nose, and burning, acrid tears ran down the cheeks; the eye was excessively tender; he was forced to remain in a totally dark chamber; the light caused him the greatest agony; tearing, throbbing pains were felt in the forehead, bottom of the eye and back of the orbit, and occasionally became so severe that they forced piercing cries from the patient; he could only get a little relief in a kneeling posture with his head resting on the bed, and bent down almost to his knees; his pulse was frequent and sharp; there was much heat of the head, great thirst, and no sleep, with extreme general agitation; he was excessively irritable.

Treatment.—Mercurius, Hepar. s., Pulsatilla, Spigelia, and Lachesis were given; Hepar. and Lachesis contributed most to the cure, which was effected in 10 days.—*Clinique Homœopathique*, p. 41.—DR. MALAISE.

LEDUM PALUSTRE

Is most useful in gouty and rheumatic ophthalmia, when the lids stick together; with great itching at the angles of the eyes; lachrymation, acrid and smarting, corroding the lower lid and cheek; painful pressure behind the eye, as if it would be forced out, without inflammation; tearing pains in the head and eyes, with inflammation; swelling and great inflammation of the sclerotica and conjunctiva; tearing pains and burning pressure in the eyes.

LYCOPODIUM.

HAHNEMANN found it useful in inflammatory affections of the eye, with nocturnal agglutination, and lachrymation by day; it is homœopathic to inflammatory affections of the conjunctiva, especially of the lids, and of a catarrhal, scrofulous, or blennorrhagic character. In the two former affections, it has frequently been used with advantage, and DR. GOULLON attests to its efficacy in the ophthalmia of new-born infants. It has also been used successfully in most obstinate cases of scrofulous ophthalmia.—DR. DUDGEON, (*Brit. Jour. Hom.* Vol. 6, p. 483.)

MERCURIUS

Is indicated when there is agglutination of the lids in the morning; pressure, shooting, burning, and smarting in the eyes, with heat and lachrymation; inflammation of both eyes, with many red vessels on the whites, with intolerance of light.

Inflammation around the edge of the cornea of a peculiar lilac color, with aching in the eyes.

Inflammation of the conjunctiva of the lids and ball; redness and swelling of the lids; excoriation of the angles of the eyes; burning and itching of the lids, with thick muco-purulent secretion, and agglutination; ulceration and eversion of the lids.

Fluory inflammation of the membrane of the aqueous humor, and of the substance of the iris.

Retinitis with burning, pressing pain deep in the eye, great intolerance of light, constant lachrymation, colors, sparks of fire before the eyes.

DUDGEON says, it is homœopathic to catarrhal, scrofulous and exanthematous ophthalmia; while rheumatic, arthritic, syphilitic, and gonorrheal inflammations have all been treated successfully with this remedy.

CASES 66 to 70.—A mother and four children were attacked with inflammation of the eyes; there was inability to open the lids; slight inflammation with smarting pains; much lachrymation; feeling as if a foreign body were under the lids; intolerance of day and candlelight; stools slimy and acrid.

Treatment.—They all took Merc. Sol. 2, and recovered in 8 days, without relapse.

CASE 71.—An apprentice had had inflammation of the eyes for 3 weeks. Both eyes were reddened, especially the left; the cornea was red and dim, and surrounded by a raised swelling of the conjunctiva, (*chemosis;*) the eyelids were dry and swollen; the inflamed parts burned violently; and there was in tolerance of light; it seemed to him as if fiery sparks flew from his eyes; there were stitches of pain in the eyes and temples; the sight was dim.

Treatment.—Puls. 12, was given without effect; then Merc. 30 and 18, produced so much relief in 9 days that he could go to work again.

CASE 72.—A woman, aged 67, who had frequently suffered with erysipelatous inflammations, was attacked with violent inflammation of the eyes; the sclerotica was very red, and swollen up into a high ridge, (*chemosis;*) the cornea was quite dim, and pus was already forming between its layers; she had headache, dizziness, slimy, yellowish and whitish coated tongue, loss of appetite, much thirst, high fever, with congestion to the head, with intercurrent chills, inclination to perspire, moist skin, fleeting stitches of pain here and there in the limbs and body, restlessness and sleeplessness at night.

Treatment.—Mercurius 1st and 3d, was given internally; and a solution was also applied externally to the eye; a rapid cure was effected.—*Hygea.* Vol. 17, p. 372. DR. SCHELLING.

NUX VOMICA.

CASE 73.—A youth, aged 22, had suffered for several years, every spring and fall, with ophthalmia, which generally lasted several weeks.

There was a burning, itching pain in the eyelids; collection of matter in the angles of the eyes; inflammation of the eyes, with intolerance of light, especially in the morning; rending pains at night; constipation; hæmorrhoids.

Treatment.—Nux 24, removed the whole attack in 4 days. —SCHRETER.

CASE 74.—A child, aged 6 weeks, had bleeding from the eyes, which seemed protruded; there was swelling of the lids; the vessels of the sclerotica were much enlarged; small drops of blood exuded from the surface of the eyes; eructations and regurgitations after eating or drinking; attacks of twisting and screaming, relieved by the expulsion of flatulence; constipation, with hard stools, great straining, and prolapsus of the rectum; perspiration on the head; coldness of the limbs; restless sleep; great restlessness.

Treatment.—Nux 30; on the 3d day the constipation was removed; the rectum did not prolapse; the sleep was more quiet, and the turgescence of the blood-vessels had disappeared.—*Archiv.* Vol 6, part 2, p. 42. HARTMANN.

PHOSPHORUS.

DUDGEON thinks it indicated in some cases of catarrhal, scrofulous, rheumatic, and perhaps arthritic ophthalmia. KNORRE found it useful in inveterate catarrhal ophthalmia, when both the eyes and lids were inflamed; the edges of the lids raw and sore; constant lachrymation, causing smarting and burning; copious secretion of thin, muco-purulent matter; itching, and burning in the eyes; sticking together of the lids; dimness of vision.

PULSATILLA.

LOBETHAL recommends it when there is decided inflammation of the meibomian glands, with great lachrymation and profuse mucous secretion. In catarrhal ophthalmia, with agglutination of the lids in the morning, it is the principal remedy; it is also useful in scrofulous and syphilitic ophthalmia, and is the best remedy in O. morbillosa, the most severe cases of which it suffices to cure.

It is most indicated when there is a smarting pain in the eyes, with dryness, and feeling as if some foreign substance were in them; swelling of the eyes, and sensation, as if one were squinting; red, inflamed spots near the cornea; burning and itching of the eyes; sensation as if hair or sand had got into the eyes; sensitiveness to light, with excessive tearing, boring, and cutting pains; inflammation, swelling, and redness of the lids and their edges; styes upon the lids, with inflammation of the whites of the eyes.

CASE 75.—A delicate lady, aged 28, was attacked with acute, bright-red inflammation of the *left* eye; she had pricking, burning, and biting pains in the balls; lachrymation and dimness of vision; there was a spot on the edge of the cornea; fever, anxiety, and oppression of the chest.

Treatment.—Pulsatilla 4, in solution, was used internally and externally, and effected a cure in 8 days.—*Hygea.* Vol. 13, p. 59. DR. SCHELLING.

CASE 76.—In the autumn of 1845, an epidemic of ophthalmia occurred, in which there was profuse lachrymation, by day and night, excessive secretion of mucus, which stuck the lids together at night, with feeling as if grains of sand had got between the eyes and lids.

Treatment.—Pulsat: 2, 3, or 6, never failed to afford relief, except in a few dyscratic subjects, in whom Sulph. 6, was required in alternation.—*Genl. Hom. Jour.* Vol. 30, p. 110. DR. WEBER.

CASE 77.—A healthy woman, aged 36, had suffered for many years with ophthalmia and trichiasis, (see page 14;) the lashes were pulled out, but she had profuse lachrymation whenever she went into the open air; her eyelids stuck together in the morning, and she had aching in the eyes, and a sandy sensation, also simple cataract.

Treatment.—Pulsatilla 9, removed the inflammation.—*Archiv.* Vol. 3, part 3, p. 70. CASPARI.

CASE 78.—A gentleman, aged 30, had inflammation of the eyes for 5 or 6 days, with dryness, and burning heat, worst in the evening; the edges of the lids were red and swollen; muco-purulent matter glued the lids together; the conjunctiva was lax, flaccid, and unequally red, as if mottled.

Treatment.—Pulsat. 3, and lotions of tepid water cured him perfectly in 18 days. DR. Y.

CASE 79.—Mrs. F., about the change of life, had suffered with purulent ophthalmia for 3 weeks; she had acute pain, especially towards evening; her pulse was hard and full; and she had annoying pains in the region of the kidneys.

Treatment.—Aconite 24, was given 3 times a day, and in 6 days the pains were all gone; and the eyes were in a satisfactory state, except in the evening. Pulsatilla 12, then cured her in a few days. MALAISE.

Dose.—The 2d, 3d, 4th, 6th, and 9th potencies have been used with success.

RHUS TOXICODENDRON

Is one of our most important ophthalmic medicines, especially in the catarrhal, scrofulous, exanthematic, and erysipelatous varieties.—DUDGEON.

HERING thinks that it is useful in the inflammations of the internal surface of the lids in new-born children, when the lids are closed spasmodically, become everted when they are opened, and exude a thick, yellow, purulent mucus.

HARTMANN says, the inflammation against which Rhus is most serviceable is never very bright red in color; the meibomian glands are apt to be involved; and there often is swelling, not only of the lids, but also of the neighborhood of the eye.

CASE 80.—A child, aged 2½ years, had redness of both eyes, with lachrymation by day, and agglutination at night; he had been restless and sleepless for 2 days; there was an œdematous swelling extending far down on the cheek to the wings of the nose.

Treatment.—Rhus, 30 effected a cure in 2 days.—*Annals.* Vol. 1. MSCHK.

CASE 81.—After excessive use of the eyes by candlelight, the following eye-affection set in: frequent styes, first on one lid, then on another; burning pains in the eyes, with dimness of sight; œdematous swelling of the left lids, extending to neighboring parts and preventing the opening of the eyes; the cervical and parotid glands became enlarged.

Treatment.—Rhus 12 and 18, of each one dose, and Pulsat. 12, removed the whole attack in 10 days.—*Genl. Hom. Jour.* Vol. 12, p. 22. DR. HARTMANN.

CASE 82.—An infant, aged 6 weeks, suffered with ophthal neonat., and received Rhus 9, 2 doses daily; the eyes improved continuously, so that they were quite well in 14 days. Two other similar cases were cured in the same way.—*Hygea.* Vol. 20, p. 359. DR. MALY.

CASE 83.—A scrofulous child, aged 6 months, suffered with ophthal. neonat., in full development; the inflamed lids were perfectly closed, but from time to time a gush of purulent matter poured from them; attempts to open the eyes caused eversion of the lids, the swollen internal surface of which prevented all inspection of the eyes themselves.

Treatment.—Rhus 6, in 3 ounces of water, was given in teaspoonful doses once a day, and the lids were also bathed with it. A cure was effected in 4 days.—*Archiv.* Vol. 16, part 2, p. 94. DR. GROSS.

CASE 84.—A pale, delicate, and weakly man, aged 54, frequently suffered with inflamed eyes every winter. He had been sick for a month with inflammation of both eyes, extending from the conjunctiva over the cornea, which was opaque; he had piercing pains in the eyes and temples, dizziness, pains in the arm-pits and arms, frequent eructations, pains in the stomach, yawning, and nausea; his pulse was irritable, quick, and small; his skin dry.

Treatment.—Rhus 200, in solution, was given, and in 2 days the redness of the eyes and pain in the head had almost subsided; sleep and perspiration had set in; on the third day the pains in the limbs were removed. A relapse, 10 days after, was cured by Rhus 200, in 24 hours.—*Genl. Hom. Journ.*, Vol. 46, p. 136. Dr. SCHELLING.

CASE 85.—A woman, aged 75, who had suffered much with gout, had suffered for 22 *years* with intolerance of light, so that she could only open her eyes at twilight; every attempt to open the eyes was followed by a profuse gush of tears; the cheek was covered with a red, burning eruption, extending as far as the wings of the nose; the violent burning disturbed her sleep at night.

Treatment.—Rhus 200, was given every night and morning; in 8 days the eruption and burning had ceased, but the intolerance of light returned after a marked improvement.—*New Archiv.* Vol. 3, p. 52. Dr. NEHRER.

DOSE.—The 6th, 9th, 12, 18th, and 200th dilutions, have all been used successfully.

SEPIA

Is supposed to be most useful in scrofulous ophthalmia; according to RUECKERT, it has been used successfully in the following cases of simple (?) inflammation of the eye.

CASE 86.—A strong and hearty child, aged 4 years, had suffered for a year with repeated attacks of inflammation of the eyes; the lids stuck together at night, so that they had to be softened and moistened apart in the morning; there was great intolerance of light, and much pain in the eye; pustules formed upon the cornea, broke, and left dim spots for a long time.

Treatment.—After taking Sepia 30, he had no more attacks.—*Annals*, Vol. 2, p. 202. Dr. TIETZE.

CASE 87.—In an epidemic of asthenic inflammation of the eyes, attended with intolerance of light, especially in the morning, dingy redness of the conjunctiva, lachrymation and swelling of the lids, with much heat.

Treatment.—Two or three doses of Sepia 30, generally sufficed to effect a cure.—Dr. SCHMID.

CASE 88.—A man, aged 24, had suffered with inflammation of the eyes for 4 days; he had violent piercing pains in both eyes; the lids were swollen, and could not be opened on account of intolerance of light; profuse lachrymation; heat in the eyes; obstruction of the left nostril; confusion and emptiness of the head.

Treatment.—Sepia 30, caused some improvement in one day; and 2 doses more effected a cure.—*Genl. Hom. Journ.* Vol. 10, p. 203.

CASE 89.—A boy, aged 12 years, had suffered in consequence of styes, with a hard tumor upon the lower eyelid, which had persisted for almost 2 years; it was of the size of a small pea, adherent to the tarsus, and prevented the free motion of the lid.

Treatment.—Sepia 30, 1 dose every 8 days; after the 2d dose, pain sat in, in the induration, and inflammation and suppuration commenced; after the 3d dose the swelling broke, and the whole disorder was permanently removed.—*Vehsemeyer*, Vol. 2, part 1, page 52.

STAPHYSAGRIA.

This remedy is useful when *styes* occur frequently upon the lids, or leave indurated spots behind them, or do not suppurate and discharge properly, but become hard; also, when the eyelids are apt to stick together, with biting and burning pains, especially in the angles of the eyes, and when crusts form between the lashes.—HERING.

CASE 90.—A man, aged 44, had frequently suffered with ophthalmia; he had been in the following state for 9 weeks: both lids of the right eye were somewhat swollen, and of a bluish red color; the white of the eye was reddened, especially at the inner angle; both lids were covered with styes in their first stage of development; the lids were also stuck together with hard yellow crusts; he complained of aching pains when the eye was not covered, and at times of burning in the lids; his pulse was hard and quick, and his bowels constipated.

Treatment.—Staphysagria 15, 3 doses of 1 drop each, removed the whole disorder perfectly.—TIETZE.

SULPHUR

Is recommended by HERING when there is great swelling, inflammation, and redness of the lids, with violent burning pains, and profuse discharge of mucus and pus.

Another physician says, that in many very old and *chronic* cases, a somewhat large dose of Sulphur will often effect a more certain cure, even if it is preceded by a previous aggravation.

A third physician always gives Sulphur before he administers Calcarea, provided other symptoms do not contraïndicate it, or it has not already been taken in excess; he has observed from abundant experience that it is as useful in chronic affections, as the previous use of Aconite is in almost all acute inflammatory diseases.

KALLENBACH has given Tinct. Sulphur in the 1st or 2d dilution in ophthalmia neonatorum with the most decided benefit; it cures acute cases in 4 or 6 days; sub-acute attacks in 10 or 14 days.—*Genl. Hom. Journ.* Vol. 21, p. 88.

CASE 91.—A child, aged 6, suffered almost habitually with inflammation of the eyes; it had but few free intervals; the last attack had persisted for 6 weeks; there was great redness, swelling, and pain of the lids; intolerance of light, and outbreak of numerous small itching pustules.

Treatment—Tinct. Sulphur 5, every 3 days, increased the eruption at first; but it began to dry up after the 3d dose, and a cure was effected in 18 days.—*Hygea*, Vol. 18, p. 40. Dr. SEGIN.

CASE 92.—A woman, aged 47, had suffered from her youth with weak eyes, which often became inflamed and painful; the white of the eye and meibomian glands were swollen and inflamed; acrid tears flowed from the eyes whenever the lids were opened; both eyes were painful, as if salt had got into them; the cornea was dim; there was intolerance of light, imperfection of vision, and the patient was discouraged and tearful, fearing to lose her eyes.

Treatment.—1 dose of Tinct. Sulphur 1, produced a 3 days' aggravation, which was followed by a permanent cure.—*Annals*, Vol. 3. p. 5.

CASE 93.—A previously healthy man, aged 43, had suffered for 5 days with itching and burning pains in the eyes; the lids were swollen; the conjunctiva reddened, swollen, and projecting like a bag over the lower lid; there were cutting pains in the eyes, and constant lachrymation.

Treatment.—Two doses of Sulphur, 3d trit., cured him entirely in 8 days.

CASE 94.—An apprentice, aged 18, had suffered since his 5th year with ophthalmia; the right eye only was involved; the conjunctiva was bright-red and inflamed; the cornea very dim, dingy, and dusty-looking, as if a skin were over it; vision was much impaired, so that he saw every thing indistinctly as if through a thick mist; the eyelids were very red and burning, they adhered together at night, and secreted a viscid, acrid, and biting fluid, which excoriated the neighboring parts; the eyes watered constantly, especially in damp weather.

Treatment.—In 8 days after taking Sulphur 400, there was a marked improvement; the redness of the conjunctiva had much lessened, the cornea was less dim, vision more certain, ready, and extended, the burning pains were lessened, and the lachrymation diminished. At the end of 8 weeks the patient was entirely well, with the exception of some watering of the eyes, which was removed by Euphrasia 200.—*New Archiv.* Vol. 2, part 1, p. 73. STAPF.

CASE 95.—A man, aged 48, had a staphyloma of the right eye, after an attack of ophthalmia; during the next year the left eye became afflicted; the whole of the white of the eye was bloody-red and swollen; the naturally brown iris had a reddish hue, (*Iritis,*) and a whitish spot of the size of a pea on its base; the eye was intolerant of light, watered much, and stuck together at night; the ball of the eye was painful when in motion; there were drawing pains about the orbits; the lids of the right eye were reddened; there was pain in the occiput on lying down.

Treatment.—Bellad. 30, did but little good; but after taking Tinct. Sulph. 3, a rapid recovery set in.—HARTLAUB.

CASE 96.—Madam B., aged 30, had been afflicted for 12 days with diarrhœa and ophthalmia; she had violent cutting pains at intervals, attended with diarrhœa and bearing down pains, worse at night; both eyes were affected, and the lids everted; the pulse was febrile and frequent.

Treatment.—Sulphur 2, effected a cure in 5 days.—*Archiv.* Vol. 3, part 2, page 117. SCHNIEBER.

CASE 97.—A child, aged 1½ years, had been troubled for 8 days with inflammation of the left eye; the white of the left eye was much reddened, that of the right somewhat so; the eyelids were greatly swollen, and could only be opened with difficulty and imperfectly; there was great intolerance of light, lachrymation, and agglutination of the lids; general febrile heat, rapid changes in color of the face, gritting of the teeth during sleep, and constipation.

Treatment.—Aconite 24, was followed by Sulphur 2, half a grain; the child improved steadily up to the 10th day, when it was entirely restored.—*Archiv.* Vol. 19, part 3, page 162. TIETZE.

CASE 98.—A man, aged 54, had already had several attacks of ophthalmia, attended with ulcers on the cornea; after much allopathic treatment with mercury, he was left in the following state: the left eye wept constantly, and could not be kept open on account of intolerance of light; the ball of the eye as far as visible was violently inflamed, and the dark-red vessels unusually filled. There was an ulcer on the lower segment of the cornea, from which bundles of red vessels radiated; sight was lost; there were piercing and burning pains about the orbit, and pus apparently had formed in the interior of the eye.

Treatment.—One dose of Acon. 2, every night and morning for 3 days; then Sulph. 2, was given in the same way for 3 more days; in 8 days the inflammation was all removed. Then Sulph. 2, 6 doses was given, 1 dose every other night; afterwards, only every 4th night; constant improvement of the sight occurred, attended with a progressive healing of the ulcer of the cornea. At the end of 4 weeks, Silex 6, was given, 1 dose every 4th night. He remained well for 5 years, when a new attack was quickly cured by Sulphur, Silex, Euphras., Calc., and Hepar.—ELWERT, p. 117.

CASE 99.—A boy was operated upon for cataract, and an obstinate inflammation of the eye was the consequence; at the end of many months he looked sickly, was weak, and had but little appetite, with a quick pulse. The eye watered, was constantly inflamed, perfectly disorganized internally, and atrophied, with entire and permanent loss of vision. The well eye began to be affected.

Treatment.—Sulphur 4, 1 dose every 4th night, was given for 6 weeks; the inflammation subsided greatly, and finally was entirely removed by Bellad. 4, 1 dose every other day.—ELWERT, p. 123.

CASE 100.—A man, aged 27, had suffered for years with periodical attacks of ophthalmia, which sometimes lasted for 3 months; had been treated allopathically for 4 weeks without benefit. The whole conjunctiva of the *left* eye was blood-red; there were aching, tensing, burning, and piercing pains in the eye; mist before the sight; rending pains on the *left* side of the head; chilliness during the day, fever at night, with quick and hard pulse.

Treatment.—Aconit. and Pulsat. were given without much effect; but Sulphur 30, produced a rapid improvement, followed by a cure in 14 days.—*Practical Contributions*, Vol. 1, p. 202. Dr. TIETZE.

CASE 101.—A young man, aged 20, had suffered for 14 days with ophthalmia in consequence of injury to the eye with a spear of corn; the ball was slightly reddened; there were burning and piercing pains; a small, white pustule close to the edge of the cornea; intolerance of light, and lachrymation.

Treatment.—Sulphur 6, cured the inflammation, and Calcarea the intolerance of light.—*Annals*, Vol. 2, p. 198. Dr. HARTLAUB.

CASE 102.—A man, aged 25, had had a violent ophthalmia for 3 weeks; the whole right eye was inflamed in the highest degree, and looked like a piece of fresh bloody meat; the conjunctiva was dark red; there were ulcers on the cornea; severe piercing and boring pains in the interior of the eye; excessive photophobia; the lids greatly inflamed; the lower one everted; and there was a profuse discharge of an acrid, excoriating fluid.

Treatment.—Bellad. 400; in 9 days the inflammation, photophobia, and pains were essentially relieved; but the ulcers, eversion, and discharge were unaltered. Ten days after taking Sulphur 400, the ulcers were healing rapidly, the inflammation and discharge from the lower lid materially lessened, and the disturbed vision improved; in 35 days there was only a little opacity of the cornea remaining. Euphrasia 200, then effected a perfect cure in 14 days more.—*New Archiv.* Vol. 2, part 1, page 85. STAPF.

CASE 103.—A woman, aged 30, had suffered for a long time with redness and swelling of the edges of both lids; the meibomian glands secreted pus; the lids stuck together in the morning; there was a burning sensation as if sand were under the lids; the patient could not work in the evening, nor read; it was even difficult to do this by day; the pains increased in the evening, lessened while in the free air, when the eyes watered more than in the house. Constipation; menstruation only every 6 weeks, and then habitually scanty.

Treatment.—Three doses of Sulphur removed the whole disorder.—*Hygea*, Vol. 3, p. 13. GRIESSELICH.

CASE 104.—A man, aged 52, received a blow over the right eye, followed by inflammation, which had been treated allopathically without success for 3 months; the conjunctiva was greatly inflamed; the cornea dim, with an ulcer upon it, and the anterior chamber of the eye was half filled with pus.—(*Hypopion.*)

Treatment.—Arnica and Senega did no good; Sulphur 6, one dose every other day, was then given, and in 14 days the pus had entirely disappeared, the ulcer had healed, and the dimness of the cornea much lessened.—VEHSEMEYER, Vol. 1, part 1, p. 18.

CASE 105.—A woman, aged 68, had been successfully operated upon for cataract in both eyes, 6 months ago; a subsequent inflammation of the right eye was followed by an effusion of pus in the anterior chamber, (*Hypopion.*) The sclerotica and conjunctiva were inflamed, and the cornea so hazy that the iris and pupil could not be seen; there was no ulceration of the cornea, but a deposit of yellow matter could be seen at the bottom of the anterior chamber; both eyelids were puffy and swollen, and their edges inflamed; there was lachrymation, heat in the eye, feeling as if the eyeball were swollen, and burning and piercing pains increased at night.

Treatment.—In the course of 11 days, 80 drops of Tinct. Sulphur were administered, followed by entire cessation of the inflammation and swelling of the lids, and the pus was partially absorbed; after taking cold, a relapse was followed by a visible increase in the quantity of pus; but Sulph. 3d trit., 3 doses per day, effected a perfect cure.—*Genl. Hom. Journ.* Vol. 19, p. 70. KNORRE.

CASE 106.—A woman, aged 38, was attacked with a swelling at the internal angle of the right eye, which discharged matter, succeeded by a flow of clear, limpid fluid; the eyelids were inflamed, the eye watered, and at the internal angle there was a sore of the size of a small pea, from which pus and tears exuded; pressure on the lachrymal sac caused the same fluid to pour out of the punctum lachrymale; the right nostril was dry.

Treatment.—The continued use of Sulphur cured the *fistula lachrymalis* completely.—*Genl. Hom. Journ.* Vol. 37, p. 249.

Review.

Of the 15 patients cured by Sulphur, 7 were males and 5 females, of the ages from 20 to 68 years; and 3 were children, 2 of which were less than 2 years old.

The causes of the disease were repelled itch, in 1 case; mechanical injuries in 2 cases; operation for cataract in 1 case; and small-pox in another.

The inflammations were violent, although often chronic; the *lids* were greatly inflamed, swollen, and even everted; the *meibomian glands* inflamed and swollen; there were *discharges* of acrid, corroding matter; the *conjunctiva* was bright red, swollen, sacculated, and resembling raw flesh; the *cornea* was dim, dirty, and apparently cuticulated, or beset with ulcers, and surrounded with a radiating vascular net-work; the *Iris* had become altered in color, reddened and marked by a white spot of lymph; there was great intolerance of light; the *sclerotica* was inflamed and ulcerated, with violent cutting, burning, piercing, and boring pains; and there was effusion of pus in the anterior chamber in 3 instances.

In 5 cases out of 15 the *left* eye was alone effected; in 3 cases, the *right.*

Dose.—The 2d and 3d triturations were used twice; the 3d dilution of Spt. Sulph. also twice; the 2d, 3d, and 4th dilution, 4 times; the 6th, twice, in repeated doses; the 30th, once; the 400th, twice.

The *Sulphur* alone effected cures in 10 cases; in others, Acon. and Bellad. were given previously with but little effect; while Euphrasia, Calc., and Silex were used 3 times to perfect the cures.

The *duration* of the disease varied from 5 days to 13 years, and more; the *time of cure* varied from 5 to 14 days, or 8 weeks.

GENERAL REVIEW OF THE TREATMENT OF SIMPLE INFLAMMATIONS OF THE EYE.

THE preceding chapter embraces 106 cases of disease, in which 18 or 20 different remedies were used.

In the more *acute* attacks we find that Merc. and Sulph. were used 7 times; Arsenicum 4 times; Arn., Bell., Cham., Hepar, and Rhus, each 3 times; Acon., Nux, and Sepia, each twice; Conium, Puls., and Staphysagria, each once.

In the *chronic* cases, Calcarea was given ten times; Sulphur, 9 times; Arsen., Bell., Euphrasia, Rhus, and Sepia, each twice; Conium, Hepar, and Puls., each once.

When the attacks were *typical* and *periodical*, Bellad. effected a cure in one case, Arsenicum in another, while Sepia proved specific in one epidemic, and Pulsat. in another.

In Affections of the Eyelids.

Aconit., Arsen., Bellad., Calc., Cham., Hepar, Merc., and Sulphur, were useful when the lids were *swollen* and *inflamed.*

When they were shining, Acon.;—red, Sulph.;—red and dry, Merc.;—*everted*, Merc. and Sulph.;—forcibly contracted, Merc.;—spasmodically closed, Arsen., Bell., and Rhus;—the internal surface only inflamed, Arsen., Bell., Rhus;—redness of the edges of the lids, Con. and Sulph.;—crowded with blood, Cham.;—swollen, Conium;—ulcerated, Merc.;—itching, Bell.;—burning and biting, Calc.;—cutting, Calc.;—as if sore and bruised, Hepar;—œdematous swelling, Rhus and Sulph.;—inflammation of the meibomian glands, nocturnal agglutination, profuse secretion of purulent mucus, Acon., Calc., Euphras., Hepar, Puls., Sepia, and Sulph.;—*Styes and Tarsal Tumors*, Puls., Sep., and Staphys.;—inflammation and *blenorrhœa* of the conjunctiva of the lids, Euphras., Acon., Hepar., Lycopod., Puls., and Rhus;—*Erysipelatous inflammation*, Hepar.;—inflamed and ulcerated angles, Hepar.

Inflammations of the Conjunctiva of the Eyeball.

When it is *inflamed and red*, Bell., Graph., Hepar, Sulph.;—when slightly reddened with varicose vessels, Puls.;—bright red, Acon., Ars., and Sulph.;—bluish red, Arsen.;—as if injected, Arsen.;—with net-like bundles of vessels, Arsen., Merc., Rhus;—spongy, Bellad., Sulph.;—*bloated*, Rhus;—with *chemosis*—a dropsical wall around the cornea—Acon., Arsen.;—*granulated*, Arsen.; —swollen, Acon.;—hanging down like a bag, Sulph.

Of the Sclerotica.

When it is blood-red, swollen, and spongy, Merc., Sulph.;—rose-red, with great development of the blood-vessels, Euphrasia;—swelled, Nux.;—ulcerated or sore, Sulph.

Of the Cornea.

When it is *conical*, Euphrasia;—when it is protruded like a vesicle or bladder, and has broken internally, Hepar.;—surrounded with a vascular zone, Arnica;—with tortuous vessels, Rhus;—with vesicles on the edges, Hepar.;—with pustules, Sepia.

When it is *dim*, Arnica, Calc., Merc., Rhus, and Sulph.;—when it is dingy, Sulph., Bell.;—when it is veiled and misty, Arsen. and Sulph.;—as if covered with a membrane, Sulph.; —when it only admits a little light, Calc.

When there is pus between its laminæ, Hepar. and Merc.;—open ulcerations, Arn., Ars., Calc., Con., and Euphrasia;—when the ulcers are surrounded by a vascular net-work, Sulph.

Of the Iris and Pupil.

When they are *contracted*, Arsen., Bell., and Euphrasia;—when the iris is reddened and covered with lymph, Sulph.

Against *intolerance of light*, Bell., Con., Calc., Graph., Hepar., Merc., Nux., Sepia, and Sulph.;—increased by crying, dust, or draughts of air, Bellad.;—especially by candlelight, Calc., Merc.

Lachrymation, Arsen., Bell., Euphras., Hepar., Merc., Sepia, Sulph.;—especially when in the wind, Calc.;—when the tears are salt and biting, Pulsat.

When *blood* flows from between the lids, Cham., Bell., Nux.

When the attending *pains* are *burning*, Arsen., Bell., Calc., Hepar. ;—when biting and burning, Merc., Puls. ;—burning and piercing, Arsen., Bell. ;—as if sore or ulcerated, Arnica ;—when there is a feeling as if the eyes were being torn out, or had not room enough in the orbits, Arsen. ;—aching pains, Bell. ;—especially when looking at the light, Euphras. and Hepar.

Among the accompanying affections, Bell., Hepar, and Arsen. were used against drawing and rending pains about the orbit ;—Calc., against deafness ;—gastric affections, and diarrhœa, Merc. ;—feverishness, Merc. and Pulsat.

Doses.—These varied from the lowest to the highest potencies; still the latter were used less frequently, and sometimes were so inefficient that more material quantities had to be used. Bellad. was used in a few cases in quite strong doses; the same remedy that was given internally, was also occasionally applied externally, a procedure which certainly should be employed more frequently, especially in obstinate and chronic cases.

The above cases were furnished by 44 different physicians. The *lower* potencies, up to the 3d dilution, were used in 31 cases; of these, 1 dose sufficed in 15 cases, repeated doses were required in 12, and solutions in 4. The *higher* dilutions, namely, from the 4th to the very high, were employed in 62 cases; single doses sufficed in 22 cases, repeated doses in 24, solutions in 6 instances. The very high dilutions were given in 10 cases, and repeated doses were required in 4.

OPHTHALMIA OF NEW-BORN CHILDREN.

Ophthalmia Neonatorum.

LAWRENCE says, this is a disease of considerable consequence, and the more so from its commencing in a way not calculated to excite the attention, or alarm the fears of the mother or nurse. It causes more blindness than any other inflammatory disorder that happens to the eye; and the number of children is very considerable, whose sight is partially or completely destroyed by it. Still, there are milder and severer varieties of it; the milder forms are caused by cold, by exposure of the tender eyes of the infant to too strong a light, or to dust, or some other transient or mechanical cause. In the great majority of the severer cases, there is a vaginal discharge from the mother, such as leucorrhœa, or some other less simple affection; the eyes of the infant are exposed to the contact of these morbid secretions during labor, while passing through the vagina.

The inflammation commonly comes on about 3 days after birth, and in the first stage is confined to the mucous membrane of the lids; the edges of the lids stick together a little when the child wakes from sleep, they are redder than natural, especially at the corners, and if they be everted, their inner surface will be found red and villous, and a little white mucus is seen on the inside of the lower. The ball of the eye is at first in a natural state.

In the second stage, all the symptoms are increased; the inflammation extends from the conjunctiva of the lids to that of the ball of the eye; the congestion and redness are augmented; the lids swell and become red, even externally; there is a copious secretion of purulent fluid from the inflamed membrane, which agglutinates the edges of the lids, then accumulates between them, and finally pours over the face, staining the cap and linen. The lids are apt to become everted when we attempt to examine their inner surface, or even when the child cries; this eversion is generally temporary, but it may be more permanent.

If the inflammation should continue, and not be checked by suitable treatment, it soon extends to the cornea, and thus may reach the interior of the eye.

Sloughing of the cornea is one of the most common of its effects; when this change is about to take place, the cornea at first becomes whitish and dusky, then loses its polish and firmness of texture, being converted into a dirty grayish, or brownish slough. The entire cornea may thus perish and separate, and then the iris may protrude through the aperture, presenting an irregular brownish prominence. Or *ulceration of the cornea* may occur more or less considerable in depth and extent, followed by adhesion of the iris; or *opacity of the cornea* may ensue from a deposit of lymph into the substance of the corneal conjunctiva, producing a thin grayish film; or, between the layers of the cornea, causing a dense opacity.

These several diseased processes occur very quickly, and go on rapidly; there is a singular contrast, however, between the violence of this disorder in newly-born children, and the serious consequence to which it so rapidly leads, and the readiness with which it yields to suitable treatment. Hence, LAWRENCE says, if we see a case of purulent ophthalmia before any injury is done to the cornea, we may assure the parents that the sight will not suffer.

Treatment. — KLOTAR MULLER says, at first it is advisable to give a few doses of Aconite; as soon as a considerable secretion of mucus occurs, *Ignatia* should be administered and followed by Hepar. Sulphuris, if improvement does not set in, in a day or two. TESTE prefers Aethusa Cynapium and Kreosote in the severer forms. HARTMANN prefers Aconite, followed by Sulphur, or Hepar. Sulph., when the secretion of muco-pus becomes excessive. He also advises Ignatia in the simpler forms; and Mercurius when the ophthalmia has been caused by an ordinary leucorrhœal discharge, irritating the eyes of the infant. Nitric acid and Thuya should also be thought of in severe cases. LAWRENCE depends almost entirely upon the local application of Alum to the eye, from 2 to 4 or 6 grains to the ounce of distilled water, aided by an occasional dose of Magnesia; out of many hundred instances he can hardly recollect one where the eye suffered in any respect, if the cornea was clear when the infant was first seen; using no other means than Magnesia internally, and the solution of Alum externally.

ACONITE.

GROSS says that Aconite 30, if used early, will frequently break up attacks of oph. neonat.

In one case, Aconite 200, broke up a recent case in 24 hours.

WESSELHŒFT used to cure ophth. neonat. very quickly with Dulcamara; lately he gave Aconite, Pulsat., and Calcarea without benefit; after a dose of Dulcamara the whole attack subsided in 24 hours.

LYCOPODIUM.

CASE 107.—A babe, aged 6 days, was attacked, from taking cold during the jaundice, with an extremely violent inflammation of both eyes; purulent matter exuded by the teaspoonful, on the 5th day of the attack, from the œdematous and extremely swollen lids; the conjunctiva looked like raw flesh; the cornea was dim.

Treatment.—Sulphur was given without benefit; Lycopod. 30, internally, and Lycop. 9 applied externally produced rapid amendment, and in 10 days the eyes were entirely saved.—*Archiv.* Vol. 20, part 3, p. 54. GOULLON.

RHUS TOX.

HERING and HARTMANN recommend this remedy, especially when eversion of the lids takes place when the eyes are opened; or when a red swelling protrudes.

MALY cured 3 cases with 2 doses of Rhus 9, per day; and GROSS 1 case with Rhus 6, in solution, applied internally and externally. In these cases a dark-red swelling projected between the lids.

SULPHUR.

When the disease has made great progress, Tinct. Sulph. or Calcarea given in alternation, will often be found useful.—GROSS. A relapse of the disease was cured in 24 hours by Sulph. 400.

KALLENBACH effected cures of acute cases in 4 or 6 days, with Tinct. Sulph. 1st and 2d dilutions; chronic cases required 10 or 14 days.

HYPOPION.

This name designates the presence of pus in the anterior chamber of the eye; it is an occasional effect of inflammation of the aqueous membrane; but more frequently it proceeds from the bursting of a corneal abscess, and then is seen in conjunction with more or less opacity of the cornea, and acute inflammation of the external tunics of the eye. Abscess of the iris breaking into the anterior chamber may produce hypopion; it may also occur in iritis not proceeding to suppuration; in inflammation of the internal tunics; and in general inflammation of the ball of the eye; all depending upon concomitant inflammation of the membrane lining the chambers of the aqueous humors.

Treatment.—Some of the most eminent allopathic oculists, such as RICHTER, LANGENBECK, BENEDICT, and BEER, once strongly recommended operative measures to let out the pus. In his early writings, BEER recommended letting out the matter; he appeals to his great experience, and will hardly condescend to notice objections. "Any one," he says, "who has successfully and completely cured by incisions so many cases as I have, will not think it worth while to hear or read, and much less to refute such objections." But subsequent experience induced him to change his opinion completely, and to reprobate the incision in equally strong terms. It is now regarded as an invariable rule, not to puncture the cornea in hypopion, for when the inflammation is arrested, the pus will be rapidly absorbed. Even BEER finally says, when matter shows itself in the anterior chamber, the surgeon must on no account think of opening the cornea; for the eye will certainly be much injured. It is surprising how many centuries of malpractice are tolerated before physicians and surgeons learn to place a little reliance on Nature.

In 10 cases of violent ophthalmia with especial affection of the cornea, an evident deposit of pus was observed in the anterior chamber of the eye. The following homœopathic remedies were used successfully:

ARSENICUM.

See case 23, page 64. A violent inflammation of the eye, with effusion of pus in the anterior chamber, was cured by Arsenicum 4, given every 4 hours; the whole disorder was gradually removed in 14 days, the absorption of the pus going on all the time.

HEPAR. SULPH.

CASE 108.—A woman, aged 38, of weakly and relaxed constitution, had suffered much from scrofula in her youth, and for 14 days with corneitis of the right eye. In the centre of the dull, dim, and very protruding cornea there was a pustule of the size of a pin's head, which had broken into the anterior chamber, which was filled with pus up to the level of the iris. There was fever, aching, burning, and bruised pain in the eye, extending over the head.

Treatment.—One grain of Hepar. Sulph. was given for 3 days in succession; then foot-baths containing 1 drachm of the same remedy were used for 5 days. The disease gradually yielded, only a slight scar remained on the cornea, and the pupil was perfect in color and shape.—*Genl. Hom. Journ.*, Vol. 15, p. 4. BICKING.

Two more cases were successfully treated with the same remedy; see article, Hepar. Sulph., page 82; also chapter on scrofulous ophthalmia.

MERCURIUS.

Merc. solub. was given in 1 case; see chapter on rheumatic ophthalmia; also Merc. corrosiv. in 1 case; see chapter on scrofulous ophthalmia.

SULPHUR.

See case 98, page 97; also case 104, page 99; case 105; and the chapter on arthritic ophthalmia.

RUMMEL says that it accomplishes extraordinary results in hypopion, even when it arises from gonorrhœal ophthalmia; in one case it caused resorption of the pus in a few days.

In all these cases, although the quantity of pus was large in some, a cure was effected in from 8 to 14 days.

The *doses*, in every instance, were of the strong triturations; Hepar. Sulph. was even given in the undiluted state.

In 2 cases, Euphrasia was given to perfect the cure.

FISTULA LACHRYMALIS.

Although WALTHER says that experience has shown that the use of all and every allopathic internal remedy is invariably fruitless, while counter-irritation, even when faithfully and patiently carried out, is equally powerless, still homœopathic remedies have occasionally removed this unpleasant affection.

For remarks on the nature and treatment of acute inflammation of the lachrymal sac, see page 18.

SULPHUR.

See case 106, page 100, in which Sulph., continued for a long time, cured a fistula lachrymalis.

CASE 109.—A teacher who had suffered from childhood with fistula lachrymalis, was cured by Sulph., Stann., and Silex.—*Genl. Hom. Journ.* Vol. 39, p. 280. Dr. WEBER.

LACHESIS.

CASE 110.—A single dose of Lachesis 12, cured a fistula lachrymalis in 14 days, together with a very disgusting and obstinate eruption upon the face, after a number of other homœopathic remedies had been used without avail for more than a year.—*Archiv.* Vol. 20, part 1, page 120. SCHELL-HAMMER.

NATRUM.

CASE 111.—A corpulent, but otherwise healthy woman, aged 50, had noticed for 3 months a considerable swelling on left side near the nose; pressure upon it forced out mucus at the inner angle of the eye.

Treatment.—Natrum m. 400, was given every 5th day; in 2 months this imperfect fistula lachrymalis was entirely cured.—*Genl. Hom. Journ.* Vol. 40, p. 14. GROSS.

CALCAREA.

CASE 112.—A woman, aged 47, had suffered for 8 years with a fistula lachrymalis of the right eye; the skin for an inch around was ulcerated; and watery pus exuded from the opening.

Treatment.—Calc. 30, effected considerable improvement for 2 months: then Lycop. 30, was given; and finally Calc. 30, perfected the cure at the end of 4 months.

CASE 113.—A maiden, aged 13, had suffered for a year with fistula lachrymalis, against which several homœopathic remedies had been given in vain. A scab frequently formed upon the unnatural opening, which then remained closed for several days; but the scab soon fell off again, and the fistula was reëstablished.

Treatment.—Silex and Petrol. diminished the size of the opening, and lessened the swelling, redness, and quantity of mucus which could be expressed from the sac. After giving 2 doses of Calc. 200, the opening closed in 14 days, and was covered with a thin membrane; all swelling about the sac had disappeared.—*Genl. Hom. Journ.* Vol. 34, p. 200. RUMMEL.

CASE 114.—A woman, aged 50, had a fistula lachrymalis for 3 years; the sac enlarged from time to time, and had to be emptied of its accumulation of pus by pressure.

Treatment.—8 doses Calc. 30, effected a perfect cure. SCHULZ. HARTLAUB and SCHOLZE were equally successful.

Review.

Calcarea effected 3 cures, two of which were accomplished by the 30th dilut., one by the 200th potency. Lachesis was successful in 1 case; Natrum, in 1; Stann. and Silex, in 1; and Sulph. in 1.

RUCKERT has noticed that this obstinate disorder will often not yield to any remedies for a length of time; but finally the right medicine will cure it.

SCROFULOUS OPHTHALMIA.

According to LAWRENCE, this is an external inflammation of the eye, occurring in scrofulous subjects. In scrofula, the morbid disposition is generally strongly marked; certain forms of disease are so easily excited, and return so readily, that it is often almost impossible to keep them off; and those membranes which are exposed to the external air are apt to suffer the most; for instance, the eyes, nose, and lungs.

"Two kinds of constitution, differing considerably in some respects, are observed in persons called scrofulous. In one, there is a pale and bloated countenance, a swelling of the upper lip and septum of the nose, and a tumid abdomen; the mucous membrane of the stomach and bowels is easily disordered by errors of diet, or by trifling causes which would have little or no effect on other persons; the nutrition of the entire body is more or less impaired; there is a languid state of the circulation, so that the skin is pale and rough, the extremities are cold, the muscles are loose and flabby, and there is a kind of torpor in all the functions, bodily as well as mental." The whole forming the so-called *torpid scrofulous constitution.*

"In another set of scrofulous subjects the skin is fine and thin, the veins distinct; there is an almost unnatural color in the cheeks; the circulation is rapid, the nervous system irritable, and both are easily excited. The various functions of the body and mind are performed quickly; a premature development of intellect is often observed in such children, and they are powerfully affected by all external influences, forming the so-called *irritable scrofulous constitution.* LAWRENCE justly says we can not suppose that the phenomena and treatment of disease will be the same in the two kinds of constitution just described, though the term scrofulous is used in both instances.

Of the remedies which have been used successfully against scrofulous ophthalmia, Arsenicum, Aurum, Belladonna, Euphrasia, Mercurius solub. et sublim., Pulsatilla, Rhus, and Sulphur, are most homœopathic to the *irritable* or acute varieties. while Calcarea, Causticum, Conium, Hepar. Sulph., Magnesia, and Silex, are most homœopathic to the *torpid* or chronic varieties.

According to ANCELL, in Scrofula, the *Red* corpuscules of the blood are deficient in number and defective in structure; the Globulin, Haematin, and Iron of the blood-globules are all *deficient*. Hence China, Ferrum, and Manganese are important remedies in the treatment of the scrofulous constitution.

The *serum* of the blood, or the liquor sanguinis is vitiated in quality; the water, albumen, and lime being in decided *excess*. Hence albuminous articles of food, and those containing an excess of lime, and lime-stone water, should be carefully avoided in scrofulous persons. The fibrin of the blood is rather below the natural standard, except when irritation, fever, or inflammation sets in, and even then the quantity of fibrin is manifestly lower than it would be if either local inflammation of the same parts, or general inflammatory action occurred in individuals whose blood was previously healthy. The *quality* of the fibrin is always *defective*. The fatty matters are often decidedly deficient, also the alkaline and earthy salts. Hence the food of scrofulous patients should contain a good deal of *fibrin*, an excess of *fat*, and of alkali. Professor SCHULTZ states that when blood is in its natural alkaline state, 2 drops of acetous acid will neutralize one drachm of serum, while in one scrofulous patient he found the serum quite neutral, and in another scrofulous subject, one drop of acetous acid neutralized 4 drachms of serum. BENNETT's theory of scrofula is, that too much albumen and too little of the oleaginous principle is conveyed into the economy; that there is a decidedly acid state of the primæ viæ, which, while it renders the assimilation of the albuminous principles more easy, by neutralizing the alkaline pancreatic juice, prevents the solution and assimilation of the oleaginous principle; hence, in a short time the blood becomes overloaded with albumen, and decidedly deficient in fatty substances. In the treatment of scrofula by dietetic means, it may be as important to avoid albuminous articles of diet, as it is well known to be to avoid sugar and all substances which may be converted into saccarhine matter, in diabetes. Acids should be avoided; the use of alkalies may be encouraged.

It is impossible to point out all the articles of diet which scrofulous persons should avoid, or prefer. The gravy from the dish of beef, pork, and mutton, should be avoided, perhaps, as the blood of ox, sheep, and pig contain from 18 to $\frac{19}{1000}$ of albumen, while the muscle of beef, pork, and deer contains only from $\frac{2.2}{1000}$ to $\frac{2.6}{1000}$, or $\frac{2.3}{1000}$; the flesh of veal and chicken, from $\frac{3}{1000}$ to $\frac{3.2}{1000}$; that of trout and pigeon, from $\frac{4.4}{1000}$ to $\frac{4.5}{1000}$; that of carp, only $\frac{5.2}{1000}$. Isinglass, white and yolk of eggs, liver of the ox, and sweetbreads are, perhaps, objectionable, as they contain respectively, from $\frac{7.2}{1000}$ to $\frac{13.5}{1000}$, 15.5, 17.47, and 20.19. Still, in practice, some of these apparently objectionable articles are not absolutely so; thus, according to MAGENDIE, the white of eggs combines a number of conditions favorable to digestion. It is alkaline, contains saline matters, and especially common salt in very large proportion; the animal matter which it contains is the same as that found in the chyle and in the blood; it is liquid, but is coagulated by the acids of the stomach, forming flocculi having but little cohesion. Lastly, white of egg contains some organized membranes, which may perform in digestion some useful and perhaps indispensable function.

Of the exciting causes of scrofula, cold is the most powerful, especially when combined with moisture. The next in order of the direct causes is insufficient or unwholesome food, excess or irregularity of diet, especially when aggravated by sedentary habits, neglect of exercise, and residence in an impure atmosphere. Hence, warm clothing, active exercise, fresh air, and proper diet, are indispensable *in the treatment* of scrofula.

To return to the consideration of scrofulous ophthalmia: The external redness of the eye is often inconsiderable, and sometimes more apparent in the lining of the lids than in the eye itself. Single blood-vessels, or bundles of them run across the white of the eye to the cornea, and either extend over its margin, or stop short at the boundary between it and the sclerotica. Where these blood-vessels terminate we observe small elevations called vesicles, pustules, or phlyctenæ. These pimples, which may have a whitish appearance, or contain a little clear or yellowish fluid, may be single, or in great number, situated on the cornea, or sclerotica, or, which is more frequent, on the boundary between them. The occurrence of these elevations, which is characteristic, though not belonging exclusively to the present affection, has led MACKENZIE to regard scrofulous ophthalmia as "an eruptive disease, affecting the white of the eye, not as a mucous membrane, but as a continuation of the skin over the eye, and to call it phlyctenular ophthalmia." LAWRENCE. "I regard these vesicles or pustules as eczematous or impetiginous in their nature, and that scrofulous ophthalmia is in reality an eruption of eczema, or a salt-rheum of the eye; often the eruptions upon the eye and skin approach eczema impetiginodes in character." ANCELL classes eczema among the scrofulous eruptions.

In scrofulous ophthalmia, the effect of light upon the eye is peculiarly painful, and the uneasiness produced by it is often carried to an extreme degree, so as to constitute a distinguishing symptom of the complaint. The head of the patient is always held down to avoid the light; the lids are spasmodically closed, and a powerful contraction of the muscles of the eyelids offers an effectual obstacle to any attempt at opening them. The spasmodic action of this muscle, (the orbicularis,) excited by exposure to light, causes actual pressure upon the eye, and makes the patient scream or wince with pain; it also makes the lids look as if they were swollen, although they are not so. The patient makes every effort to protect the eye from the painful impression of light, contracts the brows, throws the skin between them into wrinkles, draws down the skin of the forehead, elevates the lips and wings of the nose, and in short, puts into action all the muscles of the face to protect the suffering organ. Hence arises a peculiar and characteristic expression of the countenance. The painful impression of light upon the eyes, in severe cases, is such, that the patient seeks the very darkest corner of the room to escape from the light, and if in bed, it will turn the face against the pillow, or hide it under the clothes; or if brought into the light it presses its hands against the eyes and holds the head down; great irritation, redness and eruption being often produced upon the forehead, eyelids, and nose by this cause. LAWRENCE.

This great sensibility of the retina (*photophobia scrofulosa*) is not the result of inflammation, but rather the result of an irritation similar to that of spinal irritation, which, in fact, is frequently a nervous, scrofulous irritation of the spinal nerves; nor is it in direct proportion to the increased redness of the eye, being often excessive when the eye appears almost natural. Hence this symptom need not excite any fear of injury to the eye.

There is often a copious flow of tears; thus, when the eye is exposed to light, a copious discharge of scalding tears takes place, the passage of which into the nostrils often excites frequent sneezing or redness of the lids, and excoriation of them, and of the face may ensue. These irritating tears cause itching and soreness in the parts over which they flow, and aggravate the original complaint; the patient rubs and scratches the lids and face, which become red, sore and pimply; finally, small, yellow pustules form on this inflamed skin, and produce a discharge which incrusts. The eruption may extend over the forehead, temples, and face, presenting all the characters of eczema or impetigo. LAWRENCE.

The affection of the eyes is generally attended by disorder of the stomach and bowels; there is costiveness, with white or furred tongue, foul breath, distended belly, morbid appetite, and grinding of the teeth during sleep.

The edges of the lids are often red, swollen, and painful. The mucous membrane of the nose is frequently affected; there is an acrid secretion with excoriation of the nostrils, with swelling and redness of the wings of the nose, and often of the upper lip. The ears are often red and sore, and excoriated behind, showing the wide extent of the eczematous affection; and the glands of the neck frequently become enlarged.

The inflammation of the eye will suddenly get better, and may return as suddenly. Repeated attacks often occur at longer or shorter intervals, and slight exciting causes will renew the disorder when the predisposition is strong. In this way the affection may last for months and years, and it is difficult to say when the patient is permanently recovered. The affection of the eyes often alternates with other symptoms; thus, the ears may become worse, and the eyes get better, or *vice versa*. Hence the alternations of improvement and aggravation and the obstinancy of the disease are strikingly similar to those which happen to salt-rheum in other parts.

Scrofulous inflammation of the eye often produces serious changes, especially in the cornea; and this may happen although visible redness does not exist in any great degree. The elevations of the conjunctiva, previously mentioned, under the names of vesicle, pustule, or phlyctæna, may subside, leaving merely a thin opacity, which gradually disappears; sometimes a thick opacity remains, which becomes diminished, but does not disappear. But the vesicles, pustules, or phlyctænæ more commonly ulcerate; the ulceration may spread in extent or depth; and in the latter case may not only make their way into the substance of the cornea, but even penetrate into the anterior chamber, and thus lead to prolapsus of the Iris. (LAWRENCE.)

A thick and vascular corneal covering may be formed called pannus; or general dulness of the cornea from intestitial deposition of lymph, or blood may be found; or the texture of the cornea may become so weakened as to yield to the pressure from within, and be enlarged into the external protuberance called *staphyloma*.

Scrofulous inflammation rarely affects the interior of the eye, unless the cornea be ulcerated or perforated.

ARSENICUM.

BONNINGHAUSEN with characteristic assumption and ignorance states that Arsenicum is only useful in those cases in which there is ulceration on the inner surface of the eyelids.

For further remarks on the indications for the use of Arsen. see pp. 61 to 63. This remedy not only exerts a specific action upon the conjunctiva of the eyes and eyelids, but also has a well established reputation in the treatment of many eruptive diseases, such as chronic eczema, impetigo, etc. From cases furnished by SEGIN, HERMANN, WIDEMANN and others, RUCKERT has arranged the following digest of symptoms as indicative of the use of Arsenicum in scrofulous ophthalmia, namely:

When the *eyelids* are swollen; their edges reddened; the meibomian glands secreting much mucus; the lids stuck together in the morning, loaded with crusts, and closed spasmodically, with piercing pains on attempting to open them.

The *conjunctiva*, or white of the eye, traversed with blood-vessels, degenerated and composed of spongy and bright-red cellular tissue, with many enlarged veins.

The *cornea* smoky, dim, ulcerated, with opaque spots on its outer edge, with deep ulcers about its circumference, deposit of pus between its layers, covered with bluish-gray spots, and so opaque that no trace of the iris or pupil can be observed.

The *sclerotica* spongy.

The *punctum lachrymale* swollen and inflamed.

Intolerance of light in an extreme degree, so that the patient sits in the dark, or lies upon his face.

Lachrymation copious, acrid, gushing forth when the lids are opened, attended with muco-purulent discharge.

The *pains* in the eyes are biting, piercing, or *burning* in their character, attended with violent stitches when the eyes are opened, and cutting pains deep in the orbits.

Among the *accompanying disorders* are: pimples upon the face, fine rash, eruption about the eyes, itching soreness of the lids with scabs upon them, redness of the eyes with secretion acrid, watery mucus, and general restlessness.

Review.

Of 6 cases treated with Arsenicum, all were between 2 and 11 years of age, and five were females.

Doses.—Drop doses of the 3d dilution were used 3 times daily, in one case with evident improvement, which ceased as soon as only 1 or 2 doses were given per day. In 1 case, Arsen. 6, in drop doses, was given every 2 days; the 30th dilution was administered in 4 cases; and 3 doses per day were used in another case.

The disease had lasted in most cases from 1 to several years, and the cures were effected in from 1 to 6 weeks.

Arsenicum was used alone successfully in 1 case; Conium was required in addition in one case; Sulphur was given in 3 cases without marked benefit, while after the cure of the inflammation, Euphrasia, Calc., Cann., Crocus, and Nitric Acid were given to remove the remains of the disease.

AURUM.

See page 66.

CASE 114.—A girl, aged 7, with scrofulous ophthalmia and excessive intolerance of light, was quickly cured by the internal use of 1-grain doses of Aurum 3, and external use of a solution of the same. LOBETHAL.

BARYTA.

See page 66.

BELLADONNA.

(*a*) FRANK remarks that Belladonna is the most useful of all remedies against *intolerance* of light, both in scrofulous and catarrhal ophthalmia. But he saw very little good effect from infinitesimal and occasional doses; while drop doses, 2 or 3 times a day, of the 1st or 3d dilution, or even teaspoonful doses of an infusion of 10 grains of the herb to 2 ounces of water, 2 or 3 times a day, coupled with the free external use of the same preparation, proved eminently useful.—*Genl. Hom. Jour.* Vol. 18, p. 293.

(*b*.) HARTMANN says that Bellad. is beneficial in scrofulous ophthalmia when frequent relapses occur, and the attack approaches catarrhal inflammation in its nature, and is attended with much intolerance of light. Still, Hepar. Sulph. was often required to bring back the patient to the state he was in before the relapse, and then some other antipsoric remedy was required.

(*c*.) SCHREON says that he has often used Bellad. against scrofulous ophthalmia with benefit, especially when aided by Sulphur. When there was great intolerance of light and profuse lachrymation, he gave the 3d or 6th dilution, from 3 to 6 drops in a tumbler of water, in spoonful doses every 12 hours, with evident benefit, which was carried still further by drop doses of Tinct. Sulphur, also every 12 hours. Still in many other cases these same remedies and doses proved of no avail. If they had been used in more massive quantities and at shorter intervals, they would probably have proved more useful, as Bellad. is *antipathic* both to intolerance of light and excessive lachrymation. (See page 67, P.)

(*d.*) HERING advises Bellad. when there are aching pains in the eyes, increased by opening them; when the eyes are red and much congested; when vesicles and ulcers are present upon the cornea; when catarrhal symptoms are present, and the attack has been brought on by taking cold.

CASE 115.—A scrofulous youth, aged 19, with swelled upper lip and nose, who had suffered with sore eyes when a child, was attacked anew.

Symptoms.—The eyes were much inflamed; the lids were red and swollen; the lashes of the lower lids had fallen out; there was great intolerance of light, profuse lachrymation, abundant secretion of muco-pus, and the lids stuck together at night.

Treatment.—One dose of Bellad. 30, lessened the photophobia and intolerance of light considerably; and then a dose of Aurum 6, removed the disease in so far that the patient was able to resume his occupation as a tailor.—*Genl. Hom. Journal.* Vol. 28, p. 23.

CASE 116.—Bellad. 12, several doses, removed a scrofulous photophobia in a few days, which had resisted many allopathic remedies for a long time. An attack of measles, shortly afterwards, did not bring back the scrofulous ophthalmia. DR. FIELITZ.

CASE 117.—A girl, aged 3, suffered with scrofulous ophthalmia, great intolerance of light, profuse lachrymation when the eyes were open; her eyes were slightly reddened, many blood-vessels ran to the outer edge of the cornea; and there were small ulcers on both eyes.

Treatment.—Bellad. 6, almost cured her in 6 days; the remainder of the intolerance of light was removed by Ignat. 6.—*Annals*, Vol. 4, p. 401. DR. MALY.

CASE 118.—A little girl, aged 6, suffering with scrofulous ophthalmia was not relieved by Bellad., Conium, Calcarea, Sulphur and other remedies administered in various dilutions for several weeks. Then 1 grain of Extract of Bellad., solved in 4 ounces of water, and applied freely to the eyes, produced such good results that the patient was able to open her eyes in 2 days, and the intolerance of light ceased entirely in a few days more.

In similar cases, the 2d and 6th dilutions of Bellad. produced like good effects when applied externally.—*Hygea.* Vol. 8, p. 6. DR. OHLHAUTH.

CASE 119.—A man who had suffered for 2 years with scrofulous soreness and inflammation of the edges of the lids, was quickly relieved of an acute attack by Bellad. 200. But a long continued treatment of the primary affection, with the high potencies, was entirely without benefit.—*Genl. Hom. Journal.* Vol. 31, p. 218. DR. CLOTAR MULLER.

Review.

It is remarkable that in the above cases the *lower* potencies of the remedy and even the Infusion and Extract of Bellad. had to be used; especially as many of them were rather slight than severe; and that Bellad. only removed some of the symptoms of the disorder, and then that other remedies had to be employed. In obstinate and chronic cases, RUCKERT himself has seen but little benefit follow the use of Bellad. against intolerance of light, although it is thought more useful against this symptom than any other, especially when used externally. [The explanation is contained in the fact that Bellad. is not particularly homœopathic to intolerance of light and lachrymation.] (See page 67.) P.

CALCAREA. CARB.

(*a.*) STAPF says that Calc. has almost always proved the most reliable remedy in his hands against scrofulous ophthalmias, even of the worst description, in which ulcers and specks had been present on the cornea for a long time.—*Archiv.* Vols. 7 and 8.

(*b.*) LOBETHAL says, that it is an admirable remedy against morbid growths upon the cornea, resulting from scrofulous ophthalmia, especially when aided by Nitric Acid and Cannabis. *Genl. Hom. Jour.* Vol. 13, p. 6.

(*c.*) Calcarea has been used with great benefit in obstinate and chronic cases of scrofulous ophthalmia when attended with great intolerance of light, profuse secretions of tears, mucus, and pus, with which the lids become glued together, and when there are aching pains deep within the eyes.—*Annals.* Vol. 4, p. 139.

(*d.*) LORBACHER says that he only succeeded in curing obstinate and chronic cases of scrofulous ophthalmia perfectly and permanently when he gave Sulphur and Calcarea in alternation for a long time. He even found the high dilutions useful.—*Quarterly Journal.* Vol. 1, part 2, p. 256.

(*e.*) See HAY'S experience, p. 18. P.

(*f.*) See page 71.

From 13 cases reported by Drs. MULLER, DIEZ, KNORRE, and TIETZE, RUCKERT has arranged the following *clinical indications* for the use of Calcarea in scrofulous ophthalmia, namely:

When the *eyelids* are red, inflamed, itching, closed and stuck together, especially in the morning, and covered with pustules, or closed spasmodically from intolerance of light.

When the *conjunctiva* and sclerotica are inflamed and injected.

Ulcers on the *cornea*, with specks and pustules, when there is great intolerance of light, so that the patient lies upon his face; when the pupils are altered in color, and grayish, and vision is almost lost; dilated pupils; gushing of acrid, corroding tears, stitches, aching, and burning in the eyes, especially in the morning, violent piercing in the eyes, especially in the evening, by candle-light.

Accompanying Complaints.

Swelling of the face, most evident about the nose; much perspiration on the forehead; inflammation, and many pustules about the eyes; pustules and other eruptions upon the face, scalp and body attended with itching, oozing and formation of thick, yellow crusts; swelling and redness of the nose, with acrid discharge; obstruction of the nose; swelling of the upper lip; eruption upon, and swelling of the lips; eruptions and scabs upon the lips, even upon the inner surface; eruption behind the ears; swelling and hardness of the abdomen; *constipation;* hard, glandular swellings about the neck and under the chin; bloating of the whole body; inclination to profuse perspirations; irritability and obstinacy of temper.

Review.

Of the 13 patients 9 were between 2 and 10 years old.
" " 4 " " 13 and 20 " "

Nine were females.

Dose.—Calc. 4, was used in 2 cases; the 6th dilution in 1 case; the 15th in 1 case; the 30th in 8 cases; the 200th in 1 case.

Calcarea effected cures alone in 5 cases; it was assisted by Sulphur in 6 instances; by Arsenicum, in 1 case. A single dose sufficed to cure in 10 cases; repeated doses were required in 3 cases; it was given in solution in 1 case.

In 5 cases, the disease had lasted from 2 to 12 weeks; in 5 others, from 1½ to 5 years.

The cures were effected in from 2 to 6 weeks.

Almost all the cases were characterized by the severity of the symptoms, and by the presence of many of the signs of general scrofula, especially of the torpid variety.

RUCKERT substantiates LOBACHER's experience with Sulphur in alternation with Calcarea; still he only gave the doses at intervals of 4 days. Calcarea 6, often proved useful when higher dilutions were entirely inefficient.

CANNABIS.

WEBER and LOBETHAL have recommended this remedy against specks and growths upon and in the cornea, and against ulcerations of the cornea after scrofulous ophthalmia. It does not seem to have effected cures unaided by other remedies, but as an alternate remedy it has often been used with benefit.—*Genl. Hom. Jour.* Vol. 13, p. 6 and 83.

CAUSTICUM.

It is remarkable, says RUCKERT, that this remedy which offers so many indications in its pathogenesis against scrofulous ophthalmia, and which has been recommended by KREUSSELER as a wonderful remedy against this disease, is only reported as having cured one case.

CASE 120.—A boy, aged 3, was attacked with scrofulous ophthalmia, which resisted all remedies; both pupils became invisible; the cornea became bulging; and the child was entirely blind.

Treatment.—In 8 days after the first dose of Causticum 30, a remarkable improvement occurred both in the eyes and in the general health of the patient. An intermediate dose of Puls.

and a second dose of Causticum effected a cure in 4 months.—*Archiv.* Vol. 17, part 1, p. 27.

See page 72. P.

CONIUM MACULATUM.

This remedy has a well-established reputation against scrofulous affections; it acts powerfully upon the venous and glandular systems, and is even supposed to have caused atrophy of the breast and testicles.

It occasionally produces an eruption upon the skin somewhat similar to acne.

As it is apt to cause paralysis of the voluntary muscles, it may prove antipathic and palliative to spasmodic closure of the lids from irritability of the eyes in scrofulous ophthalmia.

As it produces general torpor of the brain, nervous system, and muscles, it is more homœopathic to torpid scrofula than to the irritable variety.

Finally, it is more homœopathic to chronic and torpid affections of the eyes than to acute or irritable disorders. In one case after taking Conium in large doses, the patient fell asleep, and when he awoke he could not see; in another case there were sparks before the eyes, with hiccup; fixedness and glittering of the eyes; dimness of vision; a sensation in the eyes as if they were pressed out, is characteristic of Conium; which also produces a headache, with sensation as if a large foreign body were in the anterior half of the brain. It is said not to produce dilatation of the pupils, even when introduced into the eye or by any other internal or external application of it. —PETERS.

KNORRE found it useful in purely nervous and scrofulous photophobia, when attended with spasm of the eyelids; when there was only a pale redness of the white of the eye, a narrow edge of redness around the cornea, or single large large red vessels traversing the conjunctiva. He says it is wonderful, in such cases, how quickly and certainly Conium will act; but he gave the undiluted juice of the plant in frequent doses, and often noticed that moist eruptions would then break out upon the face and head, followed by a marked diminution and speedy cessation of the intolerance of light.

When inflammation was present, and the photophobia was

only an accidental symptom, Calcarea, Graphite, and Lycopodium were more useful than Conium.

It does not prevent relapses.

Dr. Fielitz says: It is remarkable that Conium is not very serviceable against scrofulous photophobia when administered in homœopathic doses, even when the undiluted tincture is given, 1 drop at a time; while, when given in large and increasing doses of the Extract, according to Dczondi's method, it will remove the disease far more frequently, and even with a certain degree of certainty.—*Genl. Hom. Journ.* Vol. 17, p. 246.

CASE 121.—A scrofulous, portly-looking girl, aged 16, who had menstruated for about 1 year, was attacked with ophthalmia.

Symptoms.—Swelling of the upper eyelids, so that the lower lids were entirely covered by them; the swelling also extended above the eyebrows and was attended with itching and burning; the edges of the lids were violet-red in color, hard; the rest of the outer surface was pale red, shining, doughy, and very sensitive to touch; on attempting to open the lids, they became everted so that the thickly-swollen, dark-red conjunctival surface was exposed. The white of the eye was but little inflamed; the cornea sound; there was great intolerance of light; profuse secretion of a thin, yellowish muco-pus, and of tears. She complained of itching, burning, and piercing pains in the inflamed lids, aggravated at night.

Treatment. — This case was cured in 4 days with 20-drop doses, 3 times a day, of a solution of 1 scruple of Extract Coni. Mac. in 1 ounce of water.—*Genl. Hom. Journ.* Vol. 19, p. 56. Knorre.

CASE 122.—A girl, aged 6, of scrofulous constitution, had suffered for a long time with ulceration about the teeth; 7 months after the cure of this, ophthalmia set in and was treated allopathically for 4 months, without success.

Symptoms.—Great intolerance of light in both eyes, redness of the sclerotica, dimness of the cornea, redness of the eyelids, profuse discharge of mucus and tears, secretion of a mucous and acrid fluid from the nose, eruption of small and large pustules upon the right side of the face, want of appetite and sleep.

Treatment.—Conium 12, $\frac{1}{8}$ of a drop per dose, repeated every 3 or 6 days, effected a perfect cure in 14 days.—*Hygea.* Vol. 18, p. 37. DR. SEGIN.

CASE 123.—A boy, aged 6, had suffered for a year with scrofulous photophobia, inflammation of the white of the eye, with discharge of acrid tears, itching and sticking together of the lids, especially in the morning; with the remains of an eruption on the scalp, and with suppressed foot-sweats. The neighborhood of the eyelids and nose was corroded by acrid tears.

Treatment.—Sulphur 1st in the morning, and 15 drops of Tinct. Conium in the evening restored the patient in 3 months. —*Genl. Hom. Journ.* Vol. 30, p. 282. DR. MARSCHALL.

CASE 124.—In a scrofulous eye affection in a child, aged 3 years, Conium 1, in repeated 1-drop doses, acted very beneficially against considerable intolerance of light, not arising from inflammation.—*Genl. Hom. Journ.* Vol. 16, p. 134. DR. FRANK.

CASE 125.—In a case of photophobia which resisted all internal remedies, Conium 30, 2 drops in $\frac{1}{2}$ oz. of water, applied externally, proved very quickly serviceable. DR. THORER.

CASE 126.—DR. LIDER relieved scrofulous photophobia with Tinct. Conii. diluted with water, and applied directly to the eye.

Review.

The patients were all from 3 to 6, or 16 years of age.

Considerable intolerance of light was present in every case; in many instances there was a discharge of mucus and of acrid tears; also an inflammatory state of eyelids, and in one case an acute blenorrhœa, which was relieved with unusual rapidity.

The majority of the cases required the lower dilutions, or even the use of the Extract or Tincture, and the local application of the remedy. Conium deserves particular attention when intolerance of light is present without decided inflammation.

The cases were mostly chronic in their nature, and the cures were accomplished in from 14 days to 3 months; in 1 case, in 4 days only.

EUPHRASIA.

See page 79.

CASE 127.—A scrofulous little girl, aged 4, had suffered from her birth with inflammation of the eyes, attended with specks upon the cornea, and great intolerance of light. Internal remedies were of no avail; but the juice of Euphrasia dropped into the eye removed the disease so thoroughly that in a few weeks the eyes could even be used in the sunshine.—*Genl. Hom. Journ.* Vol. 1, page 40. KRETSCHMAR.

CASE 128.—A little girl, aged 6, had suffered with scrofula since she was vaccinated, when 10 months old, and with ophthalmia for 1 year.

Symptoms.—The neighborhood of the eyes was red and swollen; the edges of the lids thick and knobbed; the lashes were stuck together in bundles; the white of the eye was covered with an unevenly reddened and swollen vascular tissue; the cornea was dim; the patient could not see distinctly; there was great intolerance of light, spasms of the lids, lachrymation, discharge of purulent mucus, adhesion of the lids at night, burning and piercing pains in the eyes, emaciation, swelling of the glands of the neck, and frequent attacks of colic.

Treatment.—Five drops of a solution of 3 drops of Tinct. Euphrasia in water, was given 3 times a day; at the end of 3 weeks the patient was comparatively well, having merely some redness and lachrymation of the eyes when in the open air. Then Euphrasia was given every 3 days, and several doses of Mercurius 3, also at intervals of 3 days, completed the cure.

This remedy was also used in several cases to perfect the cure of opacities of the cornea.

HEPAR. SULPH. CALC.

(*a.*) BICKING found this remedy most useful in scrofulous ophthalmia when the patients were of a phlegmatic temperament, stout, with a fine, white skin, light hair, large bellies, thick necks, and troubled with enlarged glands, eruptions and ulcers. And when their eyes in their healthy state were surrounded with a blue circle, and a plexus of venous vessels; when the eyelashes were long, the white of the eye of a dirty gray or bluish color, the cornea very conical, and the pupils unusually large.

When there was chronic inflammation, great intolerance of light, profuse discharge of tears and mucus, ulcers, and aching, burning pains as if the eyes were bruised; the more decided these symptoms were, the larger were the doses which were required to effect a speedy cure. If the attack had not lasted long; if it did not occur as a relapse of previous disease; if the eyelids were particularly swollen and covered with crusts; the eye itself but slightly inflamed; the cornea free from vascularity, and only slightly dim and smoky in places, then he almost always saw evident improvement in 8 or 12 days, from drop doses of Hepar. 12, every 2 days.

If the blood-vessels had already spread over the cornea, especially if vesicles or phlyctænæ, or ulcers had already formed, then he could only attain the same results by 2-grain doses of the 1st or 2d trituration, daily. In still further advanced cases, he was obliged to give 1-grain doses of the crude article, every day, for 3 or 4 days.

In those cases in which the alteration of the structure of the cornea proceeded rapidly, when ulcers were on the point of perforating, or exudations threatened to obscure the entire cornea, or the anterior chamber was filled with pus, then he applied Croton Oil as a counter-irritant behind the ears and on the neck, and only administered Hepar. after the Croton-eruption had made its appearance.—*Genl. Hom. Journ.* Vol. 15, p. 1.

(*b.*) GROSS corroborates the benefit of Hepar. Sulph. Calc. in corneitis scrofulosa, and adds that in desperate cases the dilutions are not sufficient, but that 1 or 1½-grain doses of the crude article must be given.—*Archiv.* Vol. 18, part 2, p. 50.

(*c.*) SCHROEN often used Hepar. s. with excellent effects against scrofulous ophthalmia, with burning pains in reddened edges, and inner surface of the lids, intolerance of light and lachrymation, profuse secretion from the meibomian glands, sticking together of the lids, pustules on the sclerotica and cornea, and a red zone around the edge of the cornea; still relapses were apt to occur, and Bellad. often had to be used in alternation, against the excessive photophobia.—*Hygea.* Vol. 3, p. 166

(*d.*) HERING says that Hepar. is often useful after Bellad. or Merc. Viv., when the children have already taken much mercury; when the lids and eyes are red and sore, tender to touch, close spasmodically, can scarcely be moved, intolerant of light at night, and are at times quite dim, and then again bright and clear; when the eye feels as if it would be forced out; when there are ulcers or specks upon the cornea, and small pimples or pustules about the eye. But daily doses of the 2d trit. must be given for several days.

(*e.*) VOGT says that this is one of the most excellent sulphurous remedies; it acts more quickly, penetratingly, and powerfully than any other preparation of sulphur, and affects the lymphatic and glandular systems in particular, although it has its influences upon the assimilative processes, and the organic cohesion, while it diminishes the plasticity of the fluids. It exerts a less irritating influence upon the circulation, and is rather apt to depress than excite the heart and arteries. It was first recommended by DOUBLE and SENF against membranous croup, from its decided action in lessening the plasticity of the blood; they even thought that it was superior to Calomel, in this respect, and that it might be used to facilitate the secretions of the skin and mucous membranes, even of the lymphatic, glandular, and serous systems in cases in which Mercury was not allowable; hence, it has been employed to remove retentions, obstructions, accumulations, deposits and indurations of the most obstinate, chronic, and deeply-rooted nature, in feeble and cachectic and dyscratic constitutions. In short, it is a most profoundly alterative remedy which has cured many chronic inflammations, old and chronic eruptions, obstinate coughs, catarrhs, and lung-affections, suppressed menstruation, glandular obstructions, and indurations. PETERS.

(*f.*) According to SOBERNHEIM it renders the pulse softer and slower, the blood darker and *considerably deficient in albumen;* its effect in this respect is so decided that HARTWIG asserts that in $\frac{1}{4}$ of an hour after taking Hepar. Sulph. in massive doses, that the blood of horses in from $\frac{3}{4}$th to $\frac{4}{5}$ths deficient in albumen. If this be the case, it must be a powerful antipathic remedy against scrofula, in which we have seen there is a great excess of albumen. PETERS.

CASE 129.—A scrofulous child, aged 7, formerly stout, but now emaciated, was attacked with ophthalmia after hooping cough, and which had resisted all remedies.

The eye was extremely painful, much swollen externally, a bluish substance projected between the lids, and a watery, offensive fluid which excoriated the cheeks, was discharged in abundance. There was lachrymation and intolerance of light; the white of the eye seemed converted into a red mass of flesh, and formed a raised wall (chemosis) around the quite opaque cornea; pus was effused on the inner side of the cornea.

Treatment.—Two-drop doses of Tinct. Sulph. fort. were given for 8 days, when an offensive tinea capitis made its appearance, and an eruption upon the breast and neck, attended with fever and obstinate constipation. The Sulphur was continued for 8 days more in connection with cold baths; the eruption declined, but the tinea increased; the painful irritation of the eye subsided so that it could be examined.

In the anterior layer of the opaque cornea, opposite the pupil, there was an effusion of pus, forming a small projection; there was also a larger effusion deeper in the substance of the cornea at its lower portion, and a semi-lunar deposition of pus in the anterior chamber of the eye, (hypopion.)

Now ½-grain doses of Hepar. Sulph. Calc. were given for 6 days in succession, at the end of which time the eye was almost free from pain, and secreted a thicker and less acrid but still offensive mucus. No remedies were given for six days more; then as the cornea was almost disengaged from the swelling of the conjunctiva, and was brighter and more clear, as the secretion of mucus had almost ceased, and the pain had nearly disappeared, 4-drop doses of Tinct. Euphrasia were given daily for 14 days, when the eye was perfectly restored. —*Genl. Hom. Journ.* Vol. 23, p. 353. DR. BICKING.

CASE 130.—A scrofulous boy, aged 4, and suffering with scald head, had had ophthalmia for several weeks, during which he had been treated allopathically without success.

Symptoms.—The neighborhood of the eye was inflamed; the eyelashes encrusted, edges of the lids swollen; the left eye could only be opened with difficulty, and then a quantity of tears gushed forth; the conjunctiva was traversed by a number of bluish-red blood-vessels; the cornea was hazy and covered with ulcers; the right eye could be opened more easily, but was generally inflamed; the cornea was grayish and spotted, and perforated by a penetrating ulcer; the iris had fallen forwards into the perforation, (prolapsus iridis.)

Treatment.—Grain-doses of Hepar. Sulph. were given for 3 days; on the 4th day, the eyes could be opened in a darkened room, the lachrymation was less profuse, the redness of the conjunctiva paler, the cornea clearer. At the end of 4 days more, the prolapsed iris had withdrawn, and the ulceration of the cornea was in process of healing. Sulphur and Euphrasia were given to perfect the cure.—*Genl. Hom. Journ.* Vol. 16, p. 118. BICKING.

CASE 131.—A child, aged 6, of delicate and weakly constitution, with relaxed muscles, bloated face, swelled upper lip, deep-set eyes, irregular stools, frequent swellings and indurations of single glands, was attacked with ophthalmia and treated allopathically for a long time with Mercury and Antimony.

The eyes were much reddened, the lids swelled, red, and burning hot; there was great intolerance of light.

Treatment.—Hepar Sulph. 30, 4 doses at intervals of 6 days, removed the affection entirely in 2 months.—*Archiv.* Vol. 19, part 1, p. 78. ARGENTI.

CASE 132.—A child, aged 7, markedly scrofulous, suffered with ophthalmia of the left eye; the sclerotica was violet-red, the cornea dim, the eye watered profusely, the lower lid was swollen, and there was great intolerance of light.

Treatment.—Bellad. 200, was given without benefit; 10 days after, Calc. 200, relieved the photophobia somewhat, but an ulcer formed upon the cornea, and the patient wept and complained of much pain. Then Hepar. Sulph. 200, was given without benefit; finally, Hepar. 3, 4 doses was given with relief from pain in 3 days; and the cure was perfected in 9 days more, under daily doses of the same remedy; the ulcer commenced to heal on the 5th day after the stronger doses of Hepar. began to be used.—*Genl. Hom. Journ.* Vol. 33, p. 101. KALLENBACH.

Review.

The above 4 patients were all children from 4 to 7 years of age, and suffering with the torpid form of scrofula, although the ophthalmia sat in with great violence, attended with decided disease of the conjunctiva, cornea and lids, and even with effusion into the anterior chamber of the eye, (hypopion,) and prolapsus of the iris.

Dose.—In 2 cases, the crude Hepar. Sulph. was given with

good effect; in one case, Hepar. 200, failed, while Hepar. 3, succeeded; Hepar. 30, was used in 1 case. Repeated doses were required in every case; and the lower dilutions were generally most successful. HARTMANN found Hepar. to act most beneficially after the previous use of Bellad.

The cures were effected in from 10 days to 2 months, even in the most unpromising cases.

MAGNESIA CARB.

CASE 133.—A girl, aged 11, suffering with scrofulous ophthalmia, was left, after the use of several remedies, with dimness and opacity of the cornea, so that she could scarcely distinguish any thing clearly; the ball of the eye was inflamed, and the lids swollen.

Treatment.—After taking Magnes. c. 24, the inflammation abated and the cornea commenced to be more transparent, so that the little patient could see almost every thing, although somewhat indistinctly. Nitric Acid 30, removed every trace of disease in the cornea.—*Archiv.* Vol. 10, p. 1, page 157. RUCKERT.

MERCURIUS SOLUBILIS.

HERING with characteristic complexity and impracticability of advice says that Mercurius is suitable especially after the previous use of Bellad. when the pains in the eyes of little children are cutting, especially from using the eyes, aggravated in the evening by the warmth of the bed; with burning, biting, and lachrymation while in the open air; intolerance of light, with dimness and mistiness of the eyes; or when small pustules or pimples are present upon the ball of the eye; and when relapses occur after every taking cold.

CASE 134.—A little girl, aged 2, had suffered for 3 months with ophthalmia.

Symptoms.—The eyelids were swollen; there was a pimply eruption upon the lids and cheeks; crusts formed between the lashes; there were whitish-gray specks upon the cornea of both eyes; intolerance of light, so that the little patient lay upon her face; the nose and lips were swollen; there was a discharge of much greenish, thick, and acrid mucus from the nose, which had excoriated the nostrils and upper lip; the backs of the hands and the fore-arms were sore from wiping off the nasal mucus; the parotid glands were swollen; and the child was irritable, impatient, and tearful.

Treatment.—Several remedies, and among them Arsenicum, were given without benefit; then Merc. Sol. 2, 1 grain every night and morning, relieved the whole disorder in 5 weeks.—*Genl. Hom. Journ.* Vol. 31, p. 152. DR. HAUSTEIN.

CASE 135.—A scrofulous child, aged 2, had suffered more than a year, after being vaccinated, with disease of the eyes, and swelling of the glands of the neck.

Symptoms.—The lids of both eyes were reddened and swollen; the left eye was considerably inflamed and intolerant of light; there was a white spot on the outer side of the cornea; frequent and acrid discharge of tears, especially from the left eye; adhesion of the lids at night; during the day the child lay constantly upon its face, and was exceedingly fractious; her nose was obstructed with mucus.

Treatment.—Acon., Bell., Sulph., Merc., and Calcarea, all in the 30th dilutions, and Euphrasia in the 6th were given without benefit; but Merc. Sol. 3, one dose every 2 days for several weeks, produced a rapid improvement and effected a cure by the time that 14 doses had been taken.

In a similar case, the author saw no good results from the high dilutions, while Hepar. 3, and Merc. 3, soon effected a cure.—*Genl. Hom. Journ.* Vol. 28, p. 24.

CASE 136.—A girl, aged 8, had a sore eye for a week.

Symptoms.—The conjunctiva was reddened, there was constant lachrymation and intolerance of light, with piercing pains; there were several pustules on the edge of the cornea, which had burst and formed ulcers.

Treatment.—Merc. v. 3, 1 dose, effected a rapid cure; the scars and specks disappeared in a few weeks.

MERC. SUBLIM. CORROS.

BÖCKER used this remedy internally and externally in scrofulous ophthalmia; for external use he solved 1 grain in 1 ounce of pure water. He treated 34 patients in one year; the majority were children from 2 to 14 years of age; many had ulcers on the cornea; very few had pannus; and in these the cure was delayed for several weeks. In 3 cases, after using the remedy for 6 weeks, he was obliged to omit it, as a very copious flow of saliva sat in; but these patients soon recovered without the use of any other remedy.

Most of them recovered in a short time; and he had opportunities of seeing many of them afterward, and of convincing himself that they remained perfectly cured.

Relapses occurred in 5 cases, but these were cured by the same remedy.

In another year, he treated 28 additional patients; he only found Merc. useful in the *erethistic* form; in the *torpid* variety, the remedy was not only entirely useless, but even proved injurious in 3 cases.

In the 3d year, he treated 6 cases. All were cured.—*Hygea.* Vol. 21, p. 480.

From these cases the following *clinical indications* have been obtained for the use of Merc. Corrosiv., namely:

When the *lids* were greatly swollen and spasmodically closed; the upper lid projecting far down and over the lower; much dried mucus upon the edges of the lids.

The meibomian glands much inflamed; discharge of thick pus and mucus from the eyes; great intolerance of light; and necessity to remain in the dark.

The *cornea* covered with red vessels; also with ulcers, which threatened to perforate it; chalk-white specks; and commencement of staphyloma.

The white of the eye greatly inflamed, swollen, velvety, and covered with papillæ.

The anterior chamber filled with pus, (hypopion.)

The neighborhood of the eyes and the cheeks red, swollen, and covered with small pustules; the glands of the neck hard and swollen; eruption on the back of the head.

Doses.—Half a grain of Merc. Sub. was solved in 5 scruples of water, and 2 or 3 drops given 3 or 4 times a day; in 1 case, the 1st dilution was used 4 or 5 times daily. In some cases, an external application of 1 grain to 4 ounces of water was used.

Some of the patients had suffered from 1 to 3 weeks; others from 1 to 3 months; and several for 2 years.

The cures were effected in from 4 to 9 days; or in from 10 to 15 days; or at the latest in 6 weeks.

This remedy deserves every consideration and confidence. It is peculiarly homœopathic to scrofulous eczematous ophthalmia.

NITRIC ACID.

(*a.*) LOBETHAL says that it is an excellent remedy against vegetations on the cornea from scrofulous inflammation.

(*b.*) GROSS gave it in the very high dilutions, after the previous use of Calc. 200, and saw it cure ulcers of the cornea, and partially remove opacities.

(*c.*) BONNINGHAUSEN recommends it in alternation with Pulsatilla.

(*d.*) WEBER thinks it is the most useful of all remedies against opacities of the cornea.

PULSATILLA.

CASE 137.—A child, aged 4, was attacked with a purulent and offensive eruption upon the head and face, and then with a scrofulous ophthalmia, which had already lasted for a year.

Treatment.—Sulph., Bell., Calc., and Euphrasia did not help. Pulsat. 12, in alternation with Nitric Acid 12, produced an aggravation for some days, followed by so rapid an improvement that the cure was entirely perfected in 20 days. No relapse occurred for 7 months. HAUSTEIN.

PSORIN.

STAPF says that this remedy has proved most useful in his hands against scrofulous ophthalmia.—*Archiv.* Vol. 19, p. 6, p. 148.

RHUS TOXICOD.

FIELITZ says that it is an important and useful remedy against scrofulous ophthalmia, with intolerance of light, when the eyes can not be opened, even at night; but it must be given at least as strong as the 2d or 3d dilution, as the high potencies are entirely inoperative. It is most indicated when the meibomian glands are swelled, and secrete much mucus; when relief ensues in the evening, and the eruption appears in the form of tinia capitis, but extends down upon the face in the form of crusta lactea, attended with swelling of the glands of the neck. It should not be given alone, but in constant alternation with Bell. or Sulph. or Calc.—*Genl. Hom. Journ.* Vol. 17, p. 246.

(*c.*) Another author says that Rhus is an indispensable remedy in scrofulous ophthalmia, being most indicated, however, when the scrofulous disease has manifested itself not only upon the eyes, but also upon other parts of the body, especially upon the head in the shape of tinia favosa; and when the inflammation of the eye is attended with the formation of pustules, great intolerance of light, and biting, aching pains.

The inflammation is generally not very active; still the piercing pains in the ball of the eye are often very acute, and the pains are usually increased by exposure of the eye to light, so that the patient fears to open it, and a false photophobia is produced.

Swelling, not only of the eyelids, but of the whole neighborhood of the eye, is often present, and then forms a farther indication for the use of Rhus.—*Genl. Hom. Journ.* Vol. 37, p. 308.

(*c.*) LOBETHAL says that he is convinced that the high dilutions of Rhus are entirely inefficient, and that it is even not prejudicial to the little patient to bring on the primary effects of the remedy by means of strong doses, in order to produce a powerful alteration in the disordered lymphatic system.—*Genl. Hom. Journ.* Vol. 14, p. 325.

(*d.*) THORER says he has lately treated several scrofulous ophthalmias, in all of which, vesicles and pustules were present. Rhus 30, 1 or 2 globules, every 2, 4, or 6 days, always afforded the most excellent result, and either perfected the cure alone, or at least removed all danger from the ulcerations on the cornea. Experience proved to him that Rhus 30, was always sufficient if the remedy was indicated.—*Practical Remarks*, Vol. 3, part 2, p. 25.

(*e.*) Rhus is particularly homœopathic to erysipelatous, eczematous, and pemphiginous eruptions. It has been used successfully against obstinate herpetic eruptions, and DELILLE FLAZAC has even seen warty vegetations disappear under its internal use. Some allopathic physicians, such as GESCHEIDT, ELSHOLZ, and SCHEIBLER have given it with brilliant success against scrofulous ophthalmia when attended with very obstinate and excessive photophobia. Also PEITHNER and WEITENWEBER found it very curative against scrofulous conjunctivitis, inflammation of the cornea, with ulceration of the cornea, inflammation of the meibomian glands, spasm of the eyelids, and intolerance of light; especially when these were complicated with scrofulous herpetic eruptions upon the face and head. It has also been used successfully against amblyopia and amaurotic weakness of the eyes. DUFRESNOY, RAYER, MATHAI, and WILLEMET have confidence in it against herpetic and scrofulous affections.

The Rhus eruption is erysipelatous in its nature, attended with great and inflammatory-œdematous swelling, with outbreak of pemphigous, or itch-like vesicles and pustules. PETERS.

From cases furnished by THORER, LOBETHAL, and HAUSTEIN, RUCKERT has arranged the following *clinical indications* for the use of Rhus in scrofulous ophthalmia:

Great or moderate swelling of the eyelids; conjunctiva swollen and inflamed; red vessels running toward the cornea; the cornea covered with phlyctænæ or vesicles; small ulcers on the cornea, supplied with blood-vessels from the white of the eye; vesicles on the edge of the cornea; ulcers upon both eyes; specks and dimness of the cornea; loosening of the sclerotica at the outer edge of the cornea; considerable lachrymation and intolerance of light, forcing the patient to lie constantly upon his face; acrid, hot discharge of tears; sticking together of the lids.

Accompanying Complaints.

Eruptions upon the head and face; large pustules on the face, which change to superficial ulcers; the whole face is covered with a thick, whitish-yellow crust, which exudes moisture at some places; new vesicles spring up upon the red skin where the scabs have loosened and form offensive scabs; swelling of the face and nose, with roughness of the skin; scrofulous eruptions upon the internal surface of the thick and swollen nose; discharge of a thick, greenish, acrid mucus from the nose; watery discharge from the nose; suppuration of the glands behind the ear; thirst; hard and difficult stools; emaciation; irritability and inclination to weep.

Review.

The patients were from 1½ to 10 years of age; one was 19.

Doses.—In one case, the first dilution was given in solution;

the 3d was given in solution in one case, and in two-drop doses in another; the 30th, in repeated doses in 3 cases; the 200th failed in one case, which was relieved by Rhus 3d and 18th. Rhus alone effected cures in 5 cases; Arsenicum was given as an intermediate remedy in one case, and followed by Calc.

The disease had lasted in 3 cases from 5 to 8 days, and was *cured* in from 5 to 9 days; 2 cases which had lasted each 1 and 4 years, were *cured* in 5 weeks.

The above cases, even the chronic ones, do not seem to have been of the most violent kind, although attended with eruptions upon the head and face, and pustules upon the eye. Some physicians prefer the lower dilutions, and RÜCKERT has seen the 3d succeed when the 30th had failed.

SILEX.

CASE 138.—A girl, who had suffered for a long time with ophthalmia scrofulosa, was cured by Aqua Silic. 10 drops 3 times a day, contined for several months.

SULPHUR.

(*a.*) KNORRE says that it is most useful when the eyelids are most involved; when small vesicles are present upon the edge of the cornea and nourished by vessels running from the conjunctiva; the photophobia not great; and the inflammation of the eyes is not as severe as that of the lids.—*Genl. Hom. Journ.* Vol. 6, p. 21.

(*b.*). HERING says that it is most useful when the lids are spasmodically contracted in the morning; when the eyes do not bear day-light well, or the patient is quite blind by day, and can only see in the dusk; when the sight is dim and misty, the cornea dull and dusty; and when the lids are most affected, especially after the previous use of Bell., Merc., or Hepar. Also, when the white of the eye is reddened and crowded with blood, with small vesicles upon it, attended with lachrymation, intolerance of light, and violent aching in the ball of the eye, increased by sunlight. The 3d dilution should then be repeated every day, or every other day.

(*c.*) According to BALLY, in the earlier stages of scrofula, when there is a general coldness of the extremities and skin, vast quantities of Sulphur are sometimes separated from the blood through the kidneys, also from the bowels, and from open sores, as is evident from the blackening of lead-plasters and silver instruments when brought in contact with scrofulous pus; clearly showing that sulphur is thus unnaturally discharged from the system. Again, cystine contains no less than 26 per cent. of sulphur, and is occasionally produced in excess in the urine of scrofulous persons.

It accelerates the capillary circulation, the patient often feeling a degree of warmth in the extremities; in fact it plays an important part in the production and maintenance of the animal heat. It is most useful when there is a tendency to coldness of the hands, feet, and limbs; when eruptions are present upon the skin, and vesicles, or pustules, upon the eye; when there is much flatulence of the stomach and bowels; and large quantities of sulphur are expelled from the system, through the skin, bowels, and kidneys. PETERS.

From cases supplied by TIETZE, KNORRE, FLEISCHMANN, SEGIN, ELWERT, and NEGIDI, RÜCKERT has arranged the following *clinical* indications for the use of Sulphur.

When the eyelids are more or less swollen, especially in the morning; the meibomian glands red and swollen; the edges of the lids inflamed, thick, knotty, ulcerated, and covered with thick and hardened matter.

When the conjunctiva is injected, showing a convolution of fine red vessels, which run to the edge of the cornea, and is reddened and swollen. The outer angle of the eye red and swollen.

When the cornea is surrounded by a pale-red circle, with lymph effused between its layers; when it is dim, traversed by red blood-vessels, vascular at its upper half, with specks, ulcers, and pustules upon its surface and edges.

When there is a profuse and hot flow of tears on opening the eye; great intolerance of light, especially of candlelight; pain and aching in the eye; stitches, shooting through the eye into the brain; double vision; inability to see small objects, while large ones seem enveloped in a mist.

Attending Disorders.

Eruption of itching pimples over the whole body; pustules about the eyes and ears; lips swollen and covered with scabs; nettle-rash and scald-head.

Swelling of the glands of the neck, behind the ears, and on the nape; suppuration of the glands of the arm-pit; distension of the abdomen; loose and chalky stools; emaciation; general want of development.

Review.

Of 14 patients, 2 were males, 8 females, and 4 unknown; 10 were between 1 and 9 years old, 4 between 14 and 17.

The inflammation was generally great in extent and severity; the cornea had generally suffered severely; the eye affection was often accompanied by a general scrofulous condition, marked by eruptions upon the head and body, and swellings of the glands.

Doses.—The 2d and 3d triturations were given in $\frac{1}{2}$ grain doses in 4 cases; one dose sufficed in 3 cases; repeated doses were required in 1. The tincture was given in single doses in 1 case; in repeated doses in 2. The 2d dilution, in single and repeated doses, each in 1 case. The 5th dilution in repeated doses in 1 case. The 30th dilution in repeated doses in 3 cases. The 30th dilution in single doses in 1 case.

Sulphur alone proved sufficient to cure the disease, in 8 cases; in 5 cases, Acon., Bell., and Conium were given with but little effect; in 5 cases, Sulphur was required to complete the cure, after the previous use of Calc., Lycop., Bell., and Hepar. After the use of the trituration of Sulphur aggravations occasionally occurred, at times of the general inflammation, at others of the photophobia, but then a rapid cure followed in a few days.

In 4 cases in which the disease had lasted from 2 to 14 days, *cures* were effected in from 2 to 8 days; in 4 other cases, of from 1 to 3 years' standing, cures took place in from 1 to 4 weeks. In cases of many years' standing, from 6 to 10 weeks were required.

CLOTAR MÜLLER'S TREATMENT.

Hepar. Sulph. is the principal remedy in all ordinary cases, but it must often be given for a long time together. In recent cases, when there is considerable redness, swelling, and pain, it will be advisable to give several preceding doses of *Aconite* or *Bellad.*

Intolerance of light is generally soon improved by *Bellad.*; still, *Conium* is the most important remedy in those cases in which there is no visible inflammation, either of the eyes or lids. *Viola Tricolor* often removes this very troublesome symptom.

In the severest forms of this disease, in which the pain, swelling, and ulceration are very considerable, and the whole course of the disease quite acute, the *Merc. Sublimatus* is the most reliable remedy.

If the tears are so acrid that they excoriate the cheek, and eruptions make their appearance upon the face, head, or ears, then *Rhus Tox.* is the most important remedy.

Conium and *Cannabis* are the best remedies against the scars, specks, and dimness of the cornea, left by recent attacks; but Sulphur, Calcarea, or Silex are necessary in very old and chronic cases.

HARTMANN'S TREATMENT.

HARTMANN says that although the management of such a disease should be principally conducted with anti-scrofulous medicines, yet he has frequently commenced the treatment with *Euphrasia* 3d to 6th dilution, with great benefit to the patient, especially when there is redness of the sclerotica, which is traversed by red blood-vessels; specks, vesicles, and ulcers, on the inflamed cornea, profuse discharge of tears and mucus, which corrode the surrounding parts; swelling of the eyelids; sensitiveness of the eyes, and intolerance of light, with spasmodic contraction of the eyelids; stinging and aching pains in the eyes; profuse discharge from the nose. He knows that Euphrasia is not the principal remedy in this disease; but it will be found excellent, provided it is chosen in accordance with the symptoms, and especially when the ophthalmia is complicated with catarrhal symptoms.

If the inflammation should become very acute, and the pains intolerable, especially when the eye is dry, with excessive sensitiveness, then a few doses of *Aconite* should be given.

Next to Aconite, *Belladonna* is the best remedy; but these two remedies are not sufficient to effect a complete cure; there will remain a certain degree of inflammation, and the intolerance of light may be particularly distressing toward evening, and will sometimes increase so as to induce spasmodic closure of the lids. Then *Hepar. Sulph.* 3d, may be given with great effect; the higher attenuations are not as efficient as the lower.

Before giving *Hepar.* s., it may be advisable to give a few doses of *Mercurius solubilis*, especially if the swelling and spasmodic closure of the lids render it impossible to obtain a correct view of the state of the eye. The Mercurius will diminish the inflammation sufficiently to enable Hepar. s. to act with promptitude and decided effect. When the inflammation runs very high, and burning and corroding tears are discharged whenever the eye is opened, *Mercurius Corrisivus*, 2 or 3 times a day, will act admirably.

In some cases, Hepar. s. will effect a partial improvement only, and some other remedy must be given, after which Hepar. will again act favorably. HARTMANN then usually gives Sulphur and Calcarea.

Sometimes all the efforts of art are baffled by the obstinacy and virulence of the disease, especially when new ulcers break out on the cornea as fast as the old ones heal; then Cannabis, Mercurius, Silex, or Sepia, may be used. But in obstinate cases, where no other medicine seemed to do the least good, *Arsenicum* will finally overcome it, especially if given in alternation with Euphrasia.

THORER has recommended *Rhus*, and HARTMANN has given it with good results in some cases, especially when scrofulous and herpetic eruptions on the head and face were present.

ALLOPATHIC TREATMENT.

LAWRENCE says that we must first endeavor to remove the unhealthy condition of the digestive organs and skin, which is so prominent a feature in the complaint, and to invigorate the constitution.

The bowels must be completely cleansed from the accumulated load of ill-digested food and unhealthy secretions; 2 or 3 purgative doses often afford the greatest relief to the sufferings of the child. Then Mercurius should be given until the tongue is clear, and the motions of natural consistence and color. Finally, in the state of debility to which the young sufferers are frequently reduced by this painful and obstinate complaint, tonic medicines may be used. MACKENZIE recommends

Quinine strongly; he has found no remedy so useful as this; it exercises a remarkable power over the constitutional disorder which attends scrofulous ophthalmia, and thereby over the local complaint. In most instances, its effects are very remarkable; in most cases, it acts like a charm; abating commonly in a few days, the excessive intolerance of light, and the profuse lachrymation; promoting the absorption of the pustules, and hastening the cicatrisation of the ulcers of the cornea.

Belladonna has been strongly recommended against intolerance of light and spasmodic closure of the lids; if the dose be increased until dilatation of the pupil is produced, the photophobia invariably disappears.

GENERAL REVIEW OF THE TREATMENT OF SCROFULOUS OPHTHALMIA

In the preceding chapter, we find 75 cases of scrofulous ophthalmia cured by 15 different remedies, in which Sulphur was given with decided advantage in 14 cases; Calcarea, in 13; Merc. Subl., in 10; Rhus, in 7; Arsenicum and Conium, each in 6; Bellad., in 5; Hepar., in 4; Merc. Solub., in 2; Aurum, Caust., Euphrasia, Magnes., Acid. Nitric, Pulsat., and Silex, each in 1 case; while Baryta and Psorin have been merely recommended.

When the disease occurred in a *chronic* form, we have found that Arsen., Aurum, Calc., Conium, Hepar., Magnes., Merc. Sol., Pulsat., and Sulphur, have been relied upon. In the more *acute* attacks, Bellad., Subl., Rhus, and Sulphur. In the *slighter* cases, Bellad. and Rhus. In the more *severe* attacks, Arsen., Calc., Hepar., Subl., and Sulphur. When there was an *effusion of pus* in the anterior chamber, (hypopion,) and prolapsus of the iris, Hepar. Against specks, ulcerations, and vegetations of the cornea, Cannabis, Euphras., and Nitric Acid. In the more *torpid* forms, Hepar.; in the erethistic, or *irritable* varieties, Sublimate.

Doses.—In these we find very great differences of opinion and practice. The *lower*, or stronger preparations of Bellad., Hepar., Conium, and Rhus, were used, and these were even found practically, more preferable to the higher potencies. Aurum,

Euphrasia, Merc. Sol. and Subl., Silex, and Sulphur were also used in the lower dilutions. The 30th dilution of Ars. and Calc. was occasionally relied upon, and also of Sulphur, Rhus, Hepar., and Causticum. The high potencies of Calc., Hepar., and Rhus were employed, but at times without effect.

The 75 cases were furnished by 34 different physicians, the majority of whom are in favor of the *lower* dilutions, namely, Böcker used them successfully 13 times; Tietze, 6 times; Bicking, in 4 cases; Lobethal and Hanstein, each in 3 case; Frank, and Frelitz, each in 2 cases: in all, in 31 cases. The *higher* dilutions were relied upon by an anonymous physician in 9 cases; by Thorer in 5; by Tietze in 4; by Gross and Segin, each in 3; by Hermann in 2; by Bicking and Haustein, each in 1 case; in all, in 29 cases.

The *local* use of the appropriate remedies was employed with Aurum, Bellad., Conium, Euphrasia, and Subl.; the external use of Conium was found especially useful against nervous photophobia. Rückert says, that the external and local action has been too little brought in play; when the watery solution does not avail, an ointment may be applied with benefit.

The *results* of the treatment were necessarily very variable, although they were often both rapid and decided even in the most refractory cases. Thus, of 11 cases in which the disease had lasted from 1 to 4 weeks, cures were effected in every instance in from 2 to 6 or 10 days.

In 4 cases in which it had persisted from 1 to 4 months, 3 cures were effected in from 4 to 14 days, and in 1 case, at the end of 5 weeks.

In 21 cases, in which the duration was from 1 to 5 years and longer, 3 cures were accomplished in from 4 to 20 days; 14 cures in from 1 to 6 weeks; and 4, in from 8 to 12 weeks.

In contrast to these results we find in Fischer's Clinical Guide, that of 20 cases treated *allopathically*, 9 had lasted from 4 to 14 days, and 3 of these were cured in from 14 to 18 days; 3, in from 3 to 4 weeks; 2, in from 7 to 8 weeks; and 1 at the end of 8 months.

Of *nine* other cases which had lasted from 4 to 6 weeks, 6 were cured in from 3 to 8 weeks; and 3, in from 11 to 20 weeks. In 1 other case of 12 weeks' standing, a cure was accomplished in 4 weeks; and 1 of 3 months' duration, in 3 months.

In 15 cases out of the 75, it is expressly stated that they had been treated allopathically for a long time unsuccessfully.

HARTMANN recommends Hepar., after the previous use of Bellad.; while SCHROEN and HERING both recommend Sulphur, and the latter, Merc. Calcarea is often indicated after Sulphur, and HARTMANN and LOBACHER advise them in alternation. Calc. is recommended by LOBETHAL, as equally useful as Nitric Acid and Cannabis, against vegetations of the cornea. GROSS recommends Nitric Acid after the previous use of Calcarea.

In excessive intolerance of light, SCHROEN gives 1 dose of Bellad. between each 2 doses of Hepar. HERING is afraid to use Sulphur after Hepar.

BICKING thinks Hepar. most indicated in patients of the torpid scrofulous constitution; also Conium and Calcarea. BÖCKER thinks that Sublimate is more useful against the irritable than the sluggish forms of inflammation.

The parts of the eye involved in the disease, and the *kind* of pains which prevailed, and the signs of general scrofula which were present in the different cases, will be found most easily by reference to the following TABLES, of which No. I. contains the disorders of the tissues, and the varieties of the pains; while No. II. includes the other more distant affections.

TABLE II.

	Arsenicum	Bellad.	Calcarea.	Conium.	Hepar.	Merc. Sol.	M. Subl.	Rhus.	Sulph.
Swelling of the Head			Calc.						
Eruption on the "				Con.	Hep.		M.Subl.	Rhus.	Sulph.
Do., with Scabs			Calc.					Rhus.	
Perspiration of the Forehead			Calc.						
Inflam. & Swelling ab't Eyes			Calc.		Hep.			Rhus.	
Eruption on the Face	Ars.		Calc.	Con.		M. Sol.	M.Subl.	Rhus.	Sulph.
Nose, Swollen and Red	Ars.	Bell.	Calc.			M. Sol.			
Acrid Nasal Discharge	Ars.		Calc.	Con.		M. Sol.		Rhus.	
Swelling of Parotid Glands						M. Sol.			
" Upper Lip		Bell.	Calc.		Hep.	M. Sol.			Sulph.
Eruption on Lips			Calc.						Sulph.
Scabs on Lips			Calc.						
Salivation			Calc.						
Thirst for Water			Calc.						
Swelling of glands of Neck			Calc.		Hep.		M.Subl.	Rhus.	
Thick, Hard, Abdomen			Calc.		Hep.				
Constipation			Calc.					Rhus.	
Bloating of the Body			Calc.						
Inclination to Perspire			Calc.						
Pimples on the Body									Sulph.
Suppressed Foot-Sweat				Con.					
General Restlessness	Ars.								
Irritability and Obstinacy						M. Sol.			

TABLE I.

	Arsenicum.	Aurum.	Baryta.	Bella-donna.	Calcarea.	Causticum.	Conium.	Euphrasia.	Hepar.	Magnesia.	Merc. Sol.	Merc. Sub.	Acid Nit.	Rhus.	Sulph.
Eyelids Swollen	Ars.			Bella.			Con.		Hep.		M. Sol.	Sub.		Rhus.	Sulph.
" Inflamed				Bella.	Calc.		Con.				M. Sol.				
" Conjunctiva							Con.								
" Spasmodically Closed	Ars.				Calc.		Con.		Hep.		M. Sol.				
" Covered with Pustules					Calc.										
" Itching of							Con.								
" Sticking Together	Ars.				Calc.		Con.		Hep.		M. Sol.	Sub.			Sulph.
" Piercing Pains when Opened	Ars.														
Edges of the Lids Inflamed and red	Ars.			Bella.			Con.		Hep.			Sub.			
" " Knobby and Ulcerated							Con.								Sulph.
Meibomian Glands, Secreting Mucus									Hep.						
" " Red and Inflamed	Ars.											Sub.			Sulph.
" " Swollen	Ars.														Sulph.
Conjunctiva Inflamed							Con.					Sub.			
" Swollen												Sub.			
" Red and Injected	Ars.			Bella.	Calc.		Con.		Hep.						Sulph.
" Flesh-Red	Ars.								Hep.			Sub.			
" Spongy															Sulph.
" Bag-Shaped												Sub.		Rhus.	
" Granular, or covered with Papillary bodies												Sub.			
" of Cornea surrounded with a Convol. of Blood vess.				Bella.			Con.					Sub.			Sulph.
" " Degenerated	Ars.														
Angles of the Eyes red															Sulph.
Pupils Dilated							Con.								
Cornea hazy and dim	Ars.				Calc.		Con.	Euph.	Hep.	Mag.			Ac. Nit.		Sulph.
" with bluish-gray Specks	Ars.														
" Puffed up						Caust.									Sulph.
" covered with Vesicles			Bary.						Hep.					Rhus.	
" " Pustules				Bella.	Calc.				Hep.		M. Sol.				
" " Ulcers	Ars.				Calc.				Hep.			Sub.			Sulph.
" Layers of filled with Pus	Ars.								Hep.						
" " Lymph															Sulph.
" Vascular									Hep.			Sub.			Sulph.
Anterior Chamber full of Pus									Hep.			Sub.			
Sclerotica Injected					Calc.		Con.		Hep.						
" Spongy	Ars.														
" Swollen and Knobby															Sulph.
Caruncula Lachry. Swollen	Ars.														
" " Inflamed	Ars.														
Intolerance of Light	Ars.	Aur.		Bella.	Calc.		Con.	Euph.	Hep.		M. Sol.	Sub.			Sulph.
" Candle-Light									Hep.						Sulph.
Lachrymation	Ars.			Bella.					Hep.						Sulph.
Tears, Hot															Sulph.
" Acrid	Ars.				Calc.		Con.		Hep.		M. Sol.			Rhus.	
" with Pus	Ars.			Bella.			Con.		Hep.						
Aching Pains				Bella.	Calc.										Sulph.
Biting "	Ars.														
Burning "	Ars.				Calc.		Con.		Hep.						
Piercing "	Ars.				Calc.		Con.								Sulph.
Cutting "	Ars.										M. Sol.				

RHEUMATIC OPHTHALMIA.

See page 49.

(*a.*) RÜCKERT says that in this dangerous form of eye-inflammation, the homœopathic literature has several very interesting cases of cure to present.

The following remedies have been used most frequently, namely, Acon., Bryon., Clematis, Coloc., Natrum, Mer., Puls., Merc. Sol., Rhus, Spigelia, and Sulphur.

ACONITE.

KREUSSLER says that Aconite deserves particular attention in rheumatic ophthalmia; it often effects cures unaided by any other remedy.

(*b.*) It is a decidedly homœopathic remedy to rheumatism, (see Treatise on Apoplexy, p. 67.) It causes pains, especially in the bones and joints. VOGT. Painful sensations in the bones and joints, which disappear after the breaking out of a profuse sweat, and abundant flow of urine. SOBERNHEIM. It acts decidedly on the fibrous system; causes the most violent pains in the bones and joints. HARNISCH. General painfulness of all the joints. KÜTTNER. (PETERS.)

BRYONIA.

(*a.*) DUDGEON says it is an efficient remedy in rheumatic ophthalmia, when the sclerotica, and membranes of the aqueous humor are involved.

(*b.*) HERING says it is useful after Pulsatilla when the pains have lessened, but the redness remains; also when the eyes burn or smart as if sand were in them, aggravated in the evening and at night; when the lids are swollen, and the pain shoots into the head, when they are opened.

(*c.*) Bryonia resembles Colchicum in its action; it acts principally upon the serous and fibrous tissues, and upon the liver, and is perhaps most serviceable in the rheumatisms of bilious persons, who are also subject to derangement of the stomach, nausea, and diarrhœa. PETERS.

CLEMATIS.

(*a.*) HARTMANN says it is the most important remedy, and its place can be supplied by no other, when the aching in the eyes, intolerance of light, and lachrymation are especially increased in the open air; when the eyelids stick together in the morning, with great heat in them, and the iris is inflamed.

(*b.*) It is allied to Rhus and Corrosive Sublimate in its action, causing an efflorescence upon the skin and a vesicular eruption; and curing chronic headache when seated in the fibrous tissue of the scalp, secondary syphilis, venereal ulcers, and bone pains, also fungus excrescences, and various chronic humid exanthems. PETERS.

COLOCYNTH,

(*a.*) Acts with peculiar power upon the nerves and other portions of the very lowest parts of the bowels, and neighboring organs, such as the kidneys, lumbar plexus of nerves, etc.; and is especially homœopathic in affections of the eye and head, which arise in connection with, or from sympathy with these parts, both neuralgic and inflammatory.

CASE 137.—A man, aged 34, had suffered for 8 days with pain in the right eye, returning periodically every morning; the conjunctiva was red, the edges of the lids irritated, the eye watered and seemed smaller, with the sensation as if it would fall out when the patient stooped. The attack commenced with piercing pain in the forehead over the eye; followed by rending pain extending from the eye into the right temple, aggravated by coughing, shaking the head, looking at a bright light, and by touch. There was a discharge of purulent nasal mucus; obstruction of the nose and loss of smell; the patient was chilly, irritable, and weak. The paroxysms lasted until 2 P. M., with entire relief during the evening and night.

Treatment.—The attack was cured in 4 days, by Colocynth 3, 1 dose every night and morning.—*Genl. Hom. Journ.* Vol. 34, p. 323. HAUSTEIN.

NATRUM MURIATICUM.

See Treatise on Headaches, p. 55.

The use of common table-salt, as a medicine, was for a long time confined to the homœopathists; now it is used in the dominant school as a tonic and nutrient remedy; it is supposed to improve the blood, to diminish the quantity of serum quite decidedly, thus rendering it thicker; also to increase the quantity of blood-globules quite decidedly; augments the fibrin in a slight degree, and lessens the quantity of albumen in an equal proportion; finally, it also increases the quantity of iron and fat in the blood. It increases the appetite, but its most certain and frequent effect is increase of strength, while the heat of the body is more readily generated and exposure to cold is better borne. M. PLOUVIEZ increased in weight under its use to the amount of 13½ lbs. Troy in about 2 months, and repeatedly became so plethoric with fullness about the head, that he felt himself obliged to be bled. Hence it is regarded as an antipathic remedy to debility, emaciation, anæmia, chlorosis, and scrofula. Latterly it has been used as a substitute for Bark, Quinine, and Arsenic in the treatment of fever and ague; it succeeds in about 60 per cent. of all cases. PETERS.

CASE 138.—A man, aged 29, had suffered occasionally for several years with rheumatic catarrhal ophthalmia. The eye seemed dim, pus collected at the angles, there was profuse lachrymation, slight redness of the conjunctiva of the ball, and some swelling of that of the lids; the pupils were somewhat contracted, the iris discolored; exposure to light caused a violent piercing in both temples; there was a constant appearance of gauze before the eyes, and feeling as if it must be wiped away; change of light caused violent pain; objects disappeared while reading and writing; he could not see distant objects at all; at 10 paces every thing looked like large black bodies.

Treatment.—1 dose of 8 globules of Natrum Mur. 30, was given daily for 4 weeks; then Natrum 30 and 12, in alternation, every 2 days; the patient was cured in 4 months. LORBACH.

PULSATILLA

acts decidedly upon both the mucous membranes and fibrous tissues, and hence has a relation both to catarrhal and rheumatic affections; it also has a specific relation to the eye.

HERING says after the severity of the inflammation has been lessened by Aconite, but violent pains still remain, and are cutting, boring, or piercing, the eye being intolerant of light, all the symptoms being increased in the afternoon and evening;

when there have been frequent relapses, and the patient is inclined to weep, then Pulsatilla will be found useful.

CASE 139.—A lad, aged 13, suffered with ophthalmia attended with considerable pain about the eye; the sclerotica was traversed by fine, red vessels, which formed a rose-red circle around the cornea; there was but slight conjunctivitis, and some iritis; also œdema of the upper lids and profuse secretion of mucus.

Treatment.—Pulsat. 30, 2 doses; in 48 hours the whole disease was removed except a slight conjunctivitis. Puls. is supposed to be specific in similar cases. LINK.

MERCURIUS SOLUBILIS.

Mercury is the remedy *par excellence* in all rheumatic affections of the eye in which the iris is involved. In most cases it would be unsafe to trust entirely to any other remedy.

CASE 140.—A healthy, blooming girl, aged 19, had suffered with her eyes for 12 days. Both eyes had been attacked simultaneously, but the right one had improved rapidly, so that the pupil was only a little too widely dilated and the iris too little sensitive to light. The sight was gone, however, in the left eye.

The sclerotica was inflamed, as was evident from the peculiar redness around the cornea and beneath the conjunctiva. The centre of the cornea was transparent and free from ulceration, but its circumference was dim and grayish like ground glass; the pupil was contracted, irregular, and immovable; the color of the iris had a greenish tinge, the pupillary edge was swollen, and there was a delicate gray exudation of lymph within the circumference of the pupil, (*iritis;*) there was also a small deposit of yellow pus at the bottom of the anterior chamber, (*hypopion.*) Daylight could be distinguished from darkness with the diseased eye, but every thing seemed changed into a gray mist; there was no intolerance of light, some lachrymation, no great pain by day, but violent, rending, tearing pains sat in in the eye and its neighborhood, in the temples, forehead and cheeks, every evening and night.

Treatment.—One grain Merc. Sol. 3, was given daily for 2 weeks; in a few days, the pains had ceased, and there was only a slight redness about the cornea; but the eye was dim; still the pupil was clear, and no longer irregular; the iris blue and sensitive; the dimness and pus had disappeared, and sight was restored. A perfect cure soon followed.—*Genl. Hom. Journ.* Vol. 19, p. 68. KNORRE.

CASE 141.—A sickly, psoric woman had suffered for several weeks with rheumatic ophthalmia; the sclerotica and conjunctiva of the *right* eye were inflamed; the rosy redness of the former was visible through the latter; the conjunctiva resembled a dense net-work of blood-vessels; there was an ulcer upon the cornea of the size of a mustard-seed, with broad, whitish-gray and opaque edges; there were rending and boring pains in the eyes and its neighborhood, especially in the frontal bones, with aggravation in the evening and at night. Shaking chills sat in when the aggravations lessened; lachrymation, photophobia, especially for candlelight, imperfect vision, as if looking through mist; rending pains in the ear and teeth of the right side.

Treatment.—Merc. Sol. $\frac{1}{12}$th, 6 doses, one per day, effected a perfect cure in 14 days, marked by cessation of the inflammation, and cicatrization of the ulcer. KNORRE.

Review.

The striking features in the above cases are: the presence of rending and boring pains, increased at night, and seated in the *bones* about the eye; the inflammation of the sclerotica, with bright rosy-redness visible through the conjunctiva; and the well-marked *Iritis.*

The *doses* were Merc. 1-12 gr., and Merc. 3.

RHUS.

(*a.*) In an epidemic of *catarrhal-rheumatic* ophthalmia, SCHELLING found *Rhus* the principal remedy; next in order, Arsenicum was found most useful, especially when the patient had a pale, delicate skin, tendency to bloating, considerable debility, with inclination to fainting.

When there was a tendency to scabious affections, Sulphur proved useful; to rhachitic or scrofulous disorders, Calcarea; to herpetic and impetiginous eruptions, Lycopodium.

(*b.*) HERING says, when Bryonia seems indicated, but does not help, and there are biting, aching, and sticking pains, with much lachrymation, and agglutination of the lids, or when they are swollen, as if from erysipelas, then Rhus is useful.

(*c.*) Rhus is most decidedly homœopathic to erysipelatous, pemphiginous and vesicular diseases and eruptions; as these stand in an almost antagonistic relation to rheumatic affections, it is exceedingly doubtful whether Rhus is ever truly and absolutely homœopathic to any decided rheumatic affection. PETERS.

From cases furnished by SCHELLING and SEGIN, the followign *clinical indications* for the use of Rhus have been arranged by RÜCKERT.

Eyelids swollen and closed on account of intolerance of light, and spasmodic contractions; œdematous swelling of both lids.

Edges of the lids reddened, and the lashes stuck together with mucus; profuse lachrymation of both eyes; pimples and red streaks upon the cheeks, excited by the acrid tears; conjunctiva of the left eye covered with a bright, *erysipelatous* redness; redness of the conjunctiva of both eyes, which is traversed with a delicate vascular net-work; sclerotica of both eyes velvety and dark-red; redness of the sclerotica and development of numerous blood-vessels; blood-redness of the right eye; a dense net-work of vessels surrounding the cornea, and forming a wall around its circumference, (*chemosis*;) dimness of the cornea, which is covered with mucus; grayish opacity of the right cornea, with two whitish and shining specks; commencing opacity on the left cornea; *dimness and smokiness of the capsule of the lens*; pupils insensible to alternations of light and shade; great sensitiveness of the eye to light; change of the color of the Iris from blue to *green*, with indistinctness of the pupillary margin, (Iritis.) The Iris oblique and somewhat contracted; excessive soreness of the ball of the right eye, so that it will not bear the slightest touch; aching, burning pains in the eyes; *intermittent* inflammation of the eyes; irritability of temper towards noon, so that the patient is apt to strike and press his head against the wall.

Accompanying Complaints.

Dizzy sensation, as if one were drawn backwards or sidewards while walking; headache often increased by day, and also at night, which, however, occasionally lessens, but never entirely ceases; piercing pains, especially in the left temple, extending into the eye; heat of the head; redness of the face during the attacks of pains, but frequent paleness at other times; dirty, yellow, and pale color of the face, with some bloating; rushing and noises in the ears; white coating of the tongue; insipid and pasty taste in the mouth; dryness of the mouth, without thirst; slimy state of the mouth; fullness of the stomach, and nausea after taking but little food; twisting, turning, and sense of emptiness in the stomach, with yawning and eructations while fasting; pressing and cutting pains in the abdomen; dry and painful stools, occasionally alternating with diarrhœa; frequent urinations, especially at night, occurring quickly and even involuntarily; then retention of urine, which is dark-red.

Limbs.—Not slight rending, piercing, and flying pains in the limbs, especially in the armpits, shoulders, hips, and thighs of the left side; excessive tenderness of the first dorsal vertebra, (*spinal tenderness*;) constant spasmodic contraction of the left thigh, with spasmodic pain in it, and tension extending from the knee to the swollen foot.

An eruption of red pimples and pustules upon the nose and cheeks becomes more severe as the eye affection improves, and *vice versa*; violent burning and rending pain about the affected eye, aggravated every night and morning, depriving the patient of rest and sleep; sleep restless, disturbed by dreams and tossing about.

Fever Symptoms.—Chilliness and cold extremities in the afternoon; skin dry and very sensitive to slight changes of temperature; incessant chilliness and shuddering, as if from a cold, moist draught of air, extending from the feet and thighs upwards; irritability and impatience; sudden fits of passion.

Review.

In 3 cases, the patients were of the sanguine temperament 4 were females; 2 were from 2 to 4 years of age; 2, 30 years; and 1, 42 years.

In 3 cases, the attacks arose from cold, and had lasted from 2 to 3 weeks; 2 cases had persisted for 10 weeks; in 3 cases, the disease was confined to the right side.

Doses.—Low dilutions were used in all cases, namely, from the 1st to the 5th; improvement began in from 4 to 6 days.

Rhus alone effected cures in 4 cases; in 1 case, in a scrofulous patient, Calcarea was given to complete the cure.

SPIGELIA.

See Treatise on Headaches, page 85.

(*a.*) RUMMEL says that it seems peculiarly suited to rheumatic and arthritic ophthalmias, and to possess the power of controlling severe inflammations of the eye and cornea. Pains about, and deep in the eyes are removed by it.

CASE 142.—A patient had suffered for 14 days with ophthalmia; the eye was greatly reddened; the crowded vessels formed a bluish-red circle deep in the sclerotica, a few lines from the cornea; the cornea, especially its lower segment, was so much dimmed that the form of the pupil could not be clearly distinguished, and all objects seemed as if enveloped in mist. The eyes were exceedingly painful, especially when moved or turned, somewhat relieved by holding the lids closed; violent aching, which extended from the bony portions of the orbit to the temples; sensation as if an ulcer would form in the eye; exposure to light was not exceedingly painful to the eye.

Treatment.—Sulphur 2, did not afford relief; then Spigelia 30, 1 drop, was given; the following night was spent without pain, the inflammation had lessened, but on the following evening, the pains had increased, with discharge of biting, acrid tears. Spigelia 30, was repeated, with progressing improvement, except that the cornea remained unchanged. Tinct. Euphrasia, 1 drop per dose, removed the dimness of the cornea in a few days. The painless congestion of the white of the eye disappeared under the use of Nux 24. RUMMEL.

CASE 143.—A man had had violent pain in the right eye, 2 years ago, after the cessation of which a ptyrygium commenced to grow until it extended far upon the cornea. At present there was a fresh attack of pain as if the left eye would burst, increased by stooping, and appearing regularly for a long time every morning before rising, lasting until noon, and then suddenly ceasing.

Treatment.—Nux did not help; Spigelia 30, 2 doses cured him. PULTE.

SULPHUR.

CASE 144.—A lad, aged 18, who had had suppressed itch, and lost his right eye from an attack of inflammation, was taken with ophthalmia in the left eye. Equiform, bright redness of the sclerotica, formed by minute blood-vessels; single varicose bundles of vessels on the conjunctiva; bluish circle around and slight opacity of the cornea; contraction and immobility of the pupils; acrid flow of tears; intolerance of light; violent rending pains in the supraorbital and temporal regions, and in the eye itself, increased at night; slight fever.

Treatment.—At first daily, and then bi-daily, drop-doses of Tinct. Sulph. were given; the first dose relieved the pains somewhat, and in 3 weeks, the whole disease was removed. DIETZ.

CASE. 145.—A middle-aged man had suffered for a long time periodically with attacks of ophthalmia.

Symptoms:—The whole *left* eye seemed enlarged, and its coverings swollen; the cornea was dim, as if covered with fine dust, and was the seat of a suppurating ulcer; the conjunctiva was blood-red from crowded blood-vessels; intolerance of light; constant aching pains about the whole circumference of the orbit, increased to a frightful degree by moving the eyes, or exposure to sunlight, even when the lids were closed, and almost driving the patient to despair. The pain involved the whole of the head and caused entire loss of rest and self-command.

Treatment.—1 grain of Sulph. 2, removed the whole disorder; even the ulcer healed in a few days. GROSS.

CASE 146.—A robust man, aged 27, had suffered for years with periodical attacks of ophthalmia.

Symptoms.—In a new attack, the left conjunctiva was blood-red, as if injected; there were aching, tensing, burning, and piercing pains through the left eye; rending pains in the left side of the head; but little appetite; constipation; fever in the evening, with heat through the whole body; almost constant chilliness by day; mist before the eyes; quick, hard pulse.

Treatment.—Aconite and Bellad. caused but little improvement; but 2 doses of Sulphur 30, one every 4 days, cured the whole radically in 8 days. TIETZE.

CASE 147.—In rheumatic ophthalmia, with great redness of the sclerotica, decided intolerance of light, discharge of acrid tears, rending and piercing pains in and about the eye, with rheumatic pains in other parts, Bellad. 30, with alternating doses of Sulphur 60, produced decided good effects. Several cases were cured by Sulphur alone; others by Nux. WEBER.

CASE 148.—A rough and drunken woman, aged 53, who had ceased menstruating for 1 year, had suffered for 2 years with repeated attacks of inflammation of the right eye. The present attack had lasted 4 weeks.

Symptoms.—A pale-red edge around the cornea, more decided above, where there was an extensive inflammation of the sclerotica and conjunctiva. From thence a bundle of vessels extended half across the cornea, between which the cornea appeared like ground glass, or like gelatin, and was also somewhat swollen; the conjunctiva of the ball and the sclerotica were not actually inflamed, but only traversed here and there by enlarged blood-vessels. Intolerance of light, lachrymation, heat and burning in the eyes, sticking together of the lids, rending pains in the eyes and about the face, and right side of the head, with evening and night aggravations, roaring and rushing sounds in the right ear, with deafness, periodical rending pains in the left ear, with discharge of purulent serum, especially at night; rending rheumatic pains in the right shoulder-joint, so that she can often not raise the hand to the mouth, or use it at work.

Treatment.—Sulph. 3, grain doses, one every morning; in 7 days, the inflammation had entirely disappeared; the cornea was so clear that she could distinguish large objects; 10 doses more effected a perfect cure in 3 weeks more. KNORRE.

Review.

Of the 4 cases, 3 were in males and 1 in a female, of the age ' 18 to 40 or 53 years. The disease was inclined to return riodically; one patient had already lost an eye, in a similar tack. In all cases, the disease was confined to one eye, namely, ice on the right side and twice on the left. The redness of e sclerotica and the characteristic ring about the cornea were stinctly evident. The pains in and about the eye were gravated in the evening and night.

Doses.—Tinct. Sulph. in 1 case;
Trit. 1st and 2d in 2 cases;
Sulph. 30, and 60, in 1 case.

Sulphur alone cured 4 cases, in one instance after the pre- ous ineffectual use of Acon. and Bellad. In one case, Bellad. as alternated with Sulph. Even long-standing cases were ured in from 1 to 3 weeks. In 1 case, after repeated doses of ılph. 3, a not inconsiderable aggravation preceded the cure.

General Review of the Treatment of Rheumatic Ophthalmia.

In 14 cases, Rhus and Sulph. were each used in 4 cases; erc. in 2; Coloc., Natrum Mur., Puls., and Spigelia, each in 1 se. In the more *acute* forms, Coloc., Puls., Spigel., Rhus, and erc. were relied upon; in the *chronic* cases, Sulph. and Merc.; hen there was an intermitting type, Coloc. and Rhus; conite, Bryonia, and Clematis were merely recommended.

When the *lids* were swollen, Bryon.; and when closed, hus; œdematous swelling with redness of the edges of the ls, Rhus; especial œdema of the upper lids, Pulsat.; when e angles of the eye maturate, Natrum Mur.

When the *conjunctiva* is only slightly inflamed, Pulsat.;— ight red, and traversed with a net-work of enlarged vessels, erc., Rhus, Sulph.; when there was a wall around the rnea, (chemosis,) Rhus and Sulph.

When the *scelorotica* was inflamed, Sulph.; traversed with ıall blood-vessels, Puls.; rose-red, Merc.; a bluish-red circle ound the cornea, Spigelia; a rose-red one, Puls.; red, with eat development of the vessels, Rhus and Sulph.

When the *cornea* was surrounded by a pale rim, Sulph.; by an opaque, whitish-gray circle, Merc.; dim, opaque, and glanceless, Merc., Spigel., Sulph.; gelatinous and swollen, Sulph.; covered with ulcers, Merc., Sulph.; with commencing opacity, Rhus and Sulph.

When the *iris* is inflamed, Clematis; discolored, Natrum Mur; greenish, Merc., Rhus; irregular, Rhus.

The *pupils* contracted, distorted, and immovable, Merc.; insensible, Rhus.

When the *pupillary margin* is indistinct, Rhus; swollen, Merc.; the membranes of the aqueous humor affected, Bryonia.

The *lens* smoky and dim, Rhus.

Intolerance of light, Natrum m., Puls., Rhus.; lachrymation, Merc; acrid tears, Rhus and Sulph.

Aching pains were relieved by Rhus, Spig., and Pulsat.; when aggravated by motion and sunlight, Sulph.; piercing pains, by Natrum m.; rending and boring, by Merc.; in the bones about the eye, Merc. Sulph., and Sulph.; nocturnal aggravations, by Merc., Sulph.

Rhus cured various accompanying gastric affections; pains in the limbs, fever, rending in the shoulder-joint by Sulph.

Doses.—The higher dilutions of Natrum, Puls., Spigel., and occasionally of Sulphur were used. The *lower* potencies of Rhus, Merc., and Sulph., almost always in repeated doses.

Of the 15 physicians who furnished cases, 7 used the lower potencies, and 8 the higher. Repeated doses were used in 14 cases.

Results.—In the slighter cases, improvement began in from 4 to 6 days; in chronic cases, from 2 to 3 weeks; 4 months were required in 1 case.

Calcarea was given after Rhus, and Euphrasia after Spigelia with good effect.

KREUSSLER says Aconite alone will often effect cures; Bryonia is recommended by DUDGEON, especially in affections of the sclerotica and membranes of the aqueous humor. HERING advises Clematis after Pulsatilla has relieved the pains, but not removed the redness. He also gives Pulsat. when Acon. has lessened the inflammation, but not removed the nocturnal pains. And praises Rhus, when Bryonia seems indicated, but does not help.

CATARHAL OPHTHALMIA.

See pages 27, 29, and 45 to 49.

According to KLOTAR MÜLLER, as the inflammation sets in suddenly, with great pain and some fever, it is judicious to commence with *Aconite;* it is also useful in the later stages of catarrhal-rheumatic ophthalmia, when there are insupportable pains in the whole ball of the eye, or above and about it, commencing in the evening and aggravated at night.

Belladonna is especially suitable when the white of the eye is much reddened or traversed with large blood-vessels, with great intolerance of light, discharge of burning tears, or unpleasant dryness of the eyes, increase of pain from moving them, erysipelatous swelling of the lids, violent headache, vertigo, dimness of vision, or appearance of sparks, or black, flying spots before the eyes.

Euphrasia is the main remedy when the inflammation arises in consequence of, or in attendance with, catarrh of the nose, with profuse secretion of mucus, flow of tears, and formation of small vesicles upon the edge of the cornea.

Hepar. sulph. and *Mercurius*, when there is soreness and swelling of the edges of the lids, with thick, purulent mucus, nocturnal agglutination, ulcers and specks upon the white of the eye and cornea, pimples and scabs about the eyes and eversion of the lids.

Nux Vomica is indicated, especially when the internal angles of the eye are inflamed, with aching as if from sand, or burning as if from an acrid substance, with profuse lachrymation, great photophobia, especially in the morning, catarrh of the nose and headache, great irritability and constipation.

Pulsatilla when there is a pale swelling of the lids or about the eyes, with profuse secretion of tears and mucus, agglutination of the lids, violent pains in the eyes, and aggravation of the symptoms especially in the evening and night.

Spigelia, when there are insupportable pains deep in the sockets of the eyes, especially from motion, sensation as if the ball of the eye were too large, boring, piercing, cutting, and burning pains as if from foreign bodies therein, profuse lachrymation, dull, turbid appearance of the eyes, dimness of vision, loss of sight when exerting the eyes, intolerance of light and of vision.

Against frequent and profuse lachrymation, Euphrasia, Crocus, Digitalis, Graphit., Phosphor., and Spigelia.

ACONITE.

GRIESSELICH says that he has sometimes, in catarrhal ophthalmia, seen good effects from Aconite only.

ARSENICUM.

See pages 61 and 62.

CASE 149.—A woman, aged 54, had suffered for 8 days with catarrhal ophthalmia and coryza.

Symptoms.—Redness of the sclerotica of the *right* eye, swelling of the lids, piercing pain in the ball and internal angle from moving the eye, or looking at a bright light; burning and aching as if from sand; tearing pains in the forehead extending into the eye, sensitiveness of the eyes to touch, flow of burning tears, gauzy dim-sightedness, intolerance of light, discharge of burning mucus from the right nostril, dull confusion of the head in a warm room, lassitude, chilliness, thirst, and sleeplessness.

Treatment.—Arsenicum 6, 1 drop night and morning, effected a cure in 5 days. HAUSTEIN.

BELLADONNA.

CASE 150.—A catarrhal ophthalmia in the right eye of a child, aged 2, was cured in 48 hours, with Bellad. 400.

Symptoms.—The eyelids were swollen, especially in the morning, secretion of mucus, sticking of the lids together, redness of the internal portion of the eyeball, sensitiveness of the eyes to air and light.

CHAMOMILLA

Is most useful in children when the eyes prick, ache, and burn as if heat came out from them, and are swollen, or stuck together in the morning, or else are very dry. HERING.

DIGITALIS

is recommended by KNORRE in catarrhal ophthalmia which has arisen from the sudden suppression of catarrh of the nose, when the conjunctiva of the lids and ball are swollen, with feeling as if sand were between them, and swelling and redness of the lids; aching and shooting stitches of pain, intolerance of light, constant lachrymation increased by bright light and cold, profuse secretion of pus in the corners of the eye, obstruction and dryness of the nose.

EUPHRASIA.

See page 79.

CASE 151.—A woman, aged 22, had suffered with ophthalmia for 10 days in consequence of taking cold.

Symptoms.—The white of the lids and balls of both eyes were reddened; with enlarged and congested vessels running as far as the cornea; there was an insupportable itching and pain as if from sand in the eyes; lachrymation, sensitiveness to light. The right eye was worse than the left, and the attending catarrh was also most troublesome in the right nostril.

Treatment.—After taking Euphrasia 3, a visible and progressive improvement occurred. FRANK.

CASE 152.—A young lady, aged 20, a healthy brunette, and regular in menstruation, had suffered for 3 months with catarrhal ophthalmia.

Symptoms.—The conjunctiva chemotic and reddened; profuse lachrymation; discharge of acrid water from the nose; intolerance of light, so that she was obliged to remain in a dark room; aching, cutting pains in the eyes and frontal sinuses; ulceration of the cornea.

Treatment.—Euphrasia 3, internally, and an external application of 3 drops in 3 ounces of water, effected a cure in 5 days, after a not inconsiderable aggravation. WEIGIL.

CASE 153.—A robust woman, with catarrhal ophthalmia, was cured in 5 days with Euphrasia 3, after a decided aggravation.

CASE 154.—A woman, aged 53, took 1-drop doses of Euphrasia 1, for catarrhal ophthalmia, and was soon attacked with the most violent pains in the affected eye; she only fell asleep toward morning, but then awoke almost well. FRANK.

HEPAR. SULPH.

CASE 155.—During an epidemic of influenza, many persons were attacked with catarrhal or influenza-ophthalmia; the eyes became violently inflamed, watered profusely, with excessive intolerance of light, swelling and redness of the lids.

Treatment.—After a few doses of Bellad., Hepar. acted with great rapidity and certainty.

CASE 156.—A young psoric lady had catarrhal ophthalmia with the following

Symptoms.—The eyelids were inflamed, sore, oozing, and as if cauterized, especially at the internal angles; their internal surface was bright-red and inflamed, with burning, especially in the morning; soreness, biting, and itching of the lids; redness of the conjunctiva, which was traversed with isolated large blood-vessels; intolerance of light; colored and turbid halos around the candle in the evening, and aching pains so that the eyes had to be closed.

Treatment.—Repeated doses of Hepar. 3, soon effected a cure. KNORRE.

MERCURIUS SOLUBILIS.

CASE 157.—Merc. and Rhus generally produced rapid relief in catarrhal ophthalmia with slight rosy-redness of the conjunctiva, especially at the inner angle of the eye, attended with profuse lachrymation and catarrh of the nose. Still, relapses were apt to occur unless proper care and necessary warmth were attended to. SCHELLING.

NUX VOMICA.

See page 89.

PULSATILLA.

WEBER says this remedy is useful when the sclerotica is but little or not at all reddened, or only has red spots or specks upon it; when acrid tears are secreted, and the patient believes that something has got into his eye, with aching in the eyes as if from dust, intolerance of light, redness, and swelling of the eyelids, and evening aggravations. He used Pulsat. 30, 1 dose every 72 hours, and effected cures in a few days, although Bellad. 30, or Sulphur was required at times, or Staphysagria when the lids were especially affected.

CASE 158.—A delicate, scrofulous girl, aged 15, had suffered for 12 days with catarrhal ophthalmia.

Symptoms.—The inner surface of the eyelids was reddened and swollen; on the conjunctiva there were many enlarged blood-vessels converging toward the cornea; beneath these, the sclerotica was seen uniformly and intensely reddened; there were several vesicles on the cornea of each eye; the iris and pupils were natural. Increased secretion of mucus and tears; great photophobia; piercing pains in the eyes, forehead, and temples, aggravated toward evening and midnight; scanty menstruation every 3 weeks; had previously suffered with acne.

Treatment.—Blisters had been used without benefit; after 3 doses of Pulsat. 6, 1 dose each day, the pains were relieved, and under the continued use of the same remedy every other day, a cure was soon accomplished. DIEZ.

CASE 159.—A man, aged 30, had been sick 6 or 7 days.

Symptoms.—Dryness and burning about the eyes, increased in the evening; redness and swelling of the edges of the lids; purulent mucus in the corners of the eye, with adhesion; the conjunctiva was spongy, dull, irregularly reddened and punctated.

Treatment.—Pulsat. 3, one dose every night and morning, effected a cure in 3 weeks; a similar attack, 2 years before, treated allopathically, lasted 3 months.

Review.

Ten different remedies were used in the treatment of the above 11 cases; they present little that is characteristic. But we find that Euphrasia is useful not only in acute, but also in neglected and obstinate cases; Arsenicum and Hepar. are reliable remedies in the latter class.

The lids and angles of the eyes are always most severely affected; Nux is most useful when the corners of the eyes are principally affected. Euphrasia, when there is an attending violent catarrh of the nose; Digitalis, when ophthalmia occurs after suppressed catarrh. Nux is the most suitable remedy when there is biting sensation, as if from salt in the eye.

PURULENT OPHTHALMIA.

Egyptian Ophthalmia.—This is one of the most severe and destructive diseases of the eye; it is originally and essentially an affection of the mucous membrane of the eyelids, with puriform discharge; it generally, however, extends to the conjunctiva of the ball, and sometimes, in spite of all the means that can be employed, it reaches the globe itself, producing in the cornea and iris, injurious and destructive effects similar to those which take place in the ophthalmia of new-born children. LAWRENCE.

VETCH, of 636 cases, had fifty dismissed with loss of both eyes, and fifty with that of one. In a large boys' school in Yorkshire, blindness of one or both eyes, or serious injury to the sight from corneal opacities, took place in nearly 20 instances. Of 1500 cases at Ancona, 97 lost one eye, and 49 both. Of 1604 cases treated by MULLER, 15 became blind in both eyes, 18 with impaired vision of both eyes, and 26 remained blind in one eye. Of 30,000 cases in the Prussian army, blindness followed in 1100; and in 1810, in the Chelsea and Kilmanheim hospitals, there were 2317 soldiers a burthen upon the public from blindness in consequence of purulent ophthalmia, those who had lost the sight of one eye only, not being included. All had been treated allopathically.

Symptoms and Progress.—According to LAWRENCE, in the first stage there is redness of the inside of the lids, with a coating of a little whitish mucus; some watering of the eye and stiffness of the lids. This stage is not often seen by the physician, and often is hardly noticed by the patient. But the disease soon extends to the ball of the eye, followed by high vascular action, great redness and tumefaction of the conjunctiva, and profuse discharge. The redness is uniform and bright, and there are often red patches of effused blood in or under the conjunctiva, which is besides greatly swollen and raised into an elevation called *chemosis*, often so considerable as not only to form a wall around, but also to overlap and nearly cover the cornea. At this period, the lids swell greatly, so as frequently to form two large, convex, colorless, or slightly-red protuberances, which meet and nearly close the eye, preventing in conjunction with the chemosis, all satisfactory examination of the cornea. The abundant purulent discharge not only bathes the eyes and lids, but crusts the edges of the lids and lashes, and pours out over the face, and even drops down upon the clothes; the quantity of matter discharged is said in some cases to amount to several ounces.

As the disease extends to the ball of the eye, the pain is greatly increased, becomes severe and excruciating, is deep-seated, and often attended with fullness and throbbing of the temples and headache. There are remissions and aggravations of suffering, which are sometimes periodical; and the pain often returns, particularly the sensation, as if there were a foreign body in the eye, even after it has been removed for a time by treatment.

In the early stage, there is not much fever, but when the inflammation extends to the ball of the eye, general feverishness ensues.

Nature.—A peculiar change of structure of the conjunctiva of the eyelids is the primary and characteristic effect of this contagious ophthalmia; this alteration is not the effect of inflammation, but, on the contrary, is the first manifestation of the disease, and the cause of inflammation, when the disorder spreads to the ball of the eye. The peculiar change of structure in the conjunctiva of the lids and its morbid swelling are the principal and constant phenomena; hence antiphlogistic treatment is by no means so serviceable as might be expected, if inflammation constituted the essential character of the disease. There is, indeed, high inflammation in the more severe cases, attended with chemosis; but this inflammation may be prevented by proper treatment, or may be controlled, and still the original complaint will proceed on its course and the change of structure go on. WALTHER says, that an eruption of small vesicles on the inner surface of the eyelids is always present in contagious purulent ophthalmia, and hence he considers the disease not so much an inflammation as an eruptive disease, or a form of *impetigo* of the conjunctiva.

This diseased state of the inside of the lids remains for an indefinite period after the inflammatory symptoms have subsided, and may lead, under occasional excitement, to the reproduction of the disorder in all its violence. No case can be considered cured until this state of the conjunctiva shall have been removed; it may remain dormant under each of the eyelids for months, but in a state capable of infecting whole companies of soldiers or scholars. According to EBLE and MÜLLER, the first stage of the disease consists in the presence of small serous cysts, or phlyctenæ, on the surface of the conjunctiva of the lids, soon followed by thickening and granulation of the mucous membrane. When the granulations have just commenced, the conjunctiva of the lids appears like red velvet, or as if covered with red dust; in the higher gradations, like thickly-strewn millet seeds, or rough sand, or the granulations of a healing wound; these granulations, or rather vegetations, sometimes equal a large lentil, which is their utmost size. They exist in great numbers, arising from the lining of the lids by a broad basis, being rounded at their prominent part at first, but subsequently becoming flattened by pressure against the ball of the eye. The largest are toward the middle, the smaller toward the edges of the lids and the angles, especially the outer. Sometimes they lie so close together that they seem to form one mass, but close examination will discover the fissures, sometimes tolerably deep, which separate them. This granular structure is more developed under the upper than the lower lid, the wider surface of the former possessing a great extent of mucous glands, and being less exposed to the air and contact of remedies, *The principal effects of the disease* are:

1st. *Sloughing of the cornea*, especially when the swelling of the conjunctiva of the ball, and the chemosis is very great.

2d. *Bursting of the cornea.* A paroxysm of excruciating pain is suddenly terminated by a sensation of something giving way; a little hot fluid runs down the cheek, and great relief is experienced. Just before the cornea bursts, it may exhibit no perceptible alteration, and even after this has happened it may present so natural an appearance that the fissure may be overlooked. But VETCH has discovered at times, a small line extending across the cornea; the next day, a slight opacity appeared along the line, and increased daily, till the greater part of the cornea was not only opaque, but projected in an irregular cone. In fact, the aqueous humor at first escapes by a division of the cornea, nearly as clean as if cut by a knife, and it is to the attempts of the part to effect a reünion, under the presence of disease, that future deformity is owing; as extensive disorganization of the cornea by suppuration, or ulceration, is apt to set in.

3d. *Suppuration of the cornea.*

4th. *Ulceration of the cornea.*

5th. *Interstitial deposits*, forming opacities in every degree, from the thinnest film to the most dense leucoma.

6th. *Opacity of the cornea*, from cicatrization of ulcers.

7th. *Prolapsus of the Iris.*

8th. *Adhesion of the Iris to the cornea.*

9th. Loosening, sponginess, *vascularity and thickening* of the mucous membrane covering the cornea, with enlargement of its blood-vessels, and more or less diminution of its transparency. This change occurs in various degrees from slight vascularity to pannus.

10th. *Staphyloma*, general or partial; and dropsical enlargement of the ball of the eye; or collapse of its tunics. LAWRENCE.

Prognosis.—According to LAWRENCE, the disease is less manageable in adults than in infants or children; for the affection is more formidable, the danger to the eye greater, and the issue more uncertain. If the cornea retains its natural transparency, we may hope to arrest the disease, and save the eye, by prompt and vigorous treatment. If the cornea be dim, with deep-seated pain in the eye or head, the inflammation has extended to the ball of the eye, and the result is doubtful. After partial suppuration, considerable ulceration, or interstitial deposition, recovery of sight may take place.

Treatment.—LAWRENCE, RUST, and MULLER place great stress upon the use of cold water, with which the eyes may not only be frequently cleansed, but it may also be applied with benefit as a lotion, by means of linen rags dipped in it, and laid not only over the eyes and lids, but also over the forehead. In the severer forms of the disease, WALTHER applied cloths dipped in cold water, not only to the eyes and forehead, but also to the entire head, with the greatest benefit. Confinement to the house does not seem advantageous at any period of the complaint, while free exposure of the inflamed eye to cool air, and even exercise, instead of being hurtful, as patients and their friends suppose, has been found decidedly beneficial. DR. VETCH is even disposed to recommend the trial of a journey, in the commencement of the disease, if the eye be freely exposed to the air, and the weather favorable, that is, not too exceedingly hot and sunny. He says, that when the second stage has commenced, with chemosis and purulent secretion, he has never seen any but the best effects from change of place. "Soldiers who have commenced a march with the disease completely formed, though exposed to heat, dust, and fatigue, and not abstaining even from intoxication, are invariably better at the end of the journey than when they set out." LAWRENCE can adduce innumerable observations to the same effect. MURRAY was so convinced of the beneficial effects of exposure to the air, that he was induced to march the soldiers about from one place to another, with a view solely to the good effects which he saw result from it.

Warm fluids, fomentations, poultices, and steam, increase the heat and augment the vascular disturbance; still, tepid ablutions are sometimes agreeable and useful.

The most homœopathic remedies are Rhus, Cantharides, Tartar Emetic, Clematis, Cannabis, Euphorbium, and Mezereum. Of these, Rhus and Hepar. Sulphur are generally the most useful. The Hepar. Sulph. 1st, 2d, or 3d trituration, should be given every night and morning; and the Rhus, tincture, 1st, 2d, or 3d dilution, may be given every 2, 4, 6, or 8 hours, according to the severity of the symptoms.

Euphorbium may be used when there is a severe inflammation of both lids, with violent itching and irritation, but with a rather pale swelling and profuse secretion of pus.

Local applications are said to be required at an early stage of the disease. LAWRENCE says that a solution of Alum is the first and most useful; other allopathic physicians prefer Nitrate of Silver and Sulphate of Copper, while BRIGGS has found the Oil of Turpentine to be the most effectual means of checking the profuse discharge in purulent ophthalmia; he introduces a minute quantity, on the point of a camel's-hair pencil, between the eyelids every morning, the eye being immediately afterward immersed, or bathed freely with cold water and a sponge, until the uneasiness and sense of heat which it produces in the eye and surrounding parts, is allayed, which usually requires some minutes. These applications are quite homœopathic enough, but a weak solution of Tartar Emetic is still more so, and in a few cases I have found it the most useful one; it is decidly homœopathic to pustular, purulent, and suppurative inflammation; has a well-earned old- and new-school reputation against inflammation in general, and is certainly not more irritating than Turpentine and Nitrate of Silver, which have been found very useful.

Still, I prefer, as a general rule, a solution of Kali Chlor., or Kali Carb., or Kali Hydriod., to be used several times a day for 3 days; these, although they will not decidedly check the profuse purulent discharge, will alter its character, render it less noxious, thick, and purulent; and then a weak solution of Alum, Sulph.-zinc, or Nitrate of Silver, will exert a much more rapid and permanent beneficial effect, than if they had been used without this previous preparation.

My friend, Dr. W. S. Stewart and myself treated over 40 cases of purulent ophthalmia in children, at the Home for the Friendless, without the loss of a single eye, although 3 or 4 cases proved exceedingly intractable. Two adults were not quite so fortunate, as one lost one eye, and the other had an eye partially damaged although a fair amount of vision remained.

In chronic cases, Sulphur, Hepar. Sulph., and Calcarea have proved practically useful.

ON

INTERNAL DISEASES OF THE EYE.

ARTHRITIC OPHTHALMIA.

(GOUTY INFLAMMATION OF THE EYES.)

LAWRENCE admits two varieties of this disease.

1st. *Arthritic iritis*, in which the affection is mainly confined to the iris, and is not a very serious disorder; for after a violent attack of this kind, with great diminution of sight, the symptoms subside (even under allopathic treatment), the eye recovers, and vision is completely restored. The inflammation may and does return again and again, and we are surprised to see the eyes recovering so completely as they do after these repeated attacks.

2d. *Arthritic inflammation of the internal tunics of the eye*, which is a far more serious accident, as extensive inflammation is frequently developed, affecting the internal parts of the eye generally, that is, the choroid, iris, retina, vitreous humor, lens and its capsule, and involving the sclerotica and cornea secondarily. It generally ends in loss of sight, with a dilated pupil and opaque lens. This disease almost invariably destroys sight; while the eye will recover completely from repeated attacks of arthritic iritis.

1. *Arthritic Iritis.*

In persons of a gouty habit, inflammation often attacks the iris, and is usually of an acute character. Uneasy sensations are experienced about the eye; pains occur in the forehead, brow, and orbit, often extending to the side of the head; redness of the sclerotica comes on, with pain of the eye, intolerance of light and lachrymation; in consequence of the

12

repeated motions of the lids, which become red and a little swelled, a small quantity of froth or white foam collects on their edges, particularly towards the angles. With the increase of the symptoms, the iris becomes dull and discolored, the pupil contracted, but it preserves its central situation, and becomes fixed at one or more points to the capsule. There is both headache and fever. The red zone around the cornea does not advance to the very edge of the latter, but a narrow white ring is left between them; this white border is often partial, being observed more especially towards the angles of the eye. The color of the corneal zone is also more dull in arthritic iritis than in the other varieties, and it is sometimes even livid, from varicose enlargement of the vessels. (LAWRENCE.)

As before said, the patient may recover from repeated attacks, one of Lawrence's patients had had his eye inflamed fourteen times, yet vision was unimpaired, though there were in each eye adhesions connecting nearly the whole pupillary border to the capsule. In each attack, fresh exudation of lymph occurs, the pupil becomes more and more contracted, and at last is filled up entirely with false membrane, when of course sight is finally destroyed. (LAWRENCE.)

2. *Internal Arthritic Ophthalmia.*

In this affection a severe burning or tearing pain is felt deep in the ball of the eye, with a sensation as if it were too large for the orbit. At the same time a dull or rather livid redness is developed in the sclerotica, increasing in intensity to the edge of the cornea, from which, however, it is separated by the narrow white ring mentioned in the description of arthritic iritis. Soon the vessels of the conjunctiva become distended and the cornea loses its brightness. At first there is increased sensitiveness to light and lachrymation. The pain in the eye becomes severe and almost intolerable, extends to the orbit, face, and side of the head; it entirely prevents rest, and sometimes is hardly lessened by the most active allopathic treatment. The iris is rendered darker and dull, the pupillary margin being turned backwards, and the opening itself dilated and fixed, sometimes having an oblong fissure in the transverse direction. A dull green discoloration is observed deep in the eye, and considered to indicate loss of transparency in the vitreous humor, or organic change in the retina. The posterior parts of the ball of the eye swell, and push forwards the lens into the dilated pupil, wedging it into the aperture and squeezing it against the cornea. The lens loses its transparency, turns to a dull green, yellowish green, or dull white color, forming a *green*, or *glaucomatous cataract*. This vascular congestion and the consequent swelling of the internal parts, distend the sclerotica, and give to the globe a stony hardness. The disturbance in the vessels of the sclerotica extends to the cornea, often causing considerable haziness; this change, and those in the iris and pupil, destroy all brilliance and expression of the organ, making it look like a dead eye. Sight is greatly impaired, often entirely lost from the beginning; this loss of sight may be sudden, taking place in the course of a night; Yet the patient often perceives flashes and various luminous appearances, although unable to distinguish light from darkness; and from time to time a glance of light is seen, which leads to the fallacious hope that sight may be recovered.

Finally, the pain and redness lessen, and the affection subsides leaving an iris of dull and leaden hue, a fixed and dilated pupil, either of a dull green color, or occupied by a glaucomatous cataract, with total and irreparable loss of vision. The disorder generally affects the two eyes in succession; but both may be attacked at once. The chief cause, is an unhealthy state of the constitution, and the prognosis under allopathic treatment is entirely unfavorable. When vision is lost, it is never restored; nay, if the characteristic symptoms are present, we may be tolerally certain that the disease will go on to the extinction of sight; and we cannot prevent it. The disorder indeed is so unmanageable that allopathic treatment has very little effect upon it; the pain in the eye and head continues in spite of allopathic treatment, and vision is neither restored, nor improved. (LAWRENCE.)

WALTHER and FISCHER say, it is impossible to divert the disease away from the eye by the counter-irritation, and that the treatment of the gouty diathesis comes too late to save the eye-sight.

Weber says under homœopathic treatment, if no disorganization of the eye has as yet taken place we can count with a certainty upon a cure; and even in those cases in which staphyloma, or contraction, or irregularity of the pupil has occurred we may frequently succeed in removing these, or at least in preserving sight. He probably refers to rheumatic iritis.

In well developed arthritic ophthalmia, Aconite 30, from six to twelve doses, one every four or six hours should be given; the intolerable pains, and the inflammation will either be improved decidedly, or at least checked in their course. Then Bellad. 30, should be given every twenty-four or seventy-two hours; generally after the third dose there will be a decrease in the severity of the pains and inflammation. At times Bellad. will act better, when an occasional dose of Sulphur 60, is interposed. In some cases Calc. c., 30, will produce an excellent effect, but only after the most urgent symptoms have been moderated. Weber.

If disorganization has already set in, much may occasionnally be done. Staphyloma has been removed by Bellad. 30, and repeated doses of Causticum 30. The contraction and irregularity of the pupils has yielded to Graphite, Silex, Calcarea and Sulphur 30. The remaining gouty pains have often been relieved by Bellad., Sulph., or Calcarea. Weber.

BELLADONNA,

according to Hering, is useful when the pain is severe and aching, in, around, above or near the eye, when there are violent stitches and feeling as if the eye were torn out, or pressed in; when the pains often return and go again, and flashes of light appear before the eyes, or sparks, or black specks with bright edges; or when every thing is dim as if from mist or gauze; with violent vertigo, and headache so severe that the patient is on the point of losing his consciousness.

Although Bellad. is not particularly suitable against the rheumatic or gouty diathesis, still it will often relieve the severe pains caused by the spasmodic contraction of the inflamed parts, and tend to prevent the contraction of the pupil; but then it must be used in full doses, both internally and externally. PETERS.

COCCULUS.

CASE 160.—A woman, aged 69, had had arthritic inflammation of the right eye, for four days, attended with the most violent rending pains in and about it.

Symptoms.—The right eye was generally and equally attacked with a venous inflammation; the varicose blood-vessels gave the conjunctiva a dirty-red appearance, and formed a whitish-blue ring around the cornea; the dilated pupil was oval in shape, and insensible to light, its upper edge was bent backwards; in the depths of the eye there was unmistakable greyish turbidity of the lens and crystalline body, and glaucoma had already commenced, the eye itself seemed smaller, as if it were drawn back into its orbit; the lids were inflamed and secreted a viscid, purulent fluid; there were violent pains in the brows; the left eye was sound, although the lids were already inflamed. The right eye was already totally blind.

Treatment.—Bellad. 30, was given, followed by Cocculus 12, on the next day; by the third day the inflammation and pain of the right eye were considerably lessened. Cocculus was then continued alone, and in four days more only a very inconsiderable inflammation remained, and the general condition of the patient was much improved. Nine days after, Sulphur 30, was given to remove some rending and piercing pains in the right side of the head and a slight inflammation of the lids. The patient was entirely cured in six weeks. THORER.

CASE 161.—A robust man, aged 48, had suffered for many weeks with arthritic ophthalmia preceded by rheumatic pains in the limbs.

Symptoms.—The sclerotica of the left eye was inflamed; an inflamed rose-red ring about the edge of the cornea;—cornea dim, dusty aud surrounded by a bluish white ring; the left iris was inflamed at its inner edge; the pupil drawn upwards, irregular and contracted; there was intolerance of light and contraction of the upper lid; no lachrymation; rending pains in the eye-brow, and left side of the head, aggravated in the evening and at night. There was already an angular appearance of the right pupil, and a bluish-white zone around the cornea. The patient saw as if through a mist.

Treatment.—Merc. 12 was given for four days without benefit. Then Cocculus 12 was given, with decided abatement of the inflammation, which disappeared entirely on the fifteenth day, while the intolerance of light was very slight and the pains trivial. Under the continued use of Cocculus the patient was entirely restored in a month, with the exception of some rheumatic pains in the limbs, for which he received Calc. 30. THORER.

CASE 162.—KALLENBACH also believes in the beneficial action of Cocculus in both acute and chronic arthritic ophthalmia. In one case, the almost entirely lost power of vision was restored by the alternate use of Coccul. and Sulph., one dose every eight days, in the course of six months.

CASE 163.—A woman whose fingers had been contracted by previous attacks of gout, was attacked with arthritic ophthalmia, which was soon cured by Coccul. The fingers became moveable during the treatment and remained so. KALLENBACH.

COLOCYNTH.

HERING says it is useful against inflammations attended with intolerable burning and cutting pains, extending into the head, with aching especially in the forehead or side of the brain, with drawing and rending, extending down into the nose, or spreading through the whole body, with great anxiety and restlessness.

Wine of Colchicum and Turpentine are much relied upon in the old school; drachm doses of the former, every six hours, have succeeded, when one-half the quantity had failed.

CASE 164.—An arthritic ophthalmia attended with almost permanent raging and rending pains, with burning and cutting pains in the eyes; congestion to the head, and profuse flow of acrid fluid from both eyes, was cured in a short time by two-drop doses of Tinct. Colocynth every three hours. SCHULER.

MERCURIUS-SOLUBILIS.

Lawrence says, that arthritic ophthalmia neither requires nor admits of that free use of Mercury, which is so advantageous in other forms of iritis; he has seen cases in which it was rather injurious than beneficial.

CASE 165.—A powerful man, aged 50, was attacked with ophthalmia after he had suffered with gouty pains in his limbs.

Symptoms.—Violent rending in the forehead and vertex, with severe pains shooting from the depths of the eyes, and aggravated every evening and night; considerable inflammation and sponginess of the right conjunctiva, phlegmonous swelling and inflammation of the eyelids, which were exceedingly sensitive to the slightest touch; great intolerance of light, and flow of hot tears; whitish ring about the cornea; the originally blue iris had become brownish and greenish; the pupil immoveable, and other signs of *iritis.* There was moderate fever; loss of sleep from the severe pains at night; profuse perspiration without relief.

Treatment.—Several strong doses of Acon. and Bell., produced no good effect; for every night at twelve o'clock the most violent pains set in, in the eye, and exhausted the strength of the patient; there was a bad taste in the mouth, much spitting of mucus, a pasty taste in the mouth, and some tenesmus. Then Merc. Solub. 4, one dose every night and morning was given for several days, with evident improvement to the iris and attendant pains and symptoms. Sulphur 6 and Sepia 30 were given, and the sight was perfectly restored.

SPIGELIA.

Lobethal says it is the most certain and almost only useful remedy against all gouty and rheumatic ophthalmias, when there is little external redness, but great vascularity of the conjunctiva or cornea, and when the pains in the interior of the eye are severe, boring, piercing or burning, and the feeling is present as if the ball of the eye was too large.

CASE 166.—A woman, aged 40, had suffered off and on for six years with catarrhal arthritic ophthalmia; there was an insupportable pain about the brow which deprived her of all rest and was much aggravated by changes of the weather and wind; there were enlarged almost varicose vessels on the conjunctiva, and the sclerotica was marked by a delicate, bright red net-work of vessels.

Treatment.—After Nux. had acted favorably for some time, and Sulphur 400, had been given without effect, Spigelia 30 was used with such good results that the patient was cured in three weeks. LORBACHER.

SULPHUR,

Is homœopathic to some of the varieties of rheumatism and gout.

An attack of gout is preceded in most instances by some marked disorder of the functions of the stomach and liver, such as diminished appetite, flatulence, heartburn or nausea; the stools are also unnatural, either pale, or of a dark green color and very offensive; the urine is apt to be high colored, acid and turbid. Pains and cramps may occur in several parts of the body, and shoot from thence to the arms or shoulders, and are relieved by the extrication of wind from the stomach. The bowels are apt to be irregular, colicky diarrhœa, alternating with costiveness. There is a tendency to venous conjestion of the abdomen, and to piles, with all this the patient is prone to be excessively dejected and hypochondriacal, morbidly attentive to every bodily feeling, disposed to exaggerate his sufferings and apprehensive of the worst event. WATSON.

Now, according to VOGT, Sulphur is homœopathic to weakness of digestion, discomfort in the stomach and bowels, eructations, nausea, distention of the abdomen with wind, colickly pains, loss of appetite, and tendency to diarrhœa, with more or less bilious derangement. The urine, under the use of Sulphur is apt to be thicker, darker, and saturated with animal matters.

VOGT says it may often be used successfully against some chronic and dyscratic inflammations in which Mercury and Antimony dare not be given. That is very useful against *excessive venosity*, stagnations in the venous vessels, and hæmorrhoidal affections. In chronic rheumatic affections when there is but little warmth in the skin, and sluggishness of the lymphatic and venous circulations: it is quite indispensable when the long duration, or frequent return of the affection has developed a rheumatic dyscrasia, and the condition of the system does not allow of the use of mercurials, or antimonials. HUFELAND, FRITZE and others have prevented the regular annual attacks of gout for years, by the methodical use of Sulphur persisted in for four or six weeks together, followed by China, or other remedies. It is most useful against blind piles, and its good effects are most certain when there is pain, a chronic inflammatory irritation of the affected parts, and a strongly marked hæmorrhoidal disposition, with abdominal venous congestion, although it has been used as a specific against all and very various kinds of hæmorrhoids. It acts not merely upon the piles, but exerts an alterative action upon the metamorphoses of the vegetative organs, upon the venous system in general, and tends to equalize the distribution of the blood, lymph., &c. It may even remove chronic alterations of structure, depositions, exudations, vegetations, &c. PETERS.

CASE 167.—A cachectic woman, aged 62, had suffered with her eyes, for about a year.

Symptoms.—Considerable intolerance of light, and violent pains from exposure to it; dark redness of the conjunctiva the vessels of which run towards the cornea, stop suddenly in its neighborhood, then unite and form a vascular zone with those of the other side of the eye, forming a characteristic bluish ring about the edge of the cornea. The cornea is transparent, but dim, as if covered with dust. The pupils contracted but not irregular. In the left eye a flocculent exudation extended from one edge of the pupil to the other. The iris of both eyes was swollen in places, and deficient in its peculiar radiated texture. At night the eyelids became slightly adherent with a foamy, whitish secretion, especially at its angles. There were violent pains, severe burning with piercing and pricking, increased at night, so that the patient was often obliged to sit up in bed for hours, and only obtained some sleep towards morning. Boring, pressing pains in the upper orbital margin, with great heat of the head, and sensation when moving the eyes as if they had not room enough in their sockets. Sparks and flashes before the eyes. Objects swam before the left eye in indistinct images, and the attempt to see more clearly was followed by gushes of hot tears.

Treatment.—Bellad. 6, three doses per week, produced some relief from the pains and some sleep at night, but effected no change in the local affection in the course of fourteen days. Several doses of Nux. 6, did no good. Spigelia 6, one dose every other night seemed to act beneficially at first, but not long. After the commencing the use of Sulphur 3, one dose every third morning, the whole disease was removed in three weeks. GENZKE.

CASE 168.—A robust, gouty man, aged 40, had suffered considerably with gouty inflammation in the left eye; his vision was impaired; the pupil irregular, the iris insensible. A fresh attack of gout in the upper and lower extremities was followed by an arthritic affection of the head, viz., of the left frontal bone and of the eye, aggravated at night. The inner surface of the eyelids, the meibomian glands, caruncula lachrymalis, conjunctiva and iris were uniformly inflamed, attended with swelling, intolerance of light, and inability to see.

Treatment.—Two doses of Bellad. 30, followed by Sulphur 30, on the third day, removed the inflammation by the sixth day, so that the patient could use his eye again. A relapse was quickly relieved by the same remedies, aided by Cocculus. THORER.

CASE 169.—A gouty man, of apoplectic habit, aged 50, had suffered for years with repeated attacks of ophthalmic arthritica which confined him to a dark room for weeks and months, and against which all remedies had previously been of no avail. At present he had suffered for several days with intolerance of light which prevented the slightest use of his eyes; the conjunctiva was but little reddened; the sclerotica was rose-red, and there was a bluish ring around the cornea, with pains about the eyes.

Treatment.—Four doses of Tinct. Sulph., one each day, restored the eye entirely, and no relapse had occurred at the end of one and a half years. The photophobia ceased first. GRIESELICH.

CASE 170.—A woman aged 34, who had had itch suddenly repelled several years before, had suffered for three months with violent gouty inflammation of the *left* eye.

Symptoms.—Pale redness of the sclerotica; redness of the conjunctiva of the lids and ball; dimness of the cornea, as if covered with dust, and deep, whitish spots in the centre; discoloration of the iris; pupils smoky and somewhat irregular; almost entire loss of sight in the affected eye, so that she could not scarcely distinguish colors; neither pain, nor photophobia.

Treatment.—Sulphur 6, six doses, one every other day; in five days the inflammation was considerably diminished, and vision improved. Six more doses of Sulph. 6. were given, and afterwards, three doses of Sulph. 30, one every eight days. The eye was entirely restored; the cornea became clear, the iris regained its natural color, the pupil became free and regular. HEICHELHEIM.

CASE 171.—A woman, aged 60, had been sick for eight days.

Symptoms.—Violent rending pains, first in the right eye, then in the left, extending over the brows into the forehead, and persisting night and day; both eyes were swelled; the lids erysipelatously inflamed, so that they could not be opened; violent dark red inflammation and sponginess of the conjunctiva; great swelling around the cornea (chemosis); iris inflamed and brown in color; pupils much contracted, but round in shape; great intolerance of light; ready eversion of the upper lid; the left eye could not be seen from the great inflammation and swelling of the lids; profuse effusion of mucus and pus from between the lids. Fever in the afternoon, much thirst, no appetite, night sweats without relief, constipation, scanty red urine.

Treatment.—Bellad. 24, in drop doses, for three days, with relief from the piercing pains in the balls, erysipelatous swelling of the lids; on the sixth day Spigelia 30, without benefit on the contrary the symptoms increased. Cocculus 12, in drop doses, night and morning, for four days, without good result. Then Arsen. 30, one dose every other day; after two doses the patient got some rest at night, the swelling around the cornea subsided, the gouty pains in and about the eye were lessened, and the blenorrhœa was very slight.

A relapse, occasioned by exposure to cold was followed by raging pains in and about the left eye; the cornea became milky white and turbid; great swelling of the conjunctiva; vision seemed lost; a pannus formed over the eye, and purulent mucus was discharged from it. Phosphor 30 and Staphys. 30, were given without relief; there was commencing keratocele (hernia of the cornea), and falling forwards of the iris. Lycopod. 30, for twelve days, followed by relief from the arthritic symptoms, retrocession of the organic changes, removal of the prolapsus of the iris, and almost entire restoration of sight. Finally, Euphrasia was given.

THORER.

GENERAL REVIEW OF THE TREATMENT OF ARTHRITIC OPHTHALMIA.

In the above ten cases, Sulphur was used four times; Cocculus, three times; Spigelia, Merc. and Coloc., each in one case, and Arsen., Acon., Bellad., Caust., Lycopod., and Nux. are alluded to.

When the *lids* were inflamed with phlegmonous swelling, Merc.; inflamed with erysipelatous swelling, Bellad.; inflamed, Cocc.; inflamed on their inner surface, Sulph.; inflammation of the meibomian glands and caruncle, Sulph.; foamy secretion between the lids, Sulph.; viscid moisture, Coccul.;—hot tears, Merc.

When the *conjunctiva* is dark red, as if injected, Sulph. and Spigel.;—inflamed and spongy, Merc.,—with swelling around the cornea, (chemosis) Arsenicum.

When the *sclerotica* is rose-red and inflamed, Sulph., Spigel., Coccul.:—rose-red in color, Coccul., bluish ring around the cornea, Sulph.; a white zone, Merc.;—a bluish white ring, Cocculus.

The *cornea* dim and without glance, Cocc. and Sulph.;—

with whitish and shallow excavations in the middle, Sulph.; —flocculent exudation in the anterior chamber, Sulph.

When the *iris* is inflamed, Coccul., and Sulph.;—discolored, Sulph.;—when the naturally blue iris becomes brownish and green, Merc.;—spongy, with loss of radiating texture, Sulph.;—with loss of contractility, Sulph.; prolapsed, Lyc.; —oblong, Merc.;

When the *pupils* are angular and irregular, Sulph., Graph., Silex., Calc.;—when they are actually contracted, Coccul.; —rigid, Merc.;—drawn inwards and backwards, without contractility, Cocculus.

When the *lens* is greyish and dim, with commencing glaucoma, Coccul.;—when sparks, flashes, black-spots with bright edges appear before the eyes, and everything seems dim, as if in a mist, Bellad., Sulph.

When the *pains* are boring and pressing as if the ball of the eye were too large, Sulph.;—boring, piercing and burning, Spigelia;—boring and cutting, Coloc.;—rending in the brows and head, Coccul. and Bellad.;—raging headache with anxiety and restlessness, Coloc.;—when perspiration brings no relief, Merc.

Most of the above cases were sub-acute or chronic, and Coccul., Spigel., Sulph., Calc., Caust., Arsen., and Lycopod., were the most useful remedies. In the more acute attacks, Acon., Bell., Coccul., and Merc. were used.

The Doses varied much, both high and low dilutions were employed.

In acute cases the danger of destruction to the eye was removed in six or eight days; the chronic ones required from three to four weeks to effect a cure. Even against staphyloma and irregularities of the pupil, Weber was able to do something.

DISEASES OF THE CORNEA.

Simple inflammation of the cornea has been treated of in Vol. 1., p. 51.

SCROFULOUS CORNEITIS.

It generally appears in young persons from eight to eighteen years of age; and in the female it often occurs in connection with amenorrhœa; the skin of the patient is often coarse and flabby, with the sebaceous follicles of the face much developed; it also often occurs in connection with deafness and a peculiar hoarseness of the voice; other scrofulous affections are generally present, such as swollen lymphatic glands, &c.

The redness is principally in the sclerotica and on the surface of the cornea, and is in general not very considerable; in some cases, however, the whole of the cornea is so much covered with red vessels, that it resembles a piece of red cloth, and hence has been styled pannus.

The cornea is more or less opaque and rough, and looks as if its whole surface had been dotted or pricked with a pin; it has also lost its natural polish resembling glass that has been breathed upon; in fact dimness of sight and slight opacity are the earliest symptoms of the disease. Deposits of lymph may take place, so that the whole surface becomes almost uniformly white, one patch of opaque deposition taking place after another, or else the opacity creeps slowly from one edge of the cornea over its whole area. At times these deposits of lymph also take place between the laminæ of the cornea; then although the external surface may clear, such deep-seated opacities scarcely ever are removed.

In most cases of scrofulous corneitis which have lasted a considerable time, the aqueous humor becomes superabundant, and there is more or less *hydropthalmia.* In other instances the cornea becomes somewhat conical.

Not unfrequently we find a white spot on the centre of the cornea, the rest being quite red, or in a state of pannus; as the disease proceeds the white spot ulcerates, then the pannus begins to clear, and a cure more or less perfect is accomplished. In such cases it often happens that until the central spot ulcerates, no improvement is effected; still the cornea is left more or less reduced in size, and with a permanent opacity.

The disease in its mildest form is always tedious; many cases are under allopathic treatment for a year or more before they perfectly recover; still the amount of recovery, by the gradual obsorption of the opaque spots is often wonderful, even when all hope seemed lost.

Allopathic Treatment.—Tartar emetic is often useful; Mercury and Turpentine are relied upon when the paroxysms of pain are severe and the iris becomes involved, and there are newly deposited thick opacities from the pouring-out of coagulable lymph; Quinine acts more slowly than in pustular ophthalmia, but is said to be very useful when there is great debility, flabbiness of the skin and night-sweats, it is most homœopathic when there is more or less deafness; Iodide of Potash, Cod Liver Oil and Muriate of Barytes are used when there are glandular swellings present. Among the *local* applications, a solution of Bi-chloride of Mercury with Bellad. is considered the most useful; Hydrocyanic-acid, applied in the form of vapor to the eye is said to be decidedly useful when the acute stage is over, it lessens the redness and clears the cornea.

For Homœopathic treatment, see Scrofulous Ophthalmia, Vol. 1.

ABSCESS OF CORNEA.

See Hypopion, Vol. 1, p. 106.

ULCERS OF THE CORNEA.

There are two distinct varieties, 1st, the *superficial*; 2d, the *deep*.

The former generally extends over a considerable portion of the surface of the cornea and often appears to involve little more than its merest surface.

The *deep* ulcer is usually much smaller, but it penetrates the proper substance of the cornea and often eats its way completely through all its layers, so as to open the anterior chamber, and let out the aqueous humor. The superficial ulcer is common in catarrho-rheumatic ophthalmia, the deep ulcer generally is the result of the bursting of a scrofolous pustule, or the giving way of an onyx externally.

The cicatrix which follows a superficial ulcer, is greyish or bluish white and semi-transparent; it generally can be entirely removed. The surface of a deep ulcer is usually ragged and covered with a sloughy like matter, and is apt to be covered with red vessels before it heals up; an opaque cicatrix of a yellowish white color is formed, called *leucoma*, which seldom admits of being completely removed.

Both superficial and deep ulcers sometimes assume the form

of a *transparent* pit, depression or fossula in the cornea, forming what has been called an asthenic ulcer, or very incorrectly, a transparent cicatrix; after a time, however, it becomes covered with opaque fibro-albuminous exudation and undergoes a real process of cicatrization.

Another very peculiar variety is the so-called *troughing ulcer;* it sometimes forms at the edge of the cornea, in consequence of the chimosis which attends gonorrhœal and purulent ophthalmia. Mackenzie has also occasionally met with an obstinate variety of ulcer at the edge of the cornea, which creeps on slowly, one portion healing, while the other is spreading, until at length a *deep trench* is formed around a great part of the edge of the cornea.

Occasionally it happens that a deep ulcer penetrates so far that the lining membrane of the cornea is pushed forwards in the form of a vesicle, forming what is termed *hernia of the cornea;* it is very apt to burst if touched roughly, or when the patient is blowing his nose violently, or straining at stool, or making some violent exertion; the aqueous humor is then evacuated, the iris falls forward, and too often protrudes through the ulcerated opening forming the so-called *hernia of the iris.*

Allopathic Treatment.—Mackenzie regards Belladonna as the most beneficial remedy in ulcers of the cornea; Quinine is said to be required in the asthenic ulcer, or transparent fossula.

OPACITIES OF THE CORNEA.

These are of three kinds; 1st, *nebula,* is the slightest degree; 2d, *albugo,* which arises from the deposit of lymph into the cornea, so as to present a pearly appearance; 3d, *leucoma,* which is always the result of cicatrization.

All these three kinds of specks have a natural tendency to disperse as soon as the disease which gives rise to them subsides, or is removed. In children and young persons many very dense and extensive opacities are removed in the natural progress of growth, which would be quite irremovable in adult life.

Allopathic Treatment.—Mackenzie has witnessed the good

effects of the vapor of Prussic-acid especially in nebula, in some cases of leucoma and in vascular albugo; in this last affection the action of the vapor causes the vessels to shrink, after which the speck ulcerates and disappears. The vapor of Phosphorus is much more useful. Corrosive-sublimate, Hydriodate of Potash, Sulphate of Cadmium, and the Bile of various animals, &c., &c., all cause such irritation as causes the capillaries to become turgid, and as the increased vascularity subsides, increased activity of the absorbents follows as a matter of course, and more or less of the opaque matter is removed.

HOMŒOPATHIC TREATMENT OF SPOTS AND LEUCOMATOUS OPACITIES.

CASE 172.—W. was left after ophthalmic arthritis with leucomatous opacity of the cornea; he saw before the affected eye nothing but a constant play of colors, accompanied by vertigo once or twice a day; he had boring and hammering pains in the forehead, pressure in the eye, burning and cutting pains in the lids—whizzing and buzzing in the ears.

Treatment.—Calc. 18. At the end of a week, the greyish-white opacity had changed into a lighter color, and the other symptoms were much improved—in two weeks one-half of the cornea was clear. Phosph. 30, was then given and the leucomatous opacity which had penetrated deep into the lamellæ, diminished daily in size and depth; Silicea was given to complete the cure.—*Arch.* 8, 156. SCHULER.

CASE 173.—A lady, aged 32, had opacity of the cornea of the left eye with staphylomatous excrescences on the same.

Treatment.—From August until March she took Sulph. 400, Calc. 200, Acid-nitr. 200, Euphras. 200, Cannab. 200, and Silic. 200, in solutions. Under this treatment she improved so much, as to enable her to discern objects and read print in large letters.—*N. Arch.* 2. 1. 83. STAPF.

CASE 174.—A man, aged 25, had considerable opacity of the right cornea, on the spot where there formerly had been pustule. He had also been blind in the left eye for twenty-three years from an opacity of the cornea of that eye.

After the use of Euphrasia 200 for two weeks, the opacity of the right eye entirely disappeared, and through the left he could distinguish the light of the day.—*N. Arch.* 2. 1. 85. Stapf.

CASE 175.—A boy, aged twelve, after an inflammation of the eyes, was left with greyish streaks on the cornea of the right eye, and many little spots over the whole bulb of the left.

Caustic. 30, cured the whole in six weeks.—*Arch.* 17. 1. 26. B. in D.

CASE 176.—A child, aged ten, after having had an attack of inflammation of the eyes, was left with the cornea changed into a greyish-white mass, perfectly opaque, and somewhat more prominent.

Caust. 30, several doses, with other remedies removed the leucoma in five months.—*Ibid.* 26.

CASE 177.—A man after having had inflammation of the eyes, was left with a greyish speck on both corneæ, which weakened his sight very much, so that in looking at objects they appeared as if enveloped in a mist.

Caust. 30, two doses, and one intermediate dose of Sulph. 30, every fourth week one dose, improved the condition very much—subsequently Caust. and Pulsatilla cured the patient entirely.—*Ibid.* 29.

CASE 178.—Vaccinin 1st, four doses, cured a young lady, aged 17, of opacity of the cornea, which had come on after a vaccination in her earliest childhood,—many other remedies had been administered without any benefit whatever.—*Allg. H. Ztg.* III., *p.* 149. Batzendorf.

CASE 179.—A girl, 8 years of age, affected with nebula of the right eye, without previous inflammation.

Treatment.—Euphrasia, internally and externally, was used without improvement.—Cannab. 30, one dose internally every fourth day, and externally in a solution applied to the eye, improved the affection very much in the course of two weeks. —*Pract. Beitr.* 3, 23. Thorer.

CASE 180.—Mrs. X., aged 64, after having been stung by a bee, was attacked with violent inflammation of the eye; on the day following there was considerable exudation on the cornea, and after a few days it was covered by a greyish-white spot.

After subduing the inflammation and photophobia by Bellad.—Canab. was given in one drop-doses of the Tincture every week, and daily applications of Tinct. Cannab. gutt. x. in Aq. dist. ℥j. were made,—a cure was accomplished in five weeks.—*Allg. H. Ztg.* 1, 119. SEIDEL.

CASE 181.—After an attack of gout, an old lady was seized with an inflammation of the right eye, followed by opacity of the whole cornea; after subduing the inflammation, the yellowish-white opacity disappeared in consequence of the continued use of Euphrasia, so completely, that the lady afterwards could use her eye for all purposes.—*Allg. H. Ztg.* 5, 163. KNORRE.

CASE 182.—A boy, aged 5, was subject to attacks of inflammation of the eyes, which returned monthly, leaving spots on the cornea, which finally increased so as to cause complete opacity; the densest part of which was formed by a cicatrix from a wound in the cornea, produced by a piece of wire.

Treatment.—One drop Tinct. Euphrasia once a week. The cicatrix soon disappeared, and the spots on the cornea decreased very much, but the recurring attacks of inflammation had to be cured by Antipsorics.—*Allg. H. Ztg.* 1, 40. KRETZSCHMAR.

CASE 183.—A lady of scrofulous habit, had been affected for more than a year with leucoma of the right eye; she was also troubled with humid tetters and leucorrhœa, and her menses were too profuse and frequent.

Treatment.—Diverse remedies were administered, and finally Carb.-veg., but without success.

Then Calc.-carb. 30 was given, six doses, in the course of eight days; the thickened false membrane separated, so as to expose the pupil a little; cornea became more transparent, so that the patient was enabled to see a little.—*Hyg.* 4, 127. GRIESSEL.

3. *Vascular Tumors and Warty Excrescences of the Cornea.*

CASE 184.—On the cornea of a child, aged 6 years, had formed itself, within a few months, a wart-like greyish protuberance the size of a pin's-head. Opening and shutting of the eye caused very unpleasant sensations.

After Ars. 30, in half drop-doses, it disappeared in seventeen days.

CASE 185.—A similar case to the above occurred in a child two years old.

Treatment.—Ars. 30, a half drop, diminished the growth to one-half of its size in twenty days; a second dose cured the remainder in eleven days.—SCHWARZE, 17, 18.

CASE 186.—A girl, aged 9 years, has been affected for the last year with a vascular tumor of the cornea, situated between the conjunctiva and sclerotica, from which the vessels seemed to branch out. The tumor had the appearance of a dark yellowish fleshy mass, disfiguring the looks of the patient very much. All previous treatment had been without success.

Treatment.—Carb.-an. 30 and 3d, were given every other day in alternation from October 21, to Nov. 19, also without benefit. Thuja was then ordered internally in the same way as the Carb. and an external application of Tinct. Thuja in water, was applied on Dec. 22d, the tumor had much diminished in size, and the iris became visible. The Thuja was continued, and the opacity of the cornea lessened. Then Cannab. 30. was given internally every third day, and Cannab. 1, used externally. Finally Thuja and Cannab. in alternation, until the case was cured.—*Allg. H. Ztg.* 38, 350. DRYSDALE.

4. *Sanguinous Tumor of the Cornea.*

A case of sanguinous tumor of the cornea, pointing towards the inner eye, is reported by STAPF.—*Arch.* 7, 2. 56.

On account of the lengthy description of the case we will only give an outline of the:

Treatment.—September 2d, Bellad. 30, was given and diminished the violent, burning, cutting, boring pain in the eye-ball, the photophobia, and the corrosive discharge.

Sept. 9, Calc.-carb. 12, was followed by an aggravation of the whole condition until Sept. 14th, when an amelioration sat in; towards the last of Sept. the patient could open the eye; the pain and inflammation were much less, but the fungus was quite as red in color.

Oct. 24th, Lycopod. 12, which was followed by much improvement, the conjunctiva became almost natural, the opacity was lessened, and the specks on the cornea disappeared; the fungus was much paler, and arrested in its progress.

Dec. 11, Sepia 30, was given; the inflammation subsided entirely; the fungus became smaller in size and paler in appearance.

Jan. 30, Silicea, towards the end of Feb. the fungus had almost disappeared,—the child was able to see, and even to read.

April 20, Calc. 18. By the middle of June the eye was restored to perfect health.

STAPHYLOMA.

Various protrusions, arising from the destruction or yielding of some of the coats of the eye, have received the name of staphyloma, from the resemblance they occasionally bear to a grape.

Staphyloma uveæ arises when the iris loses its natural firmness of texture, and the aqueous humor of the posterior chamber of the eye presses the uvea through the attenuated iris.

Staphyloma iridis occurs when a portion of the iris protrudes through a wound, or ulceration of the cornea; the ophthalmia of new-born children, purulent, gonorrhœal, severe scrofulous or pustular, and traumatic ophthalmiæ are the most common causes of staphyloma of the present day; before the general introduction of vaccination, small-pox used to be the most frequent exciting cause.

When the staphyloma projects so much that it interferes with the ready closure of the eyelids, the apex of the swelling may be touched with a pointed pencil of caustic potash, or nitrate of silver, then brushed over with oil; the part touched by the caustic forms a small eschar, which drops off in the course of a few days, leaving an ulcer, which in cicatrizing, causes a degree of shrinking or flattening of the protrusion; the caustic is not to be repeated until the process of reparation is perfectly completed.

When an ulcer has perforated the cornea, Belladonna, Stramonium, &c., should be used freely, in order to draw the iris out of the cornea, and prevent adhesion to it.

Choroid staphyloma is owing to a protrusion of the choroid coat through the sclerotica; it is of a dark blue color, and often has somewhat of a malignant air, so that it may be mistaken for a melanotic affection.

Single Cases.

CASE 187.—A married lady, aged 24, cachectic in the highest degree, was afflicted with herpetic eruptions, furuncles, old sores about the feet, and lastly with the following disease of the eyes.

Symptoms. Both eyes inflamed; a net-work of injected vessels surrounding the cornea; the left eye covered with a white film, increasing in density toward the lower part of the cornea, causing the opacity to be greater there; on the right eye towards the outer canthus, the margin of the cornea and upper segment of the pupil, there was a staphylomatous protuberance of the size of a small pea, of a dark greyish color; the pupil was drawn out of its natural position; the sight very much impaired; but the intolerance of light was not great.

Treatment.—May 4. Rhus 200, every two hours, followed by amelioration of pain; May 6. Lycopod. 3, three doses; after the second dose there arose a pressure in the epigastrium; uneasiness about the chest, stinging pain in the precordial region, anxiety and palpitation of the heart, violent head- and tooth-ache, swelling of the face, cheeks, neck, and salivation; —this condition lasted several days. May 10. Euphras. 6, one drop in water was applied externally. May 12. Lycop. 30, every three hours. By May 17, the cornea was more transparent, and a decrease in size of the staphyloma. On May 20, the patient was able to use her eyes.—Lycopod. 30, was given as before, until the disease of the eyes was perfectly cured.—*Allg. H. Ztg.* 36, 148. SCHELLING.

CASE 188.—A lady, 24 years of age, four weeks after her confinement, accidentally had a small chip of wood thrown into her left eye; the inflammation which it caused was treated allopathically for one month.

Symptoms.—The eye could only be opened by a great effort on the part of the patient, during which there was an escape of watery fluid and pus; the lids were much swollen, red and ulcerated; the pains were very severe, of a cutting, gnawing character; in the inner eye, night and day, there was the most violent cutting, pressing pain, increased by opening the lids, and very great intolerance of light.

Conjunctiva dark red, swollen and protruding; opacity of the cornea, with several small deep ulcers, and near its border a staphylomatous excrescence of considerable size. Pupil oblong, and one side of the disfigured iris was intimately adherent to the staphyloma. Sight was almost extinct.

Patient is cachectic, has an ashy complexion, with derangement of digestion and corroding leucorrhœa.

Treatment.—From August 24, to August 30, Sulph. 30, followed by amelioration of pain, easier opening of the lids, less discharge from the eye, and less inflammation; the ulcers had improved, and there was a decrease in size of the staphyloma.

Calcar. 30, was followed in two weeks by entire cessation of the leucorrhœa and improvement of the whole condition.

Thirty-two days after the commencement of the treatment, Nitr. ac. 30, was given, followed by steady improvement of the opacity and specks on the cornea. After Pulsat., Euphras., Senega, the sight was perfectly restored, but the iris remains a little disfigured. The staphyloma was gone and left only a discoloration of the cornea.—*Arch.* 18, 2. 45. STAPF.

GONORRHŒAL OPHTHALMIA.

According to MACKENZIE there are several varieties of this disease; the most severe is caused by inoculation from the urethra; it is comparatively rare, as the instinctive closure of the eyelids, when the finger approaches the eye, makes it actually difficult for a person to touch his own conjunctiva.

It resembles purulent ophthalmia so closely, that there are no marks which can be absolutely depended upon to distinguish the two. In general, only one eye is affected, while in purulent ophthalmia both eyes are usually involved; whenever we see one eye affected with a severe puro-mucous inflammation, the lids much swollen and of a livid color, and the discharge copious, without any affection of the other eye, we may suspect the case to be gonorrhœal.

It is often exceedingly rapid in its course; in forty-eight hours the disease may have proceeded so far that the sight will be irretrievably gone; thus, of nine cases having only one eye affected, six suffered total loss of vision of the eye affected; of five who had both eyes affected, four lost each one eye, and the fifth lost both eyes. (LAURENCE.) Still it varies much in severity, some eyes resisting the tendency to disorganization and getting well; others being rapidly destroyed.

The chemosis and swelling of the lids are often rather pale; the discharge from the eye is generally profuse and purulent. The cornea is often destroyed by an ulcerated groove forming at its edge, when it is covered and pressed upon by the chemosed conjunctiva; this groove is apt to give way about the twelfth or fourteenth day of the disease, allowing the iris to protrude in one or several points; the eye may be quite bright and clear to-day, and to-morrow we find the cornea burst, generally near its lower edge. This may happen while the patient is straining at stool, or to get on a pair of tight boots, or to lift some article. In other cases, ulceration spreads over a great part of the surface of the cornea, which seems to melt away, becoming so thin as so bulge forwards, and finally it gives way.

Allopathic treatment.—The most vigorous employment of general and local bloodletting and other antiphlogistic means will not save the eye; while the salts of Lead, Zinc and Copper will be found to aggravate the symptoms, at least in the early stages of the attack; snipping out a fold of the chemosed membrane, so as to procure a considerable flow of blood, is highly serviceable; the conjunctiva should be brushed repeatedly in the course of the day with a solution of nitrate of silver; cooling purgatives should be used.

From Metastasis.

These cases are much less dangerous; they arise without inoculation, from the suppression of gonorrhœa, by exposure to cold, violent exertions of the body, abuse of liquor, and astringent injections.

The principal point in the treatment is to restore the discharge from the urethra.

Without Inoculation or Metastasis.

These cases are generally rheumatic or catarrhal in their nature; some people are liable to rheumatism of the joints, to puriform discharges from the urethra, and irritable ophthalmia; and these diseases are apt to alternate one with the other; when one comes on, the other ceases, and vice-versa. They must not be mistaken for those frightful cases in which the eye is really clapped.

The remedies used were: Antim.-tart., Chin., Nitric-acid, Pulsat.

CASE 189.—A gentleman, aged 40, affected with gonorrhœa, from carelessness got some of the gonorrhœal matter into his right eye, after which he became affected with a violent iritis. He had violent photophobia of the right eye first, but subsequently also of the left,—severe and constant pain in the forehead, which tormented and reduced the patient very much; he had been sick six weeks. China cured him in two weeks.

CASE 190.—After suppressed gonorrhœa; a man became affected with blenorrhœa of the eye; Pulsatilla re-established the gonorrhœa and cured the blenorrhœa.

CASE 191.—An obstinate case of gonorrhœal ophthalmia, in consequence of suppressed gonorrhœa, withstood for eight weeks all allopathic treatment.

Tart.-emet. brought on the discharge again, and with the gradual increase of the same, the ophthalmia decreased rapidly.—*Allgem. H. Ztg.* 35, 26—30. ROSENBERG.

CASE 192.—A mechanic, aged 19, who had had a clap for a few weeks, became affected with gonorrhœal ophthalmia, in consequence of having brought in contact with the eye some of the gonorrhœal matter.

Symptoms.—The upper and lower lid of the right eye presented a livid, hard and painful swelling, making it almost impossible to see the eye-ball. Conjunctiva palp. et occul. highly inflamed and swollen; pain in the eye, pressing from within outward. Cornea dim, photophobia very great, with constant discharge of tears, and copious flow of yellowish matter trickling down the cheek; circumference of the eye and cheek swollen, and painful to the touch; during the day moderate, but at night severe burning pain in the eye. The left eye was not affected; duration three days.

Treatment.—Acid.-nit. gutt x, Spir.-vin. ℥j. forenoon and evening ten drops per dose in water. About the fourteenth day the inflammation of the eye gradually disappeared, though some redness and swelling of the lids and some photophobia remained for some time. The clap was subsequently cured. —*Allgem. H. Ztg.* 19, 67. KNORRE.

PSOROPHTHALMIA.

General Remarks.

a. A severe form of psorophthalmia was accompanied with considerable inflammation, photophobia, tears, sensitiveness, burning, cutting, stinging pains in the eye, and fever, with evening exacerbations, spasmodic closing of the eyelids and nightly uneasiness, and in most cases with headache; in the morning, the eyes were entirely closed from the drying of matter upon the margins of the eye-lids.

In some cases the ball of the eye presented the appearance of a raw piece of meat, covered with matter, through which the cornea was scarcely discernable. The pains were increased by cold air, and cooling collyriæ.

There was great sensitiveness to atmospheric changes, so that the patient would feel chilly in bed, with the windows closed; there was some scalding during micturition, and cutting pain in the urethra at other periods; constipation and thirst.

Treatment.—Merc. was useful, but Bryonia and Rhus still more so.—*Hyg.* 19, 85. SCHELLING.

b. The milder forms of Psorophthalmia has already been treated of in Vol. 1, p. 11.

1. *Twitching or quivering of the Eye-lids.*

In some cases this is very slight; in others it extends to the other muscles of the face, so that the eye-lids are convulsed, and the angle of the mouth drawn upwards.

It is similar to chorea in its nature; Agaricus, Stramonium,

Arsenicum, Bellad., and Actea-racemosa are the principal remedies, although Zincum and Cuprum may be required.

2. *Morbid Nictitation.*

This is a convulsive action of the orbicularis palpebrarum; sometimes the upper eye-lid is affected; in others, the lower; at times one eye only, at others both eyes.

Sometimes it is caused by a single eye-lash growing inwards so as to touch the ball; it often arises in children, whose eyes have been overtasked; or from indigestion.

The eye may be bathed with a weak solution of Belladonna.

3. *Blepharospasm.*

In this disorder the eye is spasmodically closed; it may arise from over use of the eyes; or from carious teeth, or abscesses at the root of the teeth, and is then only to be relieved by their extraction; or from a blow upon the head; or from scrofulous ophthalmia, or photophobia; or from nervousness or hysteria.

CASE 193.—A lady, aged 26, had been complaining for two months past of dryness and burning in the eye-lids and intolerance of light, painful, uncontrollable spasmodic closing of the lids, with much inclination to sleep; at other times there was nothing abnormal about the eye-lids.

Viola odorat. 200, two doses, cured the above in six weeks perfectly.—*Arch.* 2. 1. 75. STAPF.

CASE 194.—Mrs. B. was accidentally struck upon the ball of the eye, and experienced subsequently a feeling during the act of closing the eye, as if there was a protuberance upon the ball. On awaking in the morning the lids felt as if spasmodically closed.

Treatment.—Arnica and Conium were given without benefit, but Symphit.-offic. 6, a few doses, cured the patient in a short time.—*Allg. H. Ztg.* 17. 5. *Gr.*

Warts on the Eye-lids.

These are not uncommon on the external surface of the eye-lids, and sometimes grow from their edges.

If other means fail, strong Acetic-acid may be applied several times a day.

Sycosis of the Eye-lids.

To others this may seem a very trifling disease, but to the patient who is extremely desirous to get rid of it, and to the allopathic surgeon, who finds it exceedingly difficult to disperse, its apparent insignificance affords little consolation. Other hard tubucles of the same kind are generally present on the face; but those which are situated on the edge of the lid, or so close to either punctum, as almost to surround it, are more obstinate than any of the rest.

4. *Condyloma of the Eye-lid.*

Madam D., aged 28, of short, stout stature, and lively disposition became affected, a year ago, with a gradually increasing wart at the lower lid of the right eye; which by degrees hindered the closing of the lids, and impaired the sight. Allopathic treatment had been used without avail.

Symptoms.—Right eye much inflamed; intolerance of light, objects appeared dim, as if she was looking through a veil; increased secretion of tears. There was no doubt that the wart was of a condylomatous nature; it could be recognized by the specific odor, emanating from the suppurating and easily bleeding growth; it was one-third of an inch in length, and one-fourth of an inch in diameter. The whole eye presented a disgusting appearance.

Treatment.—Thuya 6. Six doses; one dose night and morning; on the third day the inflammation was less, the pain had subsided, and the specific odor much diminished;—the prescription was repeated as above; from the third to the tenth day there was no change.—Acid.-nitr. 6, was then given, the inflammation soon disappeared, also the abnormal secretion of tears, and the pain, while the wart diminished to one-half of its former size;—the sight was also improved.—Acid.-nitr. 6 was continued as before.

On the tenth day of the administration of Acid.-nitr. every vestige of it had disappeared.—*N. Archiv* 3. 1. 37. Wahle.

IRITIS.

According to *Mackenzie*, there are several varieties of this disease, viz., the rheumatic, syphilitic, pseudo-syphilitic, gonorrhœal, scrofulous and arthritic. Of these the syphilitic is the most frequent.

The iris is supplied with a quantity of red blood, large in proportion to its size, and is quite liable to inflammation; this inflammation is of the adhesive kind, and if the attack be neglected or misunderstood, the pupil may become obliterated by an effusion of coagulable lymph. Another dangerous part of the disease is, that there always attends upon iritis a certain degree of retinitis; besides there is always some sclerotic and conjunctival inflammation; finally, the anterior hemisphere of the crystalline capsule is in every case more or less affected, and often the inflammatory action involves the choroid. Still, although the case often threatens to be one of general internal ophthalmia, the iris is plainly the focus of the diseased action, and the seat of the most striking morbid changes. It is at the pupillary edge of the iris that the disease generally seems to commence, whence it spreads to the rest of the iris, to the capsule of the lens, and to the choroid and retina, while the sclerotic and conjunctival inflammation which attends it seems to be sympathetic, still the iris alone is involved in many cases.

Symptoms.—There are certain symptoms which characterize iritis, from whatever cause it proceeds; there is always more or less pain about the brow, some haziness of the cornea, contraction and irregularity in the shape of the pupil, and change in the color of the iris; a naturally blue iris becomes greenish, a dark colored one becomes reddish.

Iritis has been considered as presenting three stages: the first, characterized by increased vascularity of the sclerotica, haziness of the cornea, discoloration of the iris, inactivity and irregularity of the pupil, dimness of sight, and pain in and about the eye.

In the second stage, there is an exudation of lymph in and upon the iris, and into the pupil, contraction of the pupil, adhesions of the iris to the crystalline capsule, increase of pain, and greater defect of sight.

The third stage presents red vessels ramifying on the iris and in the pupil, the pupil closed, the lens and capsule opaque, the retina insensible, the eye-ball changed in shape, being flattened under the recti muscles, the choroid protruding through the attenuated sclerotica, and the eye boggy to the touch.

Iritis may also be *acute*, or *chronic*,

The *acute* form is attended with considerable fever, agonizing pain in the eye, severe headache, want of sleep, great redness and distension of the blood vessels, rapid and general change in the shape and color of the iris, &c.; in a few days sight may be irretrievably lost.

The *chronic* form may arise so imperceptibly, and proceed so slowly to effusion of lymph, and to diminution or even loss of sight, that no pain is felt in the eye, and scarcely any redness is visible; the patient may not be aware of his loss of sight until he accidentally closes the sound eye. In iritis of medium severity, two, three or four weeks may elapse without serious damage to vision; in the chronic form a still larger period may pass by.

Sequelæ.—Among the most striking effects of maltreated or neglected iritis are the changes which the pupil undergoes; adhesion of the pupil to the cornea (*synechia anterior*) is among the rarest results of the disease; adhesion to the capsule of the lens (*synechia posterior*) is very common; contraction of the pupil (*atresia iridis*) occurs almost as a matter of course. The inflammatory symptoms, to whatever degree of violence they may have reached, begin to abate after a time, even without medical interference, but some of the above important sequelæ remain; and occasionally even the best directed treatment may fail in preventing one or the other of these disastrous results. These are all owing to the pouring out of various quantities of fibrin, or plastic lymph.

Rheumatic Iritis.

This form can only be diagnosed by the absence of all syphilitic infection, and of scrofulous taint; and by the presence of rheumatic symptoms in other parts, and of such exposure to cold and wet as would necessarily produce rheumatism.

Treatment.—Mercury, Belladonna and Sulphur are the principal remedies, although they may require the aid of Aconite, Colchicum, Actea-racemosa or Turpentine.

Syphilitic Iritis.

This is always preceded or associated with many of the signs of secondary syphilis, such as nocturnal pains in the bones and skull, syphilitic eruptions, syphilitic sore-throat, &c. The patient will always acknowledge syphilitic contamination when these symptoms are present, and the physician tells him that he must have had the disease, as a matter of course.

Treatment.—Mercury and Belladonna, of course, must be used; Hydriodate of Potash may be required.

Scrofulous Iritis.

This is a rare form of disease, and generally associated with rheumatic, syphilitic or gonorrhœal disease. Mercury and Hepar-sulphur are the principal remedies, but may require the aid of Hydriodate of Potash or Sulphur, Graphite, Silex or Calcarea.

Gonorrhœal Iritis.

The patient is generally troubled with gleet when this form of iritis occurs; in some cases the iritis alternates with synovitis and gonorrhœa, so that when one of them is present the others are gone. It is more rapid in its progress than any of the other varieties, and is one of the most severe and formidable, while it lasts; but it yields more promptly to decided treatment than any of the rest, and affords examples of perfect recovery, even when the aqueous chambers are filled with lymph. In no other variety of iritis is the recovery so striking and complete. The patient often suffers several severe attacks, and yet vision is preserved entire. It probably arises from the so-called syphilitic gonorrhœa; in which there is an admixture of syphilis with the gonorrhœa, but the latter predominating by far, so that the syphilitic taint of the system is but slight, and hence readily controlled by medicine.

Treatment.—Mercury and Turpentine are the principal remedies, although Pulsatilla and Clematis may be required.

Arthritic Iritis.

This form has been sufficiently described under the head of arthritic ophthalmia.

Treatment.—Mercury and Cocculus are the principal remedies.

Local and Palliative Treatment.—All the varieties of iritis require the local application of Belladonna or Stramonium to the eye itself or about the brow. In many of them the pains are so severe, that Opium must be combined with the Mercury, in order to afford the patient some little respite from pain and wakefulness.

CHOROIDITIS.

The choroid coat, although extremely vascular, possesses scarcely any nervous sensibility, and is but little liable to inflammation. But although choroiditis is not a frequent disease, it is a very severe one. We can readily conceive what must be the effects of inflammation of the choroid; when its vessels become congested, and the membrane thereby swollen, it will necessarily press outwards on the ciliary nerves, and on the unyielding sclerotica, and the consequence will be, severe pain in the eye; the swollen choroid will also press inwards on the retina, and produce, only in a much greater degree, and not transiently, but incessantly, the same sensations which arise when we press heavily upon the eye-ball with the finger, viz., flashes of light and flaming spectra. The continued congestive pressure on the retina may cause paralysis of that nervous expansion and blindness. As the disease progresses beyond the stage of congestion, effusion of serum and exudations of fibrin, lymph and pus may take place both upon the internal and external surfaces of the choroid.

When the attack is *acute* there are generally severe and throbbing pains in the eye-ball and corresponding half of the head, coming on in paroxysms and much increased during the night; the eye feels stiff, and there is a sense of fulness and distension in it, accompanied with such excessive tenderness that the patient cannot touch it, much less allow it to be touched; he complains of frequent flashes of vivid, reddish, or orange-colored light, even when all external light is excluded, or of a luminous spot in the axis of vision, increased by every thing which quickens the circulation, such as taking food, or making the slightest exertion. The eye is suffused with tears, and is highly intolerant of any exposure to light.

If we succeed in obtaining a view of the eye we generally at first find the redness of its external coverings much less than might have been expected from the sufferings of the patient; but after a while the large external vessels of the eye assume a strikingly varicose appearance and are seen winding over the sclerotica and anastomosing around the cornea; they are of a livid hue and evidently in a state of passive congestion; the edge of the cornea presents a bluish white ring, which arises from the overlapping of the cornea; the cornea becomes more or less hazy and rough; at first the pupil is contracted, then becomes fringed with pigment, dilated, misshapen, often oblong, displaced and motionless; the iris is apt to assume a slate color.

Acute choroiditis may occur suddenly in the night and abolish the sight in the course of a few hours; in such a case, vision is rarely recovered, even although the redness and pain in the eye are overcome. In other cases the sight first becomes dull and misty, the seeming mist increases rapidly, and in a few days the eye is left completely amaurotic.

The subjects of this disease are generally past middle life, much oftener females than males of a dark complexion and sanguine temperament, and more frequently dark than light-eyed. They are not unfrequently short-sighted, and often present that dichromatic state of the crystalline lens, which is termed *glaucoma*, in which there is a greenish reflection from the bottom of the eye. As the disease goes on, the glaucomatous degeneration increases, the lens appears pushed forwards into the dilated pupil, and after a time the lens becomes cataractous. The eye feels as hard as a pebble to pressure, shewing that serous effusion has taken place into the vitreous body. From this condition the eye never recovers; on dissection the sclerotic and choroid may be found adherent, with copious deposits of fibrin covering the internal surface of the choroid, and the retina no longer recognizable; in some instances, however, there is more serous effusion than fibrinous exudation; in such cases the united choroid and sclerotica, unable to support the contents of the eyeball, expand and become attenuated, so as to form one or several staphylomatous elevations.

Considerable constitutional disturbance attends acute choroiditis; the patient is in a state of incessant restlessness, and is greatly alarmed for the total loss of sight; the pain entirely prevents sleep; the head is so tender that it cannot be laid on the pillow; the face is flushed, there is giddiness and nausea; the tongue is foul, the mouth parched, and there is much thirst; the pulse is quick and hard. Mackenzie has known the long-continued pain and want of sleep to wear out the patent and lead to a fatal termination.

One eye generally suffers alone from this disease; occasionally the eyes are attacked in succession, very rarely simultaneously.

Chronic Choroiditis.

In this variety the symptoms succeed each other slowly and insidiously; iridescent vision and the sensation of undulating whirling circles of light are followed by gradual deterioration or even abolition of sight; pain is felt in and about the eye, in the forehead and temple; varicose veins of a livid hue appear on the surface of the sclerotica and on the iris, while *glaucoma* commences its slow but certain course of disorganization, attended with an irregularly expanded or distorted pupil; the eyeball is hard, *which is the reverse of what happens in retinitis*, in which the cornea and sclerotica remain flexible. Photopsia often continues after all perception of external light is extinct.

The subjects of *chronic choroiditis*, like those of arthritic iritis are often troubled with symptoms of irregular gout; they suffer from a generally depressed state of health, have a feeble pulse, deficient appetite, and are troubled with nausea, flatulence and other signs of gastric derangement.

Treatment.—This is very similar to that of iritis, no cases of cure under homœopathic treatment have been recorded.

RETINITIS.

Inflammation commencing in the retina is likely to spread *inwards* to the vitreous humor, to the capsule of the lens, and to the lens itself; *outwards*, to the choroid and iris, to the sclerotica and cornea, and to the conjunctiva; thus an inflammation of the whole eyeball may have a very limited origin.

As a matter of course the symptoms must vary very much, and the description of the disease given by authors are remarkably discordant.

In acute retinitis the inflammation is never long confined to the retina, but speedily spreads to the other vascular textures within the eye, to the choroid and especially to the iris; the iris most frequently assumes a greenish hue, and a deposit of pus may take place between its lower edge and the cornea; the nutrition of the crystalline lens is disturbed by the implication of the corpus ciliare and zonula zinnii and capsulo-lentricular cataract ensues; the pupil is generally, although not always contracted; a reddish wreath is sometimes seen within the pupil; fibrinous exudation glues it to the capsule; a yellowish deposit is sometimes visible at the bottom of the eye; *the eyeball and especially the cornea becomes flaccid*, yielding to the slightest pressure of the finger, showing that a diminution of the natural quantity of the vitreous fluid has taken place.

Diagnosis.—If the disease is limited to the retina, there may be no pain in the eye, but the patient generally complains of considerable headache; when the choroid and iris become implicated there is more or less circumorbital headache; if vision is preserved, the patient complains greatly of muscæ volitans, not of fixed muscæ, which one would expect.

But the disease with which retinitis is oftenest confounded is *hyperæsthesia of the optic and fifth nerve*, in which there is excessive sensibility to light, with spasm of the orbicularis palpebrarum, pain in and around the eye, great sensitiveness of the lids and eyeball to touch; but vision is acute and perfect when the eye can be opened; it may last for a long time, but finally recovery is sudden and complete. Pure retinitis and hyperæsthesia are easily distinguished, but in some cases there is reason to believe that hyperæsthesia of the fifth nerve is combined with retinitis, so that the symptoms are of a mixed description; still, the degree of loss of vision and of softness of the eye will mark the amount of the retinitis.

Prognosis.—This is said not to be unfavorable if a proper method of treatment be commenced before the pupil is much contracted, or the power of vision greatly impaired. If the pupil be once closed, even before the retina appears to have become insensible there is scarcely any hope of preserving sight; for even should the pupil re-open in some degree, as it occasionally does when the inflammation abates, yet it is apt to remain small and motionless, and the eye is still blind.

Chronic Retinitis

Is said to be the most frequent cause of amaurosis; it is characterized by sluggishness of the pupil, muscæ volitantes, ocular spectra, obscurity of vision, dryness of the eyes and nostrils, followed after a time by flexibility and softness of the cornea.

Retinitis Lactantium.

The subjects of this disease are females of generally upwards of thirty years of age, who have had several children and nursed them long; they may never have been robust, and are apt to be scrofulous or rheumatic; they do not take a sufficiently digestible and nutritious diet; over-work their eyes, and suffer from want of rest and anxiety.

Symptoms.—These point more to a general affection of the eye, rather than to simple retinitis, yet it is much more apt to terminate in amaurosis than in general disorganization of the eye. The eyelids may be somewhat swollen and their edges red, their edges may adhere in the morning; there is often some degree of rheumatic sclerotitis; with stinging pain in the eyeball and orbital region; there is intolerance of light; the cornea may be involved with ulceration and specks; the patient complains of muscæ volitantes and of such dimness of sight that even the large letters of a title page cannot be distinguished; the pupil is at first contracted, but after a time becomes somewhat dilated and sluggish, while the cornea and sclerotica are found to yield too readily to the finger.

The pulse is small and quick, there is debility and loss of flesh; want of appetite, derangement of the bowels, rigors, flushings of the face, headache, dizziness, dragging feeling in the back and deficiency of milk.

Treatment.—The treatment of retinitis is similar to that of iritis—Belladonna and Mercury are the principal remedies—a considerable number of cases of acute amaurosis are cases of retinitis, and vice-versa, many cases of so-called retinitis are examples of amaurosis and are not necessarily inflammatory in their character. For some of the chronic forms of retinitis and iritis we may suggest the use of Baryta-muriatica, Petroleum, Phosphoric-acid, Plumbum-acet., and Sulphur.

Hartmann suggests Aconite, Bellad., Merc., Thuya, Cannabis, Hepar.-Sulph., Conium, Nitric-ac. and Clematis; also Cina, Merc.-corros., Plumbum, Sulph., and Zincum.

AQUO-CAPSULITIS.

This disease consists in an inflammation of the lining membrane of the aqueous chambers, and especially of the membrane which lines the internal surface of the cornea, and which is partially continued in the form of fine fibres into the anterior surface of the iris. The membrane in question is known as the membrane of Descemet, or posterior elastic lamina of the cornea.

We sometimes meet with this disease in the *acute* form, attended with very considerable redness of the sclerotica and conjunctiva; but very much oftener it occurs in a *chronic* form, when a peculiar sort of opacity of the cornea is one of the most remarkable symptoms; the external surface of the cornea is at first perfectly clear and glistening, but its lining membrane soon appears more or less dim and opaque; there is at the same time a muddiness in the anterior chamber and an unusual fulness and prominence of the eye-ball from an increase in the quantity of the aqueous humor; in the more severe cases coagulable lymph is thrown out from the inner surface of the cornea; and in all cases the iris soon becomes involved and all the symptoms of iritis are added, viz., discoloration of the iris, irregularity and contraction of the pupil, &c.

Treatment.—This is very similar to that of iritis; Mercury is the principal remedy; Belladonna or Stramonium must be used externally, but not as early in the disease as in iritis. Cocculus, Sulphur, Hydriodate of Potash and Spigelia may be required.

INFLAMMATION OF THE CRYSTALLINE LENS AND CAPSULE.

Opacities of the capsule probably resemble those of the cornea; capsular and capsulo-lenticular cataracts generally present themselves to our observation after the inflammation in which they have originated has subsided; but in other cases Mackenzie and Walther think that we may be fortunate enough to meet with the disease in its acute stage. These inflammations generally occur about the middle of life and in subjects of a slightly cachectic disposition; they may be seated in the anterior, or posterior hemisphere of the capsule.

1. *Inflammation of the anterior hemisphere* of the capsule is always accompanied by a slight change of color of the iris and form of the pupil, the iris becoming a little darker, and the pupil irregular; the motions of the iris finally become sluggish and limited; the pupil is generally smaller than natural, but sometimes is irregularly dilated; there usually appears a black or reddish rim of irregular breadth all around its edges, caused by the pigmentum nigrum of the uvea coming into view, or by vascular sproutings from the iris. Along with these symptoms, a number of red vessels appear in the pupil itself, the largest of which are sometimes visible to the naked eye, but the greater number are distinguishable only by the aid of a glass, and even then the pupil will have to be dilated with Belladonna in order to see them well; fortunately in this disease the sensibility of the eye is not very great, so that the patient can bear examination of the eye in a strong light and with a dilated pupil without much uneasiness. The diagnostic feature of this form of the disease is that the red vessels in inflammation of the *anterior* hemisphere of the capsule form a vascular wreath, situated and to be seen at about a quarter of a line's distance from the pupillary edge of the iris.

2. Inflammation of the *posterior* hemisphere of the crystalline capsule is a much rarer disease than that of the anterior. It is easily recognized by the deep situation of the opacity which it presents and the stellated arrangement of the vessels in the centre of the pupil. Both hemispheres of the capsule may be inflamed at the same time; in which case, behind the red vessels seen on the edge of the iris, there also appears a net-work of more delicate central vessels which seem to be seated in the lens itself.

3. As the *lens* undoubtedly derives its nourishment from

the capsule it is not to be wondered at that the inflammation should extend from the capsule to the lens, and that enlarged vessels should be seen traversing it. In fact it is supposed that all inflammations of the lens begin in the capsule.

Coagulable lymph is poured out into the lens and upon the capsule causing opacities, or acute cataract. Mackenzie says it is a fact strongly confirmatory of the accuracy of the above description of inflammation of the crystalline capsule, that in anterior capsular cataract, the specks or streaks generally radiate from the circumference of the anterior hemisphere of the capsule towards its centre; while in posterior capsular cataract, they evidently branch out from the centre of the posterior hemisphere.

This ophthalmia almost always observes a chronic course; it proceeds very slowly, and is attended with very little or no pain; when pain does attend the disease, it is seated at the bottom of the orbit, in the forehead, or in the crown of the head. Vision is indistinct and confused, where the disease is severe, particularly when the eye is directed towards distant objects; new objects are seen as if through a fine gauze. When the dimness of sight is very great retinitis may be present.

Effusion of fluid, as in pleurisy, may take place between the lens and capsule, and the lens may be dissolved in this fluid. Pus may even be effused in the same way.

Treatment.—Acute cases can generally be cured, like iritis, with Belladonna and Mercury; but chronic cases are very obstinate; Mackenzie has had cases sent to him, mistaken and treated for iritis, in which the long-continued use of Mercury and other remedies had been productive of no benefit. All the homœopathic remedies for iritis will come in play here—in obstinate cases the remedies for cataract may be tried—finally the remedies which act specifically upon the serous membranes may be tried.

ACUTE GENERAL OPHTHALMIA.

In some varieties of *general* ophthalmia one texture of the eye after another gradually becomes affected, till the whole are involved. In the *acute* variety the disease is so rapid and extensive, that the whole internal eye-ball seems implicated at once; the inflamed eye soon seems greatly swollen and is protruded from the socket; it suppurates internally, and its functions are destroyed.

The *violence of the pain* has caused this disease to be compared to a felon, and even to be called *panaris of the eye.*

The symptoms have been divided into three stages: 1st, the stage of pure inflammation, extending from the beginning up to the loss of sight; 2d, the stage of suppuration and protrusion of the eye; 3d, the stage of spontaneous rupture of the eye, or ocular capsule. The ocular capsule is a layer of condensed areolar tissue, which excludes the eye-ball from contact with the fat of the orbit, while it affords passage to the six muscles of the eye-ball on their way to their insertions.

Phenomena of the 1st stage.—In the beginning there is only slight external redness of the eye; the conjunctiva is rather œdematous than inflamed, presenting a state which has been termed *serous, or white chemosis.* The aqueous humor seems turbid, and sometimes tinged with blood. The bottom of the eye appears reddish; the iris changes color; the pupil is somewhat contracted, and the disease may easily be mistaken for iritis; the crystalline capsule may become opaque.

There is, in general, at the bottom of the eye, and in the orbit, a severe throbbing pain, exactly as in intense whitlow or felon; the pain extends to the forehead and temple, and is attended with a feeling of burning heat, tension and fulness, as if the eye could not be contained within the orbit. The patient complains greatly of intolerance of light, and is annoyed with flaming and shining spectræ. By and by this phenomenon totally subsides, the retina having become insensible from the effects of the inflammation upon its substance, or from the compression arising from the fluids extravasated from the surrounding textures, and especially from the capillaries of the choroid.

Phenomena of the 2d stage.—Blindness, or total loss of sensibility in the retina may be regarded as a sign of internal exudation or suppuration; but the most striking appearance in the second stage, is the projection of the eye. One would suppose the eye-ball to be much increased in size, but this is an error; for, after death, the eye which appeared so much swollen, will be found nearly of its natural dimensions. In point of fact the eye-ball is merely pressed forwards by an effusion into the cavity of the ocular capsule; evacuation of this fluid, by a puncture of the ocular capsule, will relieve many of the most urgent symptoms.

But the eye is also very hard to the touch, as if it contained a considerably greater quantity of fluid than in health; that it partly does so is true, but the internal effusion is not the only nor the principal cause of the excessive tension and apparent enlargement of the eye-ball. The principal cause of these symptoms, as well as the protrusion of the eye, is effusion into the intra-orbital tissues. The protrusion of the eye sometimes appears early in the attack; at others it does not occur until later, or even till the internal parts of the eye and sight are destroyed. The earlier it appears the more quickly must the fluid be evacuated by a puncture of the ocular capsule.

In this second stage, the eye-ball becomes absolutely fixed, the state of tension and pain rendering all contraction of the recti-muscles difficult or impossible. So completely is the eye fixed that we cannot even press it from side to side in the orbit.

The conjunctiva continues to swell and becomes covered with a layer of coagulable lymph. This only occurs in acute general ophthalmia. The vitreous humor may present a greenish color from infiltration of pus within the hyaloid membrane; the iris is pushed forwards towards the cornea; and pus is deposited in the aqueous chambers.

Third stage.—The whole eye-ball, as well as the ocular capsule is filled with pus; its progress is exactly as in whitlow, and after intensely severe suffering on the part of the patient, the matter may gain the surface and be discharged spontaneously. But the patient may die before this occurs, and he runs a much greater risk of his life if the disease is left without surgical interference. The cornea may become infiltrated with pus, be converted into a slough and give way. In other cases, it is the sclerotica and tunica tendinea which give way, and this may take place into the cavity of the ocular capsule, which opening in its turn through the conjunctiva, allows a large quantity of matter to escape. Sometimes it is the ocular capsule only which bursts, the eye-ball remaining entire; but this looks so much like a rupture of the sclerotica, that it is easy to mistake one for the other. It is far better to anticipate these slow and painful processes of nature by an early puncture.

The constitutional symptoms which attend general acute ophthalmia, as might be anticipated, are generally very intense; the patient is apt to have chills, anxiety, want of sleep, delirium, intense pain, and sometimes convulsions.

Prognosis.—A complete recovery is extremely rare; a termination in blindness with preservation of the natural shape of the eye may happen; but the disease is apt to end in suppuration and rupture of the eye, with collapse of this organ.

Treatment.—This must be of the most energetic character. The remedies for intense suppurative inflammation must be promptly and freely employed. In the old school they of course depend upon the free use of bleeding, Calomel and Opium, Belladonna, &c. Mackenzie says in the only case which he has seen followed by a complete cure, the mouth became promptly affected by the use of Calomel and Opium; as soon as the Mercury began to act upon the mouth, the disease began to give way, the eyeball retreated into the orbit and a perfect recovery took place. Tartar-emetic would seem much more homœopathic to suppurative inflammation than Mercury. Aconite should be used early and freely. Hepar-sulph., Ranunculus-scel., Thuya, Cocculus, Fluoric-acid, Arsenicum, Rhus, Bromine, Mezereum, Granatum, Phosphorus and Granatum deserve more or less attention.

Probably the most homœopathic remedies against intense suppurative inflammations in general, are: Tartar-emetic, Staphysagria, Rhus-tox., Kali-bichrom., Gratiola, Clematis, Anacardium, Cantharides, Mezereum, Kreosote. It remains to be seen whether a curative remedy can be found amongst these for acute general ophthalmia.

Mackenzie truly says: an important part of the treatment consists in opening the ocular capsule. If the eye be hard and protuberant, and even indistinct fluctuation is felt we should endeavor to evacuate the fluid. For this purpose we proceed somewhat as if we were about to operate for strabismus, dividing the conjunctiva at the internal angle of the eye and towards the lower eyelid, and then pressing the lancet close to the globe of the eye, and between it and the lower internal wall of the orbit, so as to avoid the internal and inferior recti-muscles. This being done there is an immediate gush of serous fluid, mixed with pus; the ball of the eye falls back and the cornea becomes flaccid, showing that the cause of the excessive hardness and projection of the eye existed behind it and not in the organ itself.

CATARACT.

According to MACKENZIE by the term cataract is understood an opacity situated between the vitreous humor and the pupil.

Enumerating the parts so situated, we have: 1st, the posterior hemisphere of the crystalline capsule; 2d, the crystalline lens; 3d, the anterior hemisphere of the crystalline capsule. Any of these parts may lose its natural transparency, and there will then be formed a *capsular*, or a *lenticular cataract*, according as the opacity is situated in the capsule or the lens. Again, in consequence of disease the natural cohesion of the lens to the capsule is sometimes destroyed, and an opaque fluid is deposited between them, forming what is called a *Morgagnian* cataract. Any opacity situated in or within the crystalline capsule is termed a *true cataract*, and all the above enumerated come under this denomination.

The aqueous humor may become turbid, or may be displaced by coagulated lymph, pus, blood, or pigment from the urea. Such a cataract is termed *spurious*, and has its seat without the capsule.

Whether the cataract be true or false, the opacity of a part which is naturally transparent, necessarily stops in a greater or less degree the light which should be transmitted through the interior of the eye; the impression on the retina is consequently rendered imperfect, and *partial* blindness ensues. Cataract never produces total blindness.

When the simple term cataract is used, lenticular cataract is generally meant. For instance, when we say that cataract is a slow disease, occupying months or years in its progress, it is of lenticular cataract that we speak; for all the others, and especially the spurious kinds may be the product of a few days or hours. Occasionally, however, even lenticular cataract is sometimes fully developed in a short space of time.

Diagnosis.—It is of much importance that we should distinguish incipient cataract from incipient amaurosis, for a mistake of this kind may be attended with serious consequences.

In both diseases there is a difficulty in discerning objects with distinctness. In cataract, this difficulty generally increases slowly for a time, and is compared to what might be produced by a diffused mist, thin cloud, or gauze intervening between objects and the eye, and gradually becoming thicker, till at length it becomes so thick that everything seems concealed by it; whereas, in amaurosis the attack is often sudden, and being partial, is described as a dark spot, or spots occupying certain parts only of the field of view, but rendering vision altogether so confused, that small objects cannot be distinguished. With common muscæ volitantes, or *floating muscæ*, as they are often called, neither cataract or amaurosis has any connection. The dark spots seen in amaurosis are what are called *fixed muscæ*, and when the eyes are closed and shaded from light, are generally replaced by shining spectra. Still amaurosis may declare itself in the early stage by the appearance of a gauze or mist, which slowly increasing in density, at length totally deprives the patient of sight. So complete a degree of blindness never occurs in cataract.

The principal remedies for incipient cataract are: Nitric-acid, Bovista, Baryta-mur., Phosph. and Phosph.-ac., Petroleum, Thuya, Kali, Hepar-sulph., Aurum-muriaticum, Chinin-sulph., Kreosote, Sabina, Spigelia, Conium, and Ammon.-muriaticum.

We generally find that the appearance of a mist or cloud is noticed most when the cataractous patient looks straight forward, and that he sees considerably better when he looks sideways.

The different degrees of light in which those affected with

incipient cataract or amaurosis see best, are worthy of attention. In incipient amaurosis there is in general a desire for an increase of light; when the patient reads with candle-light, he brings the book close to the candle; and his period of most distinct vision is noon-day, when objects are most brilliantly illuminated by the sun. Now, this is the very time when the cataractous patient sees worst; so much light causes the pupil to contract, fewer rays of light enter the eye and hence vision is obscure; but in twilight, when the pupil is dilated, more light is admitted, and the patient finds his vision improved. If a cataractous patient looks towards a window he may see very little; but if he turns his back to the light he instantly discerns more or less distinctly every object around him.

In incipient amaurosis the flame of a candle general appears broken and confused, iridescent and spreading out into rays; while in cataract a candle or street-lamp seems expanded into a large globe of weaker light.

In incipient cataract the patient sometimes sees objects multiplied with one eye; looking at the moon, for instance, he may see three or four moons. This is not the case in amaurosis, although diplopia with both eyes open is common.

In amaurosis there is generally headache, dizziness and dyspepsia; cataract is not often attended with these accessories.

The gait and aspect of the amaurotic patient are different from those of the cataractous; the latter approaches with his eyes shaded with his hand, and his head turned downwards and to one side, so as to dilate the pupils and see past the obstruction. The amaurotic person stalks on with a vacant expression, looking forwards and upwards.

In cataract the patient is able to open, shut and move his eyes promptly and naturally; this is not the case in amaurosis.

The mobility of the pupil offers valuable signs for diagnosis; in cataract the pupil contracts and expands as extensively and promptly as in the healthy state; in incipient amaurosis its movements are limited and slow.

In amaurosis the pupil rarely presents the jet black color

of health; in glaucoma it is greenish; in cataract it is whitish, or the bluish tint of milk and water.

But the *catoptric test* is the best means of distinguishing these diseases. When a lighted candle is held before a healthy eye, at a distance of a few inches, three reflected images of the flame of the candle are seen, situated one behind the other. Of these, the anterior and posterior are erect, the middle one inverted. The anterior image is the brightest and most distinct, the posterior the least so; the middle one is the smallest. The anterior is formed by the cornea, the middle by the posterior surface of the crystalline lens; the posterior image by the anterior surface of the lens. In the formation of these images the cornea and anterior surface of the crystalline lens act as convex mirrors; the posterior surface of the lens as a concave mirror. When we move the candle the erect images move in the same direction, the inverted one in an opposite direction.

Cataract, even in an early stage *obliterates the inverted image*, and renders the deep erect one very indistinct. In amaurosis all three images are distinct.

According to Mackenzie, in order to ascertain with accuracy the existence of cataract, and the nature of any cataract which may present itself, it is necessary to attend minutely to the following circumstances.

Whiteness of the cataract denotes either a dissolved lens, or a capsular cataract; *greyness*, a lenticular cataract; *amber*, or a *dark greyness*, that the lens is hard; *light greyness*, that it is soft. If the whole extent of the pupil is uniformly opaque, the cataract is lenticular; if the opacity is streaked or speckled, it is more likely to be capsular. If opaque streaks radiate from a centre, it is probable that the exterior lamellæ are chiefly affected, or that the posterior hemisphere of the capsule is the seat of the disease; if the form of the streaked opacity is convex, the anterior hemisphere of the capsule is the part affected; if concave, the posterior. With the light concentrated on the pupil by means of a double convex glass, all these particulars may be ascertained.

The color and shape of the iris must be carefully noted to see whether there has been or is any iritis, &c. If so, the remedies for iritis may be used in conjunction with those for cataract.

If the iris is sluggish or tremulous, the remedies for amaurosis or paralysis may come in play.

If there is no shadow thrown by the iris on the cataract, the posterior chamber is probably obliterated by the pressure of a large and soft lenticular cataract. If the shadow is distinct, the lens is probably small and hard. If the iris presents a funnel shape, the pupil being drawn back, we may expect that the crystalline lens is reduced in size.

The eye-ball itself deserves close attention in the treatment of cataract. A dingy color of the sclerotica denotes general ill health, which must be attended to. A flexible cornea or sclerotica marks a deficiency of the vitreous humor, attended by amaurosis; remedies for this state must be discovered. A strong hardness of the eye to touch denotes glaucoma, with a superabundance of dissolved vitreous humor, and homœopathic remedies for these must be sought out.

The amount of sight must be carefully tested. If when turned to the light the patient can distinguish the shade cast by the hand when it is moved before him, the retina is sensible; if he sees the shadow of a single finger cast on his eye at the distance of twelve inches, the retina is quite healthy, and we have only cataract to deal with.

The whitish opacity which constitutes cataract affects principally the superficial laminæ of the lens, the interior layers being generally pretty transparent, although often presenting the amber or reddish-brown hue of glaucoma. The superficial layers are not only opaque, but appear to have undergone a peculiar change, which by some has been compared to a coagulation. The lens may also have lost its natural adhesion to the capsule, and a fluid arising from the disintegration of the superficial layers of the lens may be deposited in the capsule. In other cases the whole lens is softened, or even liquefied.

The aqueous humor exerts a coagulating influence upon the lens, even the smallest puncture of the capsule, which allows the aqueous humor to come in contact with the lens, will bring on lenticular cataract; in twenty-four hours after the puncture we may see a considerable portion of the lens opaque. It is very evident, that an accurate chemical analysis of the aqueous humor, might enable us to discover a chemical antidote for cataract. The lens is so near the aqueous humor, that it is possible, that the vessels of the lens may take on an action similar to those which form the aqueous humor and thus cause cataract.

In some instances the lens contains an excess of Phosphate of Lime in cataract; in such cases the mineral acids may be useful.

Inflammation is in some instances the proximate cause, not merely of spurious, but even of true cataract. Indeed, Mackenzie says, anterior and posterior capsular cataract may be compared to specks of the cornea. In other cases the lens from long-continued inflammation becomes opaque, dissolves into a milk-like fluid and even suppurates.

As a general rule the subjects of cataract enjoy good general health; they complain more frequently of rheumatic affections, than of any other; dyspepsia, pains in the head and giddiness occasionally precede cataract in women; it may occur in connection with diabetes.

General Prognosis. Even in the incipient stage, no means are known in the old school, if the lens itself be the part affected, to prevent an uninterrupted increase of opacity and decrease of vision, till a perception of light and shade is all that is retained. If the anterior hemisphere of the capsule be the the seat of partial opacity, the disease may remain stationary for a number of years, or through the whole of life, without affecting the transparency of the lens. But posterior capsular cataract rarely continues long without bringing on lenticular opacity. If there be a dissolution of the vitreous humor, or imperfect sensibility of the retina, a cure is next to impossible.

If medical means fail, about five cases out of eight may be cured by an operation.

When the fifth pair of nerves is cut across, the nutrition of the eye is interrupted, the cornea becomes opaque, and the humors are transformed into a substance resembling curd. As similar changes are found to arise where the nerve is unable from debility or disease to execute its functions, it is by no means an unwarrantable conjecture that cataract, which is generally admitted to be in many instances an effect of abnormal nutrition, may arise as well from a faulty action of the nerve, which controls the nutrition of the eye, as from any disorder directly affecting the source whence the lens draws its nourishment. If this be correct, Mackenzie admits that it is probable by stimulating or otherwise modifying the action of the fifth nerve, the nutrition of the lens may be influenced; so that if want of nervous influence leads to opacity, excitation may remove the tendency to cataract, or even restore, in some cases, the natural transparency.

There are many varieties of cataract, and of course there is no one remedy which will cure all curable cases. The treatment of lenticular cataract must be different from that of capsular; the medical treatment of a hard cataract must differ from that of a soft. It is probable that the management of an ash-colored, yellowish, amber, white or bluish cataract may differ from that of a black one. In some of these *black* cataracts the opacity may be so very dark, that without close examination the disease might be passed over without detection. The management of a morgagnian cataract in which there is a deposition of an opaque fluid between the lens and its capsule must be very different from that of a *siliculose*, in which there is a diminution or even entire absorption of the lens with a shrivelled capsule, so that in the adult a mere scale of the lens may remain, which is hence compared to a shrunk seed surrounded by a large withered pouch. A cataract arising from inflammation must be treated otherwise than one which is caused by impaired nutrition, or by the coagulating action of the aqueous humor.

Treatment of Cataract.—Of cures of cataract we find fifteen reported. It seldom happened that one remedy proved sufficient to cure such a decidedly organic disease.

The following cases have been classified according to the nature of the cataract.

1.	Cataracta incipiens,	viz.	Cases	197. 198. 199. 200. 210.
2.	" lentis,	"	"	196. 201. 202. 203. 209. 210.
3.	" capsulo-lent.	"	"	195. 207.
4.	" glaucomatosa,	"	"	206.

5. Cataracta congenita, Case 209.

6. Those which cannot be brought under any particular classification, viz., No. 204. 205.

The remedies used were: Bell., Cannab., Euphrasia, Lycopod., Magnes.-c., Op., Phosph., Pulsat., Silic., Sulph.

General Remarks.—MOLAN says: Sometimes we can cure a fully developed cataract by homœopathic remedies, which act dynamically on the the parts diseased, or cut short the disease in its progress; and in cases which we cannot cure, we bring the whole organism of the patient in a better condition to be operated upon. Sulph., Silic., Caust., Cannab., Phosph., Calc. and Conium are mentioned as the remedies which arrest the progress of cataracts. The principal thing, however, is to choose such remedies as tend to improve the general health, for with its improvement we will not only arrest the progress of the disease, but entirely cure the patient. Sulphur, he says, is the principal remedy, and should be given in its high attennuations.—If this medicine does not act favorably, we must then select a remedy which corresponds to the totality of symptoms, in which case the dose, or repetition of the same, is a matter of no consequence.—*Allg. H. Ztg.* 35. 333.

CASE 195.—A tailor, aged 60, affected with capsulo-lenticular cataract of both eyes,—could barely distinguish light from darkness. Magnes.-carb. 30, was given once a week in alternation with Essence Cannab.-sat.—two months from that time he could read coarse print. He received several other remedies, but no more improvement was effected.—*Allg. H. Ztg.* 5. 149. SCHRŒN.

CASE 196.—A man, 42 years of age, of bilious temperament, who had had the itch twenty years ago, had suffered for some time with lenticular cataract of the left eye, perfect loss of vision, and much headache. Sulph. $\frac{a}{30}$, cured the headache and inflammation of the eye; four weeks later Silic. 30, was used without benefit, again Sulph. $\frac{a}{30}$, pustules broke out over the whole body, and for the course of a month there was a daily improvement of the eye-sight.—*Allg. H. Ztg.* 35. 335. MOLAN.

CASE 197.—Mrs. B., aged 31, was left after typhus fever, with weakness of the eyes and eye-sight.

Every thing appeared as if she were looking through a mist; she could only see outlines of objects, and did not dare to walk out alone—the left eye was most affected; behind the pupil there was an opacity of the lens, the bulb of the eye not affected, the pupil responded to influence of the light—the menses were suppressed. Pulsat., Sep. and Cannab. were used without benefit. Lycopod., 4, was then given, and six days afterwards the menses re-appeared; in two weeks more there was decided improvement of the sight, so that she could discern smaller objects, and in three weeks her sight was entirely restored.—*Hyg.* 18. 457. Diez.

CASE 198.—A carpenter had been affected for some time with tetters about the face, which disappeared after a while without his taking any medicine, but his sight became impaired, every thing appeared in a place different from its real position, so that he was unable to use his tools properly.

The pupils presented a misty, smoky appearance, as in the forming stage of cataract.

Treatment.—Spts.-Sulph., ten drops three times a day, brought out the former eruption again,—he now saw every thing in its right position, but otherwise the sight was not improved.

Since March 22d, Aq.-Silic. seven drops daily; followed by great improvement in the sight. He perspired easily, and had much perspiration about the feet. Deposit in urine like lime. July, a rheumatic inflammation of the foot sat in.—*Hyg.* 22. 408. Becker.

CASE 199.—A lady, whose feet generally perspired freely, became very dry, after which she noticed that her sight became affected in such a manner that every thing she looked at appeared to be enveloped in a cloud; she could only read large print.

Aq.-Silic. 10 drops twice a day. The accustomed perspiration about the feet returned again in about a month. Her eye-sight became much better. Two months later, at the time of menstruation, her eyes became worse again; she then took twenty drops Aq.-Silic. 3 times per day, after which she improved very much, could read much better, and is still taking the same remedy.

CASE 200.—A man, aged 58, had been affected for the last few months in the following way.

Every thing appeared smoky and foggy; he could not distinguish objects plainly; his eyes were inflamed with copious discharge of tears; he also had a sensation in the spine, as if ants were creeping up and down, (formication.)

Aq. Silic. 20 drops 3 times a day, cured the inflammation and improved the sight very much.—*Hyg.* 22. 410. 11. BECKER.

CASE 201.—An aged gentleman, affected with lenticular cataract, had been taking Silic. 30, in granules, and also in stronger triturations without any benefit whatever, still Aq.-Silic. 7 drops three times a day had been administered for four weeks, when he began to see a little with the affected eye; but no more improvement followed.—*Hyg.* 22. 308. BECKER.

CASE 202.—Mrs. D., aged 36, had had the small-pox while a child, and her eyes have been affected ever since.

Symptoms.—Tears from the right eye of a corroding saltish nature, which caused constant irritation of the lower lid and cheek; trichiasis of the few remaining eye-lashes of the upper lid; conjunctiva pale red; varicose vessels ran to the cornea; there was sometimes a sensation as if sand were in the eye; agglutination of lids during the night; for six months past, she had simple light-grey lenticular cataract; she could still distinguish very large objects at a distance of four yards.

Treatment.—After Pulsat. 9, there was a subsidence of the inflammation and photophobia; her sight was improved; the lens became clearer at its circumference, and the pupil was distinguishable; after the use of Pulsat. for a week, there was observable only a small greyish speck on the lens; the circumference was fully transparent, and the sight only remained slightly obscured.

Essence-Cannab., and lastly Opium 6, rendered the lens perfectly transparent and sight was restored. Ref. examined the eye subsequently on several occasions, but there was no return of any of the former symptoms.—*Arch.* 3. 3. 70. CASPARI.

CASE 203.—A man, aged 51, of strong constitution, and

lymphatic temperament, had been affected for some years with cataract of the right eye, and a few months ago the left eye became similarly affected.

The right eye was operated upon three times without success; since then he had had a violent inflammation of the eye, followed by opacity of the cornea, photophobia, copious discharge of tears, fever and total loss of sight in the right eye.

Treatment.—After the use of Aconit, Bell. 30, and Merc. 15, all inflammatory symptoms of the right eye disappeared; the left eye showed a white opacity of the lens. Pupil was dilated, but moveable, he could only distinguish night from day with that eye. November 22, Sulph. $\frac{3}{30}$. December 7, both eyes were much improved, the opacity of the right eye was much lessened; he was able to see his finger; left eye was also somewhat improved. December 25, the left eye had gradually improved, and the patient could go out on business; a pustular eruption then made its appearance, attended with much itching. Cannab. 15, the patient's sight improved from day to day, and very soon afterwards he could be pronounced cured.—*Allg. H. Ztg.*, 35, 334. MOLAN.

CASE 204.—A young man, aged 20, otherwise healthy, except that he was subject to inflammation of the eye, and weak sight. During one of these attacks which had lasted for some time, I found him in the following condition: conjunctiva of both eyes much inflamed and very much swollen, resembling a raw piece of meat; great intolerance of light; lids agglutinated in the morning; pressure in the eyes, especially on opening them; sight almost extinct.

Bellad. 30, in often repeated doses, subdued in two weeks the inflammatory state of the eyes, but produced no change in the eye-sight; after a more critical examination a cataract in each eye was noticed.—Bellad. was continued without benefit; finally Silicea 30, once in six or eight days, perfectly re-established the eye-sight in three months.—*Arch.* 19, 1. 77. ARGENTI.

CASE 205.—A lady, aged 60, had lost her eye-sight from cataract in both eyes, and consequently was persuaded by her friends, to have an operation performed upon her, to which she consented, provided she could not receive any benefit from homœopathic treatment.

Treatment.—After Silicea, she took Cannab. and Sulph., and improved so much in a few months as to be able to go to Russia on a visit.

Subsequently she wrote, saying that she enjoyed as good health and sight as could be expected of a lady of her age.—*Allg. H. Ztg.* 35, 334. MOLAN.

CASE 206.—Mrs. E. became affected with arthritic ophthalmia and leucomatous opacity of the cornea, and after the gradual clearing off of the opacity, the lens was noticed to be of the color of a beginning cataracta glaucomatosa.

Treatment.—After Phosph. 30, the lens returned gradually to its former healthy state.—*Arch.* 8. 3. 156. SCHÜLER.

CASE 207.—A gentleman, aged 38, in consequence of a cold in his face became affected with an inflammation of the left eye, with the following symptoms: towards the cornea an arterial network was noticed, over which were crossing some larger vessels towards the circumference of the cornea; drawing pain between the shoulder-blades and right upper arm.—Bry. and Pulsat. were given without benefit; four days later, however, the inflammation of the eye had somewhat diminished, but was followed by nebula of the left eye, in consequence of which the patient could distinguish large letters only; behind the pupil could be noticed an opacity of the capsule of the crystalline lens; the pupil was round and the iris was also unchanged, there was no photophobia, and no secretion from the eye. The accompanying symptoms were: pressure and distention over the region of the stomach, extending as far as the right breast and lower lumbar region. Great uneasiness; pressure in the forehead; feeling of heaviness and drawing in the thigh; and sleeplessness.

Treatment.—Nux. was given without benefit; then Bellad. 3, was used night and morning for two days; with such surprizing results that every vestige of disease disappeared.—*Allg. H. Ztg.* 37. 340. LEMKE.

CASE 208.—M., aged 20, tinsmith by trade, was affected one and a half year ago with the worst kind of itch, and subsequently with fever and ague. Sometimes he had tearing pains in the left eye, and some itching of the skin, to which he paid very little attention; suddenly he noticed however that he had become completely blind in the left eye.

Symptoms.—A staring look of the left eye; pupil dilated and immoveable; in the centre of the lens there was a slight opacity; his sight almost extinguished.

Treatment.—August 2, Sulph. 6; from Aug. 9, to Sept. 23, six doses of the same.

Six days after the first dose, many pustules appeared on the face and arms; in the mean time his eye-sight improved so much, that he was able to distinguish large letters. From Sept. 13th to Sept. 23d, furuncles on the arm made their appearance, after that the skin became clear again, and the affected eye was as useful as it ever had been before.—*Arch.* 14. 3. 105. EMRICH.

CASE 209.—A girl, aged 12, had been affected since her earliest recollection with flocculent cataract, (probably congenital) of both eyes. She had had an operation performed about four months ago without the least benefit; four doses Magnes.-carb. 200, were also given without any benefit. Five months later she received Euphras. 200, four doses, one every week, which resulted in her being able to see a little with the right eye. Four doses more of Euphras. 200, in water, a tablespoonful once a day, was followed by some improvement of the left eye. The Euphrasia was continued for four months with steady improvement; as soon as the patient ceased to improve, Sulph. 200 was given, followed by Magnes.-carbon. 200, one dose every week, for five months, at the end of which time the circumference of the cataracts in both eyes were only observable.

Euphras. 200, Silic. 200, and Acid.-nitr. perfected the cure. The use of spectacles for cataract assisted, however, very much to increase the sight of the child.

How much the former operation had done towards the cure Referent is not able to say.—*Allg. H. Ztg.* 35. 205. RUMMEL.

CASE 210.—A farmer, aged 50, of small stature, and with light, brown hair, had suffered for the last few weeks with impaired sight; the patient had formerly been troubled with scrofula.

Symptoms.—Patient sees with the right eye only those objects which are above him, and with the left only those which are at his side, but in all other directions every thing appears as dark as night to him.

Partial opacities of the crystalline lenses were clearly observable; the one in the right occupied the larger and that in the left the smaller half of the pupil.

Treatment.—Cannab. 2, three drops daily in water for three weeks, was given, without benefit. Calc. 3, six doses, at first one dose a day for two days, afterwards one dose every week; before the last dose had been taken, patient had entirely recovered his sight.— *Viertelj. Schr.* 2. 426. VILLERS.

CASE 211.—A priest affected with cataract, took extract of Conium internally with benefit; finally he became tired of taking medicine, and made a cataplasm of the bruised leaves, which he placed upon his eyes at night. This enabled him to read his breviary without difficulty, and to walk without a cane or guide.—*Frank's Magazine.*

CASE 212.—A healthy and regular girl, aged 23, had had dimness of sight for two years, and complete cataract for more than one;

Treatment.—She took eight to ten grains of Conium, increased to twenty-five grains three times a day; her appetite remained good, and she seemed active and well, and the edge of the cataract seemed clearing up; she could see the window, and in October could see her hands and fingers, but all objects seemed red, and her menses became suppressed.—*Ibid.*

GENERAL REVIEW.—The remedies used were: Bell., Cannab., Euphras., Lycopod., Magnes.-carb., Opium, Pulsatilla, Silicea, Sulphur.

Of these, *Silicea* was given seven times in Nos. 196, 198, 199, 200, 201, 204, 205; only in No. 196 without benefit. Among six patients were three males, three females, two of the males were advanced in age.

Form of Cataracts.—Three were incipient, one was imperfect, two perfect, while No. 201. was lenticular and seated in one eye only.

Causes: in No. 198 previous tetters, in No. 199 suppressed foot-sweats, and in No. 204 in consequence of an inflammation of the eyes. In five cases Silic. alone affected the cure; in No. 200 was followed by Cannab. and Sulph.

Dose.—Four times Aq.-Silic. was given three times a day, from seven to twenty drops per dose, and continued for some time; in one case, Silic. 30, was repeated every sixth or eighth day. In No. 201, Silic. 30, and stronger triturations of the same remedy were used without success, but Aq.-Silic. was given with benefit.

The good results showed themselves in from one to three months; in five patients there was considerable improvement, and in No. 204, an entire cure was effected.

Sulphur was given six times, in Nos. 196, 198, 203, 205, 208, 209; in No. 209 it was only used as an intermediate remedy, and in No. 205 without any reason pointed out. In two cases there was complete lenticular cataract; in two, incipient; in No. 203, one eye had already been operated upon three times. Ringworm and itch preceded the cataract in some cases.

Dose.—In one case Spts.-Sulph., three times daily, ten drops per dose; in two cases Sulph. 30, one and two doses; and in one case Sulph. 6, in repeated doses.

In four cases after the administration of Sulphur, eruptions and furuncles made their appearance.

In case No. 198, Sulphur removed the illusion about the position of objects, and Silicea completed the cure; in No. 197 and 203, there was much improvement, and in No. 208, a complete cure was effected.

Cannabis was given five times, in Nos, 195, 200, 202, 203, 210; it was used as an intermediate remedy in No. 195. Cannab. was given in weekly alternation with Magnes. 30, in No. 202, it was interposed between Pulsat. and Opium; the essence was interposed in No. 200, between Silic. and Sulphur; in No. 203, after Sulphur, Cannab. 15, was administered, it was successful in all cases, especially in affections of the lens; in No. 210, however, it was given without benefit.

Magnes. carb. was used twice; in No. 195, Magnes. 80, was used in alternation with Cannab. against lenticulo-capsular cataract; in No. 209, after Sulph. had been given in the first case with marked success.

Bellad. was administered in one case, in No. 207, in the third dilution, and removed an opacity of the capsule of the crystalline lens, the consequence of an inflammatory attack.

Calc.-carb. was given once, in No. 210, after the previous use of Cannab. in partial opacity of the lens, in a scrofulous subject, with decided success; it had to be repeated.

Euphrasia was used once, in No. 209, four doses were given at weekly intervals in a case of congenital cataract.

Lycopod. was given once, in No. 197, against opacity of both lenses, a complete cure was effected.

Phosph. was used once, in No. 206, against cataracta glaucomatosa, arising after an attack of arthritic ophthalmia. Phosph. 30, effected a cure.

Pulsatilla was given once, in No. 197, against grey lenticular cataract, attended with inflammation of the eyes, Pulsat. 9, followed by Cannab. and Opium, completed the cure.

Opium was used once, in No. 202, with considerable success.

Hence we see, that the homœopathic treatment of the various forms of cataracts has proved beneficial, contrary to the views of the great lights of the allopathic school such as Chelius, Fischer and Walther, who admit the insufficiency of their medical agents in such cases; we have seen the cures, or relief at least, achieved in diseases of the lens by homœopathic treatment. Molan has shown us, how to prepare patients in case an operation should be deemed necessary; and finally Würzler has given us his valuable experience in the treatment after operations.

After an operation upon the eye, he considers Aconite the principal remedy, except in patients of very mild temperament; Ignatia will generally subdue the violent pains in the temples and eyes; if these are accompanied with vomiting, Bryonia will be required. If the pain is of a jerking character and attended with vomiting and lienteria, Asarum is the best remedy; if burning pain with diarrhœa sets in, Arsenic will be required; hammering and jerking pains in the eye were relieved by Crocus. Stinging pain in the temples followed by loss of appetite, was relieved by Thuya.

If the operation of depressing the lens failed, and the lens broke up in fragments, Senega accelerated the process of absorption very much; and finally, if the objects appeared as if tinged with blood, Strontiana will cure.—*Allg. H. Ztg.* 21. 6. 7. WÜRZLER.

GLAUCOMA.

This name is given to a peculiar green appearance behind the pupil. *Acute* glaucoma occasionally occurs in acute choroiditis, the patient suddenly becoming blind and the eye presenting a green reflection behind the pupil. But the disease which we are now about to consider is glaucoma proper, or *chronic glaucoma.* According to Mackenzie, it is of frequent occurrence; is in its early stages attended by no external signs of inflammation, and being slow in its progress is apt to be confounded with cataract.

It does not occur until after middle age; dark-eyed persons are more liable to it than blue or grey; short-sighted persons are apt to become affected with it, also those who suffer from irregular gout and those pains in the teeth and head which are often regarded as rheumatic.

Glaucoma develops itself slowly during a course of years, and finally involves all the structures of the eyes.

1st stage: The central laminæ of the crystalline lens becomes of a reddish or brownish amber color; but a greenish hue is reflected from behind the pupil; the iris is lively and sound, so that there need be no material deterioration of vision.

2d stage: A muddy green color of the crystalline lens marks the second stage; the pupil is sluggish, and there is more or less obscurity of vision; the eye-ball is rather firmer than natural. This stage may last for four or five years or more, vision declining by insensible degrees all the time, but without pain, or external redness of the eye. The reddish or brownish amber color pervades the whole lens, and sight is obscured nearly as in cataract. It may or may not be attended with amaurosis.

3d stage: This is marked by an unnatural hardness of the eye; immobility and unequal dilatation of the pupil; a varicose state of the in- and external vessels of the eye, and marked loss of sight. The patient now frequently has a cloud over his sight, continuing for hours or days; fiery and prismatic spectra alternating with fixed muscæ, intolerance of light, pain in and around the eye. In this stage the choroid is inflamed, effusion taking place from its internal surface, the retina is compressed by the fluid, the vitreous tissue is disorganized, and a superabundant effusion of serum supplies its place.

4th stage: The lens becomes cataractous as well as glaucomatous; the muddy green hue is changed to an opaque white color. The lens is thickened and passes forward through the pupil so as to touch the cornea. The iris is changed in color, thinned and eroded; varicose vessels traverse its surface, and red spots as if from effusion of blood form between the iris and cornea. The sclerotica also becomes thinned and choroid staphyloma may be formed. Sight is lost, but the patient is still troubled with flashes in the eye from pressure on the retina.

5th stage: The cornea is irritated by the lens, becomes hazy and rough, may inflame and ulcerate, the softened and opaque lens may escape from the eye, and the vessels of the iris and choroid bleed profusely through the ruptured cornea.

6th, stage: The eye is quiet and atrophied; this may occur without bursting of the cornea; the acute symptoms subsiding, the contents of the eye-ball being absorbed and the eye becoming smaller and softer.

It is not uncommon for glaucoma to be *spontaneously* arrested in one or the other of these stages; it often remains stationary in the first stage for a great part of life, vision being not materially impeded; when the second stage has commenced the amber-colored degeneration proceeds insensibly from year to year, sight becoming more and more imperfect, without the other tissues of the eye being involved.

In the 1st and 2d stages it is a disease of the crystalline lens alone, although occasionally amaurosis is associated with it from the commencement. In the advanced stages almost every texture of the eye becomes involved.

The Germans suppose that glaucoma is the result of a slow arthritic inflammation of the eye, especially of the choroid. When it has commenced in one eye it generally extends to the other.

Treatment.—Cocculus, Silicate of Potash, and Fluoric-acid are the principal remedies.

AMAUROSIS.

According to Mackenzie, by the term *amaurosis* is meant obscurity, or partial or total loss of vision, depending upon a morbid condition of the optic nerve, retina or brain.

This disease often arises from the pressure of a tumor, or from that caused by enlarged or congested blood-vessels pressing upon the retina, optic nerve, or from debility or paralysis of these parts.

Among the remote causes may be mentioned over exertion of the eyes; congestion to the head from forced exertion of body or mind, or from errors in diet, abuse of liquor, retrocession of eruptive diseases, suppressed discharges of blood, perspiration, suppression of menses or diarrhœa, constipation; exhausting diseases, such as typhus fever, chronic-diarrhœa, neglected leucorrhœa, prolonged nursing, excessive venery, &c.

It very frequently arises from a complication of causes, all of which have to be treated or removed.

Symptoms.—The most important is impaired vision; in some cases the patient becomes suddenly and permanently blind, while in others the sight fails gradually for months and years, without ever terminating in complete loss of sight; hence amaurosis may be sudden or slow, complete or incomplete.

In the commencement of the disease it often happens that the failure of sight only occurs occasionally, and for a short time (amaurosis vaga,) coming on after any continued exertion of the eyes.

Sometimes the patient sees confusedly with both eyes open, and better with one open and the other closed (monobleptis.)

Diplopia is often the first symptom.

Many an amaurotic patient can read with ease a few lines of a printed book, after which the letters seem so confused and the effort is so painful that he is obliged to desist. But this symptom is more common in simple morbid sensibility of the retina, which is exactly equivalent to spinal irritation in other parts; it is an exceedingly troublesome symptom, but not dangerous to sight.

Sudden and temporary attacks of blindness are often connected with gastric derangement, and then may be owing to congestion about the eye, or a diversion of the nervous energy to distant irritated parts.

The failure of sight in some cases extends to the whole field of vision; in others, to only parts of it. On attempting to read, for example, more or less of the page appears indistinct; perhaps, only a word is lost sight of here and there (visus interruptus;) or only one-half of the page is seen, while the other half is as if hidden from view (Hemiopia.)

It not unfrequently happens that an amaurotic eye will still discern certain objects, if they are placed in one particular direction (visus obliquus;) but if by the slightest movement of the eye or head the person once loses sight of the object, he finds that he cannot easily recover the same point of vision. If the patient looks towards an object, it often happens that he does not see it, it is immersed in the amaurotic cloud; but if he directs his eye to some other object, situated above or below, or to one or the other side of the first, this comes in view. This *oblique* vision is at first of but little use to the patient, but gradually the eye contrives to make it more steady and beneficial.

Sometimes he catches sight of an object while it is in motion, but sees almost nothing that is at rest.

Some see all objects disfigured, bent, mutilated, lengthened or shortened (visus defiguratus.) Thus the flame of a candle may seem very long, or as if separated into several portions.

Sometimes amaurosis may be associated with short- or long-sightedness, and may by relieved by concave or convex glasses.

Objects may seem much smaller to the diseased than to the sound eye.

As the disease advances the field of vision seems to become obscured by a cloud (visus nebulosus,) or network (visus reticulatus,) the latter generally appearing grey or black, especially in a good light or over any white substance, but sometimes becoming luminous in the dark, and assuming a bluish white color, like steel or silver; or reddish yellow, like gold. This is also the case with *fixed muscæ* arising from paralyzed or insensible patches upon the retina; they appear grey or black in the day time, but glitter in the dark. Floating muscæ form no part of amaurosis, but fixed muscæ are an index of the retina being partially insensible to light.

If only one eye is affected the patient is liable to make mistakes in those actions which require distances to be exactly distinguished, such as pouring a fluid into a glass, snuffing a candle, threading a needle, &c. If the disease be recent it is likely to yield to treatment.

Sometimes the early stages of amaurosis are attended with a morbid sensibility to light, and even with pain on exposure to its influence (ocular hyperæsthesia,) while in other cases there is from the very commencement a diminished sensibility of the retina and a constant desire on the part of the patient for a more decided illumination of all objects, or a *thirst for light* as it has been called.

An unwonted dryness of the eyes and nostrils is by no means an uncommon symptom in chronic retinitis and amaurosis; and it is observed that in general great benefit is obtained if once the secretions of the lachrymal gland, conjunctiva, and schneiderian membrane are restored. Iodine, Kali-hydriod., Baryta-mur., Pulsatilla.

Pain in the eyes, and still more frequently in the head and face, forms one of the most important symptoms in amaurosis; if there be no pain, there is generally paralysis or atrophy of the optic nerve (China, Nux, Ignatia, Angustura.

If amaurosis be attended with headache and loss of smell, there is probably a tumor in the fossa pituitaria, or over the cribriform plate.

If amaurosis of one eye be attended with loss of hearing on the same side and stiffness of the muscles of the face, there is probably a tumor attached to the posterior surface of the petrous portion of the temporal bone, or arising from the meatus auditorius internus.

If amaurosis has been followed by an affection of the mind there is probably a tumor or abscess in the brain; if mental derangement precedes the amaurosis, the disease probably commenced on the surface or in the membranes of the brain; indistinctness of the perceptions and thoughts, &c., points to disease of the cineritious substance.

The general health of the patient should always be carefully attended to. Then the first stage of amaurosis may generally be looked upon as one of congestion or inflammation, which may almost always be relieved or cured.

Sudden attacks are more manageable than slow ones. When the pupil is only slightly dilated, still moveable, and of its natural form, while the eye-ball is neither firmer nor softer than in health, and no glaucoma is present, we may give a rather favorable prognosis.

There is something peculiar in the cast of the eye of an amaurotic person; instead of converging his eyes in the natural way towards an object, it is evident that there is something vacant, and unmeaning in his look, the result of the eyes being directed paralelly, as if towards an object infinitely distant. If only one eye is affected, it appears to diverge from its fellow; this kind of squinting never fails to be present. If there be much strabismus with considerable loss of vision and pain in the head, there is probably organic disease in the brain.

The lids may be more or less paralyzed.

The eyes may be unnaturally prominent or one eye more so than the other. The color of the eye is seldom healthy, the sclerotica is frequently yellowish, or bluish or ash-colored.

A sluggish or limited motion of the pupil, or entire loss of motion, often attended with dilatation, forms one of the most remarkable symptoms of amaurosis. The early and incomplete stages of amaurosis are rarely accompanied by widely dilated pupils, but only by sluggishness and a limited degree of motion. After the perception of light is altogether extinct, the opening is generally found expanded and quite motionless. Aconite, Nux, Opium and Ignatia are the antipathic remedies to this state.

If the pupils are widely dilated and fixed, the humors clear and eye-balls of normal consistence, there is probably pressure from an enlarged pituitary gland, or from some growth far forwards on the base of the brain.

If the pupils are but moderately dilated, but irregular in shape and sluggish in motion, especially if there is glaucoma, or discoloration of the iris, there is congestion or inflammation of the retina.

If one pupil is widely dilated and does not move with the other pupil, there is pressure in or behind the orbit involving the third nerve as well as the optic of the same side.

Amaurosis with lively pupils often depends on disease of the cerebellum; the third nerve is then sound as the power of motion of the iris is derived from the third pair.

Belladonna and Stramonium may produce sudden attacks of amaurosis; while Mercury and Lead are said to cause a slow and insidious form of the disease.

Treatment.—In the old school, if any symptoms of congestion are present, bleeding, cupping or leeching are brought in play. Aconite would probably effect almost as much good.

Mackenzie says, that Mercury has long and justly maintained a high character as a remedy in amaurosis. It is probable, (he says), that it aids in the cure chiefly as an absorbefacient, promoting in particular, the removal of effusions within the cranium, and sometimes even of morbid formations. It will remove amaurosis depending upon inflammation, either acute or chronic, of the retina or optic nerve. Travers says, that he has been a witness to its power in suddenly arresting the disease in too many instances not to entertain a far higher opinion of it, than of any other article of the materia medica. Lawrence says, that when the antiphlogistic treatment and a fair trial of Mercury fail, he does not believe, that it is probable we can effect any essential good by other means.

Iodine is said to be more useful in children than adults.

Emetics are said to be useful, when the tongue is foul, mouth bitter, and the patient complains of nausea.

Bark and Quinine are homœopathic to amaurosis, as many cases of blindness and deafness have been produced by these drugs, yet Mackenzie says, that Bark, Iron and Nux-vomica are remedies of great importance, when amaurosis arises from vascular exhaustion and nervous debility.

Counter-irritation is much used, with blisters, Strychnine and Veratrine; also stimulating vapors to the eye, such as Ether and Ammonia; the vapor of Prussic-acid is said to be entirely useless. Sternutatories, especially a mercurial snuff, made with one grain of Turpeth mineral to twenty grains of powdered liquorice root are highly recommended by Dr. Ware.

Galvanism is useful in incomplete amaurosis.

Amaurosis from apoplexy of the retina.

In this disorder the blood-vessels of the retina become suddenly distended or ruptured.

It may be produced by exposure to the hot sun, suppression of menstruation, congestion to the head, violent sneezing, &c.

Confusion of sight, so that the patient is suddenly deprived of the power of discerning small objects, with a dark spectrum before the affected eye, are the most remarkable symptoms; the spectrum may be red, greenish or black; it is generally large and irregular in shape. The suddenness of the amaurotic attack with flushing of the face, full and slow pulse and dizziness, will render the diagnosis distinct.

Treatment.--Aconite and Arnica are the principal remedies at first; Mercury and Nux-vomica may be required.—*See Treatise on Apoplexy, by* J. C. PETERS.

Amaurosis from aneurism, or dilatation of the central artery of the retina.

Objects placed directly before the eyes are totally invisible, but there remains some small sense of light, so as to give a confused perception of objects sidewise; there may be photophobia and feeling of pulsation in the orbit.

Treatment.—Lycopodium is the principal homœopathic remedy and has cured or relieved several cases of aneurism.

Amaurosis from structural changes in the optic nerve.

This nerve may be indurated; then Plumbum is the most homœopathic remedy. Nux-vomica and Strychnine produce softening of the brain and spinal marrow.

There may be adhesion between the nerve and its sheath; then Merc. and Hepar-sulph. deserve attention.

The medullary substance of the nerve may be ash-colored and wasted. Plumbum.

Hydatids. Graphite and Silex, or Secale.

Calculous concretions between the sheaths. Phosph.-ac.

This variety of amaurosis is developed very slowly, and rarely in both eyes; it is attended by a sensation of a black cloud, which seems gradually to become more and more dense, and by such a degree of visus defiguratus as is extremely distressing to the patient. He rarely complains of much pain, either in the eye or head, but only of a feeling of obtuse pressure in the posterior part of the orbit, without protrusion of the eye-ball. The pupil is extremely enlarged, the iris completely immoveable and irregular in shape. Glaucoma, followed by glaucomatous cataract is apt to occur.

Amaurosis from fracture and depression of the cranium, and extravasation of blood.

Besides the usual surgical treatment, Arnica is the principal remedy to promote absorption; Conium and Mercury may be required.

Amaurosis from disease of the membranes or bones of the cranium.

Exostoses may be treated with Aurum.-mur., Calc.-phosph. and Phosph.-ac. and especially by Silicate of Potash.

Ætheromatous thickenings, with Naphtha, Ether, Terebinth. —*See Treatise on Apoplexy, by* J. C. Peters, p. 38.

Fungous tumors by Thuja.

The symptoms are exceedingly like those of disease of the brain. Severe headache, fixed pain in the top of the head, palsy of some of the muscles of the eye, weakness and stiffness of the limbs, &c. The symptoms increase for a time very slowly; first one eye is affected, then the other, then the hearing. Protrusion of the eyes may take place.

When the complaint arises after sudden cooling of the head, followed by rheumatism, which, though slight in its commencement, fixes itself obstinately in the fibrous investment of the skull, we may have recourse to Iod.-pot., Mezereum, Merc.-corr., &c.

Amaurosis from congestion of the brain.

According to Mackenzie, the first symptoms with which congestive amaurosis generally shews itself, are a feeling of fulness in the eye-balls, Op., Crocus, Paris-quad., Guaiac, Phos., Aconite (—); and almost uninterrupted photopsia (—); Valerian, Staphysagria, Bellad., Stramon.

These symptoms are speedily followed by stupefying headache, generally accompanied by dizziness, and noises in the ears, keeping pace with a striking diminution in the power of vision. In some cases the patient is deprived of sleep; in others he is lethargic. When the internal carotids are chiefly affected, lethargy is generally a prominent symptom; when the vertebral arteries, there is pain in the occiput. The patient is commonly robust and plethoric. The eye may appear fuller than natural, and seems to project unusually from the orbit; the patient moves it less than in health; the eye is suffused with red vessels; the face is flushed, the arteries throb; the pupil may not be much affected at first.

As the disease advances into the confirmed stage, the headache becomes irregular, being at times severe, at others slight. The patient now complains principally of a thick gauze or net-work which renders every object before him indistinct. In clear light the net-work seems uniformly obscure, but in the dark, it is fiery and shining, sometimes appearing reddish, and at others bluish. This symptom is increased by every cause which increases the amount of blood in the head; thus if the patient strains at stool, the net-work seems thicker for some minutes after. If the local and general plethora be not relieved, vision soon becomes totally extinguished; at last all traces of sensibility to light is lost; the patient still complains of stunning headache, also of a feeling as if the eye-balls were increasing in size, while they actually feel firmer to the touch; the pupil becomes fixed, but not much dilated; the vacant stare of the amaurotic is developed.

Treatment.—It is said that under allopathic treatment a favorable prognosis can only be given when the sight is not greatly impaired; it will accomplish but little when sight is nearly or completely extinguished, even when the disease is only a few days standing. If the patient has been several months in this state it scarcely ever happens that the usual treatment effects even the slightest restoration of sight.

The dominant school of course rely on bleeding, cupping,

leeching, purging, entire abstinence from animal food, cold applications to the head, complete rest of the eyes, followed blistering and mercury. Some of these means may be allowed in very urgent cases and when there is a great excess of blood in the whole system, but they must be regarded as palliative and of temporary use only. Aconite, Kali-nitr., Glonoine, Nitric-acid, Digitalis, Conium, Cicuta-virosa, and Plumb.-acet., may be used in the early stages. While Bellad., Quinine, Phosphorus, Strammonium, Opium, and Arsenicum may be tried in obstinate cases.—*See Treatise on Apoplexy, by* J. C. PETERS.

Amaurosis with Apoplexy.

The apoplectic effusion may be confined to the eye, or it may by seated in the brain. When it is confined to the eye the suddenness of the attack and the circumstances in which the patient is placed at the time, may lead us to conclude that the attack is apoplectic. Thus, Mackenzie relates the case of a man who became suddenly blind in the left eye, while attending a public meeting, brilliantly illuminated with gas, and when he had been overheated and excited; after a time amaurosis of the left eye followed, with partial palsy of the tongue. Also, of a man who became suddenly blind in the left eye after blowing a pair of bag-pipes for half an hour. A gentleman on a journey, suddenly found one eye amaurotic in the morning; a few months after he became paralyzed.

Treatment.—See Treatise on Apoplexy, by J. C. PETERS. Aconite and Arnica are the principal remedies.

Amaurosis from aneurism of the encephalic arteries.

Mr. WARE was of opinion, that amaurosis might not unfrequently be owing to dilatation of the circulus arteriosus. Should then the dilatation, says he, take place in the posterior portion of the circulus arteriosus, so as to compress the nervi motores oculorum, the consequence will be, that the eye-lids, and probably the eyes also, will lose the power of motion. But if the dilatation happens in the anterior portion of the circulus, as the compression will then be on the optic nerves, the sight must of course be destroyed. And should the dilatation take place in both portions, so as to occasion a compression on both sets of nerves, the eye-lids will be rendered immoveable and the eyes will also be deprived of sight and motion.

Treatment.—Dr. BALL has cured aneurism with Sulphur and Lycopodium. It is not irritational to attempt to cure some cases of aneurism by internal remedies, as this disorder frequently depends upon a peculiar morbid condition spread more or less over the arterial system. It is observed most commonly in persons who are subject to rheumatism, gout, scrofula or syphilis, or who have abused mercury and have drank spirits to excess. In these cases there frequently arise inflammation of the internal coat of the arteries, ulceration, loosening, thickening, ætheromatous deposit, or even ossification between the internal and middle coats, by which the walls of the artery yield to the pressure of the blood, and the internal and middle coats are torn or destroyed. Carb.-veg., Nitric-acid and Phosphor have been suggested as remedies for aneurism.

Amaurosis from enlargement of the pituitary gland.

According to MACKENZIE, numerous cases of amaurosis from enlarged pituitary glands are on record. In some of them, the affection of sight was one of the earliest symptoms; while in others, it did not occur till a variety of other signs of brain disease had manifested themselves. Along with the amaurosis, which generally affects both eyes, and after being incomplete for some time, suddenly becomes complete, the patient complains of pain or weight in the forehead, and severe pain in the temples, apathy, loss of memory, emaciation and general weakness. Neither convulsions or paralysis seem liable to occur from enlargement of the pituitary gland, but the parts in contact with the diseased mass may be excited to inflammation, so that at last the symptoms present a combination of those of encephalitis with those of pressure on the brain.

As the pituitary gland lies behind and beneath the chiasma of the optic nerves, it must press upon these nerves when it becomes enlarged.

According to ROKITANSKY, simple enlargement of this gland rarely or never occurs; he has never met with an instance; congestion, inflammation and abscess are not uncommon,—they require Aconite, Phosphor, and Hepar-sulph.; tuberculous disease is very rare, while cancerous is not uncommon,—then Arsenicum might come in play; an exudation of colloid matter between the layers of the gland is not uncommon.

Amaurosis from injury of the head.

According to MACKENZIE, injuries of the head, many of them appearing to be slight and at first occasioning no apprehension, are much more frequently productive of amaurosis than is generally suspected. Years may elapse before the patient becomes affected with any serious indications of brain or eye disease.

Treatment.—Arnica is of course the principal remedy.

Amaurosis from congestion or inflammation of the nervous optic apparatus, brought on by exposure of the eyes to intense light, or by over-exercise of the sight.

This is one of the most frequent varieties of amaurosis, resulting sometimes from a single, short or even momentary exposure to vivid light; in other cases, from long-continued or frequently repeated examination of luminous objects, or from intense exercise of the sight upon things moderately or imperfectly illuminated. Frequently there is as much of paralysis as congestion present. This disease must be carefully distinguished from morbid sensibility of the retina produced by the same causes.

Treatment.—Nux and Phosphorus deserve attention.

Amaurosis excited by the presence of worms in the intestines.

Among the symptoms of worms are enumerated: dilatation of the pupil, want of lustre in the eye, blueness under the lower eye-lid, watering of the eyes, paleness of face, headache, throbbing in the ears and disturbed sleep, with gritting of the teeth.

Treatment.—Cures have been effected with Spigelia, Cina and Turpentine.

Amaurosis from suppression of the menses.

When this occurs suddenly, Pulsatilla, Aconite, Strammonium and Sabina are the best remedies; when it occurs, slowly, Sepia and Ferrum or Plumbum may be tried.

Amaurosis from suppressed purulent discharge.

Hepar-sulph. and Antimony or Sabina are the principal remedies.

Amaurosis from suppressed perspiration.

Aconite, Opium, &c. are the best remedies.

Amaurosis produced by drugs.

According to MACKENZIE, Belladonna, Strammonium and Hyosciamus, when taken internally, may produce complete insensibility of the retina, accompanied by dilatation of the pupils in most instances. Belladonna renders the eye-balls red and prominent; vision is more or less affected, sometimes so much so that even the brightest light cannot be distinguished. The blindness is often a very obstinate symptom, sometimes remaining after all others have disappeared; for days and even weeks, the pupils may continue dilated and the vision disordered.

Blindness with dilated pupils also may follow the excessive use of Dulcamara, and white Hellebore, or Veratrum-album. Opium induces insensibility of the retina with contraction of the pupils, as does Aconite and Nux-vomica. The amaurosis in these cases arises from congestion and paralysis of the retina.

Bitter Almonds, Quassia and Centaurium are said to cause amaurosis; while lead colic is not unfrequently attended by amaurosis. I once witnessed at the New-York Eye Infirmary an accidental cure of amaurosis with a lead wash which was to be applied to an inflamed eye; the patient derived so much benefit from it, that he also applied it to the other eye, which was completely amaurotic; the consequence was that he entirely recovered his sight in both eyes.

In the Illinois and Indiana Medical and Surgical Journal for January, 1847, page 385, we find an article on blindness caused by the use of Sulphate of Quinine, written by Dr. McLean, Professor of Materia Medica in the Rush Medical College. We are told that Quinine, when freely administered, produces a species of intoxication, tinnitus aurium, a sense of fulness in the head, cephalalgia, and other affections; and sometimes blindness, more or less lasting.

M. Trousseau relates the case of a tailor, who, for the relief of a periodical asthma, took forty-eight grains at one dose; in four hours he experienced ringing in the ears, dullness of the senses, and vertigo; and in seven hours he was blind and deaf, his mind wandered, and he was unable to walk; these effects gave way spontaneonsly during the night. A young girl at the Hospital Cochin, in consequence of having taken freely of the Sulphate of Quinine, became affected with amaurosis which continued at the end of three weeks, notwithstanding appropriate (?) and energetic (!) means were employed for the restoration of her sight.

Rognetta says, it may cause deafness, blindness, hallucinations, hæmaturia, &c.

The blindness may be prolonged for months or even years.

Case 1st. Mr. P. of the town of Barry, Jackson Co., was in the year 1845 attacked with a low grade of remittent fever the nature of which was such as to cause the attending physician to administer Quinine in large and frequent doses. About sixteen grains were ordered every hour, until nearly one ounce was taken. Before the Quinine was discontinued, he became perfectly blind; which state, with a slow and gradual amendment, continued during the first year, and his sight is not, yet perfectly restored.

Case 2d. Mrs. R. of the town of Concord, was a few years since reduced so low that her life was despaired of; as a last resort, large quantities of Quinine were given, and while taking it she became blind and continued so for several weeks; as she recovered her health, the blindness gave way, and her sight was finally restored.

Case 3d. P. M. Everett took three grain doses of Quinine every hour for three days; in a short time he became deaf, and soon after so blind that he could not see a burning candle when placed immediately before his eyes; after some weeks his sight became partially restored, but continues more or less imperfect, even at the present time. During the greater part of the first year, he could look steadily at the sun without seeing it, or even any painful sensation being produced. When he first began to see sufficiently to read, which was during the course of the second year, he could but perceive a small luminous spot upon the paper, about one inch in diameter, within which he could distinguish letters, but all without this was cloudiness and confusion. During this time the pupils were very much dilated, and he could see objects at a distance much better than those near by; his sight has improved ever since, and at the present time, although quite imperfect, is sufficiently good to enable him to read and write, although with some difficulty: the pupils are still considerably dilated, and it is with great difficulty that he can discern objects by twilight; the direct rays of the sun upon the head produce pain there, accompanied with a painful sensation deep in the orbit, and disordered vision; exercise easily produces fatigue, by which his sight is much impaired.

Case 4th. Dr. R. took three drachms of Quinine in thirty-six hours, in doses of six grains each, at the end of which time he became perfectly blind; his hearing also was somewhat blunted, although not as much as his sight; in two days his sight was again considerably restored.

Remarks by Professor McLean.

"We think it clear that the blindness in the foregoing cases was the effect of Quinine; for we see it in each, coming on suddenly during its administration in large quantities, and at a time when no other medicine was being given that would be likely to produce such results; here cause and effect appear to be closely connected, and are so plain as scarcely to admit of the possibility of a doubt." Dr. McL. also thinks that the proximate cause of the Quinine-blindness was mainly an affection (!) of the retina or optic nerve, producing amaurosis! This supposition exhibits a decided proclivity on the part of the learned Doctor, towards astute and profound exercises of the reason, and he "records his facts and suppositions in the hope that they may be the means of causing some useful suggestions in relation to the physiological effect and administration of this medicine."

In connection with the foregoing, he mentions the case of a gentleman named Porter, who had been amaurotic for sixteen years in the left eye; for a periodical neuralgia he was ordered thirty-two grains of Quinine, to be taken in doses of four grains each, every two hours. Under its influence the neuralgia disappeared, and on the following day he could see objects quite distinctly with the amaurotic eye, much better than ever before, since it first became diseased, and he was much elated with the thought of soon regaining its sight. He, however, took no more Quinine, and in few days the benefit produced to that eye was entirely lost.

Amaurosis from acute or chronic disorders of the digestive organs.

When dyspepsia and constipation are present Nux-vomica is the most useful remedy; when diarrhœa, Veratrum-album.

Amaurosis from continued loss of fluids of the body.

Is best treated with China. Not unfrequently this amaurosis first declares itself by the sensation of a mist before the eyes in the evening; there is seldom any complaint of pain or fulness; the symptoms generally creep on slowly; the patients are often melancholic, timid and hypochondriacal; subject to dizziness, loss of memory incapacity for mental exertion, capriciousness, sleeplessness, gastralgia, want of appetite, flatulence and constipation. After a hearty meal, or a few glasses of wine, or during the influence of some unexpected elation of mind, the patient sees for a short time, much better than he did before; while an opposite effect is produced by the depressing passions, want of food, continued watching, and the like.

Amaurosis from Bright's disease of the Kidneys.

Mercurius-corrosivus is the principal remedy.

1. Amblyopia. *General Remarks.*

a. In all cases of amblyopia which were principally brought

on by excessive writing, reading or fine needlework by candle-light, Lobethal recommends the external use of Ruta in decoction of one to two drachms to Colat. ℥vi. In obstinate cases he also advises the internal use of Ruta 3., repeated every two or three days.—*Allg. H. Ztg.* 13. 338.

b. Rhus is recommended against weakness of eye-sight, which is sometimes more severe than others, going and coming; attended with the sensation as if looking through a veil, and occurring in subjects, whose feet naturally perspire much, but in whom this perspiration is suddenly checked.—*Allg. H. Ztg.* 37. 304. H.

CASE 213.—A man aged 50, naturally stout and strong, became affected with incipient amaurosis, after having indulged for years in venery, and spirituous drinks to excess. Can only see the outlines of larger objects at a distance of six yards, pupils dilated and sluggish in their action, the interior of the eye looks smokyand cloudy. Cornea without lustre, sight better in the morning after rising. Want of strength, trembling of the hands, impaired digestion, restless sleep.

After two doses China 1. and 2. such improvement followed that in the course of four weeks, patient could read ordinary print.—*Arch.* 3. 3. 74. Caspari.

CASE 214.—A lady about thirty years of age, of mild temperament, and delicate constitution, noticed for a year a gradual loss of sight in the right eye; sometimes she became almost blind without using the eye more than ordinarily; there was a considerable discharge of tears; and she could not bear the glare of light.

After the use of Merc. 12. for fourteen weeks, the whole trouble disappeared, except the morbid discharge of tears, which ceased after having taken Euphrasia.—*Arch.* 1. 113. Gross.

CASE 215.—A weaver aged 29, noticed a gradual failing of his eye-sight; he could hardly discern the threads while weaving, neither was he able to read any more.

One week after use of the Ruta-tinct. one drop, he could read again, and in a week later the whole complaint disappeared. *Annal.* 1. 440. Bethmann.

CASE 216.—A lady, aged 59, had lost her eye-sight so far, as not to be able to know her friends by sight, the eye-ball was turned upwards and inwards, and the pupils inactive; sight worse on straining the eye, and on looking downwards; better by lamp-light, and while resting the head upon her arm, and while rubbing the forehead with her hand.

The eye-balls appear enlarged to her, and difficult to move; there was trembling of the upper lids, vertigo at times, with vanishing of ideas after stooping and speaking.

Several doses Rhus 1. 2. 4. with two intermediate doses of Causticum, cured the patient in the course of two months so far as to enable her to attend to her household affairs without inconvenience. *Allgem. H. Ztg.* 34. 324. HAUSTEIN.

CASE 217.—Mrs. R., aged 24, otherwise healthy, suffered from great irritation of the eyes, which had impaired her sight so much, that she had hardly been able to see anything for eight years past.

On examination the eyes showed nothing abnormal, except the retina appeared affected and so irritable, that the least ray of light darkened all objects and caused much pain. The pupils were always contracted even in the dark.

The patient was hardly able to look at anything for a second; could only see two lines of an M, the third was invisible to her.

Treatment.—For three and a half months she received Carb.-veg., Platina, Digit., Rhus, Natr.-mur., Drosera, after which she could write about three lines,—Natr.-mur., Ruta and Sulphur, were then given for a length of time, the Ruta and Natr.-mur. in alternation. Ruta and Natr. were very useful, but Ruta, however, was never productive of benefit unless given in alternation with Natr.

Ruta 30.—3, three drops. Natr. 30.—9, several globules.

Patient became able to write letters of considerable length. —*Allg. H. Ztg.* 34. 74. BECHET.

Amaurosis.—CASE 218.—Incipient amaurosis in the case of a boy, 7½ years of age, came on after the sudden disappearance of an eruption of the scalp.—He only could see the outlines of objects, and had black spots, and spiders-webs before the eyes; some things he saw double, but indistinctly; the pupils of both eyes very much dilated. The iris was insensible even in a strong light.

Sulph. 4, was given with much benefit, although the first dose was followed by colicky pain and diarrhœa; on the seventh day after the fourth dose he could distinguish larger letters, and after two more doses, his sight was perfectly restored.—Dietz. 148.

CASE 219.—A boy, aged 9, was short-sighted ever since his earliest recollection; this myopia increased gradually until it took the form of incipient amaurosis of the left eye.

Two weeks after taking Phosph. 10. one drop, he was attacked with tearing pain over the eye-brows, lasting twenty-four hours; some time after he began to see objects at a more proper distance, with steady improvement.—*Annal.* 1. 79. Schwarz.

CASE 220.—A boy, aged eight years, was taken during the desquamating stage of scarlet fever with the following symptoms: sudden blindness, much cold perspiration, very rapid pulse, very pale face, inspirations quick and irregular, abdomen soft but burning hot, extremities cold and covered with clammy perspiration.

Treatment.—Aurum-mur. gr. $\frac{1}{16}$ every hour; two doses were only given, after which the patient began to improve so rapidly, that in a very short time he was cured entirely.

A lady on the third day after her fifth confinement, was thrown into a similar condition to the one above. After two hours' use of the above remedy, she was out of all danger.—*Allgem. H. Ztg.* 15. 38. Altmüller.

CASE 221.—Consequent upon a concussion of the brain, the patient was attacked with an amaurotic condition; the sight of the right eye became very much impaired, every thing appeared cloudy, with black spots before the eye, increasing so much that he could not distinguish light from darkness; the pupil was somewhat dilated, but otherwise normal in appearance.

Arnica 2, sixteen doses restored the sight perfectly.—*Hyg.* 19. 111. Genzke.

CASE 222.—A lady, forty-eight years of age, had been affected with tearing pain in the left side of the forehead for about four months. For a week, as the head-ache was gradually disappearing, she noticed things floating before her eye, which she involuntarily tried to wipe away; for the last four days, her sight was so much impaired, that she was only able to distinguish night from day; she had burning and tearing in the eye; the conjunctiva was somewhat reddened.

Tinct.-Sulph., one drop. In thirty-six hours the sight commenced improving, and in ten days she was perfectly cured. —*Annal.* 1. 80. BETHMANN.

CASE 223.—In a case of incipient amaurosis, in a boy, aged 15, who in the course of seven months had lost his sight to such a degree, as to be scarcely able to discern light from darkness.

A perfect cure was effected in ten weeks by magnetism.—*Allgem. H. Ztg.* 33. 74. Dr. KURTZ.

CASE 224.—A mason, aged 46, noticed during the last three years after an affection of the brain (?) so considerable a loss of sight as to disable him from pursuing his trade any longer.

Symptoms.—In the region of the left eye-brow there was a prickling sensation; the pupil of the left eye was dilated and very sluggish in its action; objects appeared as if enveloped in a mist or fog; he dared not venture out to walk alone; he had had the itch formerly; immediately after urinating he had a renewed inclination to urinate. Urine red.

Treatment.—Merc. 30, in solution, was given without benefit. May 7, Pulsat. 30. May 12, Sulph. 30. May 18, Sulphur repeated. By June 11, the sight much improved. The left eye was somewhat obscured by black threads before the eye; June 12, Pulsat. 30. June 15, Sulph. 30. By June 24, the patient could distinguish objects. After Drosera 30. June 30, and Bell. 30, July 6, he had improved so much as to be able to work at his trade again.—*Allg. H. Ztg.* 34. 71. BECHET.

CASE 225.—R., aged 26, affected with leucorrhœa, menstruation normal, however, had been troubled for eighteen months with her left, and since three months with her right eye, in the following way; violent heat and itching in the eyes, with terrible head-ache in the temple, and a sensation as if the head was swollen. Cloudiness, sparks, variegated colors before the eye; as this condition increased, the eye-sight diminished in the same ratio, attended with intolerance of light. The eye-balls appeared normal, except in the interior, there was a greenish-yellow discoloration; she could see objects, but not distinguish differences; the pupils were inactive. She had been treated allopathically without having received any benefit.

Treatment.—Two doses of Merc. 30, and Sulph. 24, every sixth day, alternately; her sight became much improved, and she could read a little. June 5, and 15, she took Silic. 30, with constant improvement. After China 30, Merc. 30, and China 30, by July 17, she was able to thread a needle, but could see only half of some objects, while others seemed double, triple, &c. Bellad. 30, Aurum-sol. 30, Dros. 12, Natr.-mur. 30, Drosera 30, were followed by a perfect cure of the patient.—*Allg. H. Ztg.* 34. 72.—Bechet.

Nux-vomica in amaurosis.—The belief that amaurosis depends on impaired energy of the nerve has been strengthened by the circumstance occasionally noticed, that patients feel and see better after the excitement of wine, or of a full meal. The failing powers of the retina may experience a momentary increase by the temporary acceleration of the circulation consequent on the stimulus; just as ideas are produced more rapidly, and thoughts and language become more powerful and brilliant, when the blood circulates more quickly in the brain, and as the enfeebled stomach of the drunkard is roused by a dram. What should we expect from a regular course of tonics, or from permanent excitement of the brain?—Hays.

Tonics and stimuli, medicinal and dietetic, occasionally find place in the treatment of amaurosis. The disease, in some cases, depends on weakness of the nerve, or is connected with general debility. In other instances the patient is reduced by our treatment, and perhaps by the distress of mind, often amounting to despondency, consequent on the dreadful calamity of blindness. Sometimes, when there is no longer any reasonable prospect of restoring sight, nothing is left for us but to enable the sufferer to bear up under his privation, by upholding the general powers, and restoring the tone of the nervous system. In these several cases there are sufficient reasons for employing medicines of the class now under consideration. My objection is to their indiscriminate use, to their being ranked as primary and principal means in all cases of amaurosis, merely because the nerve is said to be *weakened*, and to the blind empiricism which often administers them in succession, because they have been called *anti-amaurotic*.

Use of strychnia.—As this remedy both in its external and internal administration, has been found a powerful stimulant of the nervous system, in various cases of paralytic affections and impaired sensibility, its powers have been tried in amaurosis. It may be considered particularly applicable to the instances in which simple want of power, or atony of the nervous structure without vascular excitement, is the cause of the symptoms. Mr. MIDDLEMORE, who has tried the remedy in many cases, says, "If a person be suffering from loss or diminution of the power of vision from an atonic state of the retina, or other part of the nervous apparatus of the eye, or of the system generally, the local use of strychnia will be, in my opinion, the most likely means of removing the defect, more especially if it be of recent occurrence."

On another occasion Mr. M. describes more particularly the cases in which benefit may be expected from strychnia. "If a patient has over-worked the eye by long-continued action, confined to the inspection of objects of the same color and description, an enfeebled condition of retina (just as we produce an exhausted state of muscle by over-exertion,) will take place. If a man subject his eye to unnatural stimulus, by looking for many hours daily at bright substances of the same or nearly the same color, or to sudden transitions from an artificial glare to comparative darkness (as miners;) or to a diminished stimulus, as by working in dark rooms, or places imperfectly supplied with light; or to any cause allowing the visual textures of the eye to remain, for a long period, in a state of inactivity, as takes place where large opacities of the cornea, and fully-formed cataract exists, the power of the retina will be partially destroyed, its susceptibility to the stimulus of light diminished; but in none of these cases will there be found any structural change in the retina or the optic nerve, any congestion of vessels, or any discoverable alteration from a healthy and natural condition; nor will the system, in all probability, be found affected; no altered state of health, sufficient to account for the dimness of vision, will be found to exist."—"Loss or diminution of the power of vision sometimes comes on from certain causes which diminish the vigor of the system generally, as, for instance, after profuse salivation, long-continued suckling, menorrhagia, &c. In all these cases, I believe, the strychnia is calculated to produce great and permanent advantage, in combination, of course, with other remedies suited to the particular exigencies of the case: for example, if the retina be weakened in consequence of diminished vigor of the system, remedies adapted to strengthen the system, and a removal of the cause enfeebling it, might be joined to the local application of the remedy in question. But the power of the retina will not always return with the returning strength of the system; in such cases the strychnine is singularly valuable, producing with wonderful rapidity, the restoration of the organ of vision. Strychnine, given internally, does not produce the same beneficial effect upon the retina, as when applied externally."

The mode of employment is to place a blister over the eyebrow, to remove the cuticle, and then dust the remedy over the denuded surface, beginning with the sixth of a grain on each side, and gradually increasing the quantity until one grain is used on each side, or until the head becomes affected. Mr. M. considers that greater effect is produced when the substance is applied over the supra-orbitary nerve. He gives the following general directions: "Place a narrow blister over each eye-brow, which must not extend beyond a line drawn upwards from the external canthus; when it has arisen sufficiently, cut away the cuticle, and apply, for half an hour, a piece of linen to absorb the serum, which is apt to be discharged in large quantities for a short time after the removal of a blister; then dust the remedy chiefly in the situation of the supra-orbitary nerve, but not so thickly as to prevent the absorption of the whole layer of the powder, at the time of the second dressing, which should be twenty-four hours afterwards; this is a proper interval between the dressings; cover the blistered surface with a piece of linen thinly spread with ung. cetacei." "Increase the dose of strychnia very gradually until the state of vision is improved, or symptoms indicative of the injurious agency of the remedy occur. If there be much local pain, excited by the application of the strychnia, dilute it with flour, or mix it with opium; and if that do not succeed, suspend its employment, until the stomach and bowels be improved, by a plan of treatment instituted expressly for their benefit, and then resume its use. If severe pain in the head, convulsive muscular twitchings, great general nervous excitement, or other symptoms, denoting the injurious agency of the strychnia upon the constitution, supervene, and the condition of vision be not improved, it must be discontinued altogether."*

This remedy has been employed by Mr. LISTON,† in the Edinburgh Royal Infirmary. He applied the blisters on the temples, and began with a quarter of a grain of the strychnia on each side, gradually increasing the quantity to one grain and a half, which brought on headache, vertigo, debility, nausea, and muscular tremors. As other means were employed at the same time the evidence respecting the powers of strychnia is the less clear.

In his *Treatise on Diseases of the Eye*, (vol. ii. p. 290, 291,) published since the observations previously quoted, Mr. MIDDLEMORE states that his favorable opinion of strychnia has been strengthened by subsequent experience.

Mr. TYRRELL says that he has frequently tried the remedy in the cases which appeared to him most appropriate, but that he had not seen one single instance of benefit from its employment, although he had persevered until alarming mus-

---

* *Report of the Birmingham Eye Infirmary, in the Midland Medical and Surgical Reporter*, May, 1830, vol. ii. p. 158, 159; also, *On the Utility of Strychnia in certain forms of Amaurosis*, ibid, p. 481—485. The remarks are republished in the *London Medical Gazette*, vol. viii. p 434—437.

In another short notice contained in the same periodical, Mr. MIDDLEMORE mentions, that in two or three instances it has produced so much head-ache and spasm, that its employment could not be continued; whilst two or three patients, who were much benefited by it experienced so much local pain, that they would not persevere in the use of the remedy. In three cases where it was serviceable, its continued use was necessary to preserve vision, which was invariably lost, when the strychnia was discontinued.—Ibid, p. 240.

† *London Medical Gazette*, vol v. p. 541 and 575.

cular contractions were produced. He considers further that serious mischief has resulted from its indiscriminate use. (Vol. ii. p. 316.)

My own experience coincides with that of Mr. Tyrrell, in reference, not only to strychnia, but also to veratria, which he has found equally inefficacious.

The latter remedy is employed in the form of ointment, in which from ten to twenty grains of the veratria are incorporated in an ounce of lard or spermaceti cerate. The size of a large pea, or a horsebean is to be rubbed on the temples and forehead for a few minutes, once or twice in twenty-four hours. The application causes redness, heat, and tingling; sometimes with more considerable irritation; and the friction should be continued until these effects are produced. In this mode of employment the veratria may be of some service as a mild counter-irritant. I have seen it used many times, but it has never produced essential and unequivocal benefit in a decided case of amaurosis within my observation. Sometimes, in females, it has irritated excessively, causing nervous symptoms, which have excited alarm; and patients have even stated that it has injured sight.—Hays.

[The results of our experience with strychnine in amaurosis, are much more favorable to the value of this remedy, than those of Mr. Lawrence and Mr. Tyrrell. It has certainly proved inefficacious in not a few cases which seemed favorable for its employment, but in others, it has been productive of the best effects. *We have found it far more effectual, however, when applied to the eye, in the form of Collyrium, or given internally, than when applied to a blistered surface; indeed we do not remember a single cure effected by the latter method of using it.* The cases in which it shows its best effects are those attended with dilatation of the pupil; for this article has almost as decided an effect in producing contraction, as Belladonna has of causing dilatation of the pupil.

The following case is one of the most striking we have met with of the efficacy of the remedy:—Harriet Taylor, aged 12, was admitted into Wills Hospital. November 10th, 1838, with amaurosis of right eye; vision in left eye good. Her mother stated that she had first noticed her daughter's defect of sight about three years ago, since which period it had been growing gradually worse. For four months the right eye, to use the patient's own expression, had been "quite dark." She cannot distinguish a candle with it, though she has a faint perception of the light. The patient has light hair; complexion fair; irides grey, contracting on exposure to light; pupil of right eye rather more dilated than that of left; is sometimes troubled with headache. We could not learn any thing from the history of the case, as given by her mother, calculated to throw any light on the cause of the loss of sight.

There was evidently no congestion of the cerebral organs, or inflammatory excitement in the system, and we therefore ordered a dose of sulphate of Magnesia at bed-time, and the next morning a few drops of the following to be applied to her right eye. ℞. Strychnin. gr. ij.; acid.-acet. ʒj., aq.-puræ ℥j. M.—HAYS.

November 11*th*, Noon. Medicine has purged her actively. The nurse had applied the solution to the eye early in the morning, and the patient finding her vision much improved, afterwards, in the absence of the nurse, had twice used it herself. Says she can now see pretty well with her right eye. Upon trial, found she could read with that eye, the other being carefully closed with my fingers, a newspaper which happened to be at hand. Says there is some cloudiness of right eye. Continue Collyrium.

12*th*. Sight improved. She read with either eye almost equally well, the other being closed, a proof sheet of this Journal, which we had taken for the purpose of trial. Cloud before right eye diminished but not entirely gone. Continue Collyrium.

13*th*. Cloudiness of right eye entirely gone; sees perfectly well with it; is not sensible of any difference in the power of vision of her two eyes. She was discharged November 17th, and went to her mother who resides a few miles in the country.

The rapidity of the cure in this case led us at first to suspect deception; on inquiry we could not discover any ground for such suspicion. The friend who had recommended the patient to our care informed us that her mother was a respectable, industrious widow, who supported by her labor several children, of which the patient was the oldest; that the daughter was intelligent, active and obliging, and her aid was of so much importance to her mother, that he had interested himself to have her relieved from her infirmity, which much lessened her usefulness. As to the excellence of her sight, when she was discharged from the hospital, we verified this in a way that admitted of no deception.

In June, 1839, we had the gratification to learn from the friend who sent this patient to us, that the cure had been so far permanent. He informed us that he had seen Harriet frequently, and that a short time before he had inquired particularly of her respecting her sight, and was assured that it was perfect.]—HAYS.

MORBID SENSIBILITY OF THE RETINA.

This disease is generally mistaken for amblyopia amaurotica, or amaurotic weakness of sight; the one is weakness or dullness of sight, the other *is over-sensitiveness of the eye to use;* the one may be comparable to paralysis, the other to spinal irritation. In amblyopia, use or exposure may increase the defect of vision, but the patient at no time sees perfectly; in morbid sensibility he never sees imperfectly, except after the eyes have been fatigued, or subjected to some cause of discomfort, as a bright light or cold wind. Morbid sensibility of the retina is probably similar to photophobia in its nature, the one is intolerance of use of the eyes, the latter is intolerance of light; both are apt to occur in over-sensitive and in scrofulous subjects.

The intolerance of use, which has been stated to be the peculiarity of the disease, of course infers that the sight is good, or rather that the eye retains all its capability of seeing, but over-sensitiveness of the organ prevents its being exerted. Use of the eye is apt to be followed by a dull heavy pain over the brows, or deep in the orbit; sometimes by a sensation referred to the anterior portion of the globe, in which the patient is unable to say whether smarting or pain predominates; sometimes by a sensation of heaviness in the top of the head; less frequently by a sharp, darting pain through the globe of the eye; and more rarely still by a sensation of uneasiness altogether indefinable or by a mere sensation of pressure in or behind the ball, or of itching on the surface of it. An impression of weight in the lids, and a slightly painful, but, for the most part indescribable sensation upon the cheek along the lower margin of the orbit are in some cases, either singly or united, the first, and for a time the only indications of intolerance of use. The sensation of excessive weight in the lids may be so decided that the patient may seem unable at times to open them, until after repeated efforts; the time at which it is most annoying being on the morning following a day during which the eyes have been over-used. Sometimes a tired feeling in the eye, analogous to the sensation of muscular fatigue, is spoken of as the first indication. In some cases the pain induced by over-use is felt only or chiefly in turning the eyes.—Dix.

The amount of use sufficient to produce these symptoms is very various; the attempt to read a single word may be followed by one or more of these sensations. The great peculiarity of the disease is, that with all this intolerance of use, blindness does not occur; thus, a person attacked with amaurosis either recovers vision rapidly, or, if slowly, with a progress which is appreciable from month to month; in morbid sensibility of the retina, on the contrary, the absolute imperfection of vision which follows the over-use of the eyes, is the same five or ten years after the commencement of the disease, as when it was first observed. This excessive sensibility of the eye is of course followed by some redness and by confusion of vision, and tenderness of the eye.—Dix.

Morbid sensibility of the retina may be mistaken for chronic iritis, retinitis, or choroiditis, or for neuralgia of the globe of the eye, amaurosis, scrofulous ophthalmia, or granulated condition of the conjunctiva of the upper-lids. In fact it associates itself with all these diseases, but never produces them; i. e., they may exite it, but it never leads to any more serious disease of the eye than itself.

Chronic iritis presents many symptoms in common with morbid sensibility of the retina. The pain about the brow, the tenderness on pressure, the slight pinkish zonular injection around the cornea; the aggravation, and in some cases, the occurrence of these symptoms only after use or exposure, are together with a slight obscuration of vision, characteristic of both diseases. But, in chronic iritis, vision is not perfect, even when no exertion of the eyes is made; there is always a stiffness in the motion of the iris, and in most cases some irregularity of the pupil and discoloration of the irides; it will also always be found that the disease commenced and persisted for a long time in one eye only.

From *chronic retinitis* it may be distinguished by the dull, turbid look posterior to the pupil.

From *chronic choroiditis*, by the absence of the bluish tinge of the sclerotic.

And from all these diseases by the permanence and gradual increase of the imperfection of vision which accompanies them.

Neuralgia of the eye is characterized by the agonizing pain which attends it; by the regularly intermittent character of the pain; by the sudden contraction or irregularity of the pupil; by the cessation of neuralgic pains in other parts of the body; by its location in one eye only, &c.

Amblyopia, or incipient amaurosis, when attended with pain in its earlier stages, presents many features in common with morbid sensibility of the retina, but may be distinguished from it, by the permanence of the imperfection of sight which attends amblyopia, and by the difference in the character of the affection of vision in the two diseases: thus, in morbid sensibility, there is an indistinctness, a blurring, fading away, confusion, and in some cases a distortion of objects; while in amblyopia, a portion only of objects, such as the upper or lower, the right or left half may be seen; or those objects only may be visible, which are situated in a certain direction from the eye; or things may appear to be doubled, or tripled, or otherwise multiplied; or their color may be changed, or they may seem to be enveloped in a haze capable of being described as smoky, cloudy, or gauze-like. In morbid sensibility of the retina the patient can see in all kinds of light, except they be excessive; while in amblyopia the light often requires to be carefully adjusted, in order to give the patient the best vision of which he is capable. In amblyopia the imperfection of vision is the first, and in some cases the only symptom; in morbid sensibility of the retina, the disturbance of vision is generally preceded for some time by pain or suffering of some sort in the eyes.

Scrofulous ophthalmia, where no ulcer or pustule is present, may be confounded with morbid sensibility; this mistake is perhaps the less important as we are inclined to think that morbid sensibility of the retina is often a scrofulous affection.

A very slight degree of *ophthalmia tarsi*, or *tinea ciliaris*, will sometimes render the eyes incapable of long-continued use, and keep them in an irritable state, resembling very much true morbid sensibility of the retina.

A slight roughness or *granulated condition* of the conjunctiva of the upper lids, may be, and very often is mistaken for morbid sensibility of the retina. It often results from a mild attack of catarrhal ophthalmia, and is of frequent occurrence on our sea-board. It can only be discovered by everting the lids, but may be suspected, if the patient complains of an occasional gravelly sensation in the eyes, or if he refers back the origin of his complaint to an attack of "sore eyes."

Location.—Morbid sensibility of the eye is supposed to arise from disorder of the *ciliary system*. This system is contiguous to, and has connections with almost every other texture of the eye; at one and the same point it unites the sclerotic and cornea externally, and the choroid and iris internally; while at the same point the choroid adheres internally to the vitreous humor by means of the ciliary processes, the ciliary portions of the retina, being included in the same adhesion. Further, the zonula ciliaris to which these processes adhere, is closely connected to the capsule of the lens. We may therefore consider this as a common point of union, embracing all the essential constituents of the globe, viz., the sclerotica, cornea, choroid, iris, retina, vitreous humor and cristalline lens. Hence any irritation of the ciliary system, which seems in fact to be the centre of the ordinary nervous sensibility of the eye, is necessarily followed by discomfort in almost every part of the organ.

Recovery from the disease is always slow; sight is never lost or materially injured.

Treatment.—Agaricus is a most important remedy. Kali-chlor. will make the eyes feel strong and render them tolerant of use, when other remedies fail. Spigelia deserves attention.

General sensitiveness of the eyes may be met by Cuprum, Arsenicum, Quinine and Conium. Carbo-animalis and Sepia are excellent remedies in chronic cases, when ill effects constantly follow the use of the eyes. Aurum is the principal remedy, when there is a sensation in using the eyes as if the blood were pressing on the optic nerve, with tension in the eyes and confusion of sight. Crocus is a good palliative, when after reading a while, even in the day time, the eyes ache and feel sore and burning, with dimness, frequently obliging one to wink. Graphite and Ruta, when there is a constant sensation in the eyes, as if one had exerted them too much in reading.

OCULAR HYPER-ÆSTHESIA.

According to Mackenzie, this disease consists chiefly in a greatly increased sensitiveness both of the optic nerve, and of the ophthalmic division of the fifth. The chief characteristic of the affection is great intolerance of light, attended with photopsia, chrupsia, pain in the eye and head, sensitiveness of the eye-ball and lids to touch, and spasmodic closure of the eye.

It occurs both in an acute and chronic form. *Acute form:* This generally arises suddenly from some evident external cause, such as, overtaxing the eyes, reaches its greatest degree of severity in a short time, and may either subside of itself in a few days, or speedily yield to treatment. One eye is generally affected first, but by and by both may become implicated; Mackenzie, however, has seen the reverse of this, both eyes suffering at first, the disease finally concentrating itself in one eye only.

Symptoms.—In the severest cases the attack commences

with such excruciating pain in the eye, as to cause the patient to shriek aloud; he is rendered totally incapable of exposing the eye to the light, and he immediately seeks to relieve this symptom by remaining in the darkest place to which he has access, pressing his eyes with his hands, or lying on his face in bed, and pressing his eyes against the pillow. The spasm of the orbicularis muscle is such, that it is almost impossible to obtain a glimpse of the eye. The pulse is full and quick, and the head hot. The symptoms are so severe, that the patient concludes his sight to be lost, and the practitioner, if unacquainted with the true nature of such cases, perhaps adopts the same idea, and *pronounces the disease to be acute retinitis.*

Chronic form.—Called to visit a patient with chronic ocular hyper-æsthesia, we are probably ushered into a room as absolutely dark as it is possible to make it, every chink by which light might enter, being closed, and a large screen so placed as to impede any gleam, which might intrude on the door being opened. There we find the patient, in some cases sitting up, in others lying in bed, with his eyes shaded, and his head covered with a thick veil or shawl. In this state, we are perhaps informed, he has been for months. In such a case, no persuasion will convince the patient, that he might bear for a few moments, sufficient light to enable us to see his eyes; or if he yields so much as to remove their coverings from them, his terror of their being touched with the fingers prevents us from making any satisfactory examination of their state. The increased sensibility of the fifth nerve is a symptom scarcely less prominent in such cases than the excessive intolerance of light. The least touch about the eye is painful and continues to be felt for a long time.—MACKENZIE.

Both the acute and chronic varieties of this disease are generally attended with spasms of the eye-lids, flashes of light and appearance of colors before the eyes, but all of these may be absent; Mackenzie has met with cases in which though the smallest degree of light was insufferable, so that the patient remained in complete darkness, with his eyes shaded, lest any accidental ray of light might reach them, yet his eyes were open and affected neither with spasms of the lids, nor with photopsia.

Although severe pain almost always attends the acute variety, yet in the chronic form there may either be scarcely any complaint of pain, or the pain may be pretty acute and concentrated in the eye-ball, or extending to the forehead and temples.

Little or no injury happens to the sight, however long the disease may last. In chronic cases the acuteness of sight sometimes appears to be increased beyond what is ordinary, so that in a state of almost complete darkness the patients will manage to see sufficiently to take their food and to distinguish readily the furniture in their room and the persons about them.

Diagnosis.—It may be distinguished from retinitis by the presence of excessive pain and intolerance of light, symptoms which do not attend inflammation of the retina. The only other diseases which it may be confounded with, are morbid sensibility of the retina and scrofulous photophobia; as these are, however, very similar in their nature, this mistake is of no great importance.

Prognosis.—This is always good; however severe the symptoms may be, either in the acute or chronic forms, Mackenzie says, we can always promise a perfect recovery. In both forms recovery is often sudden and complete, although it may last for months and years, especially if the patient be timid, or stupid, or obstinate as regards exposure to gradually increased quantities of light.

Treatment.—Mackenzie reports acute cases as recovering in the course of a few days or weeks by the ordinary allopathic treatment of obscure affections of the eye, viz., Calomel, Opium, Belladonna, &c.

The remedies advised for morbid sensibility of the retina, photopsia and chrupsia will be found useful.

PHOTOPHOBIA. (*Intolerance of Light.*)

This generally depends upon a scrofulous irritation of the conjunctiva; the patient, generally a child, may be for months unable to bear the least accession of light, or to open the eyes in the smallest degree during the day. The inflammation during this state may be very inconsiderable, so that on forcing open the lids, scarcely a red vessel is discovered. Such, however, is the sympathy of the conjunctiva, which is the primary seat of irritation, and the neighboring parts, viz., the retina, cerebral optic apparatus, lachrymal gland and the lids, that the admitted light seems to the patient to blaze like the rays of the sun reflected from a mirror, or what might be felt on looking at a sea of molten gold. When the eyes are opened, the lachrymal gland instantly pours out a flood of tears and the spasm of the lids forces the eye to close with great violence.

A large proportion of these cases are attended with phlyctenular or more properly eczematous, or so-called scrofulous ophthalmia. (See vol. 1, p. 113.)

Treatment.—In acute cases, Aconite, Euphorbium, Rhus, Conium and Bellad., are the principal remedies; in very severe, tedious or chronic cases, Arsenicum, Merc.-corrosivus, Sulphur, Silex and Calcarea may be used.

PHOTOPSIA.

(*Visus lucidus.* Seeing of light.)

Sensations of light may be produced independently of the ordinary impressions of natural or artificial light; the flash produced by sneezing, or by gentle pressure, or a blow on the eye, are familiar instances. In like manner there are sensations of light, which are altogether the result of irritation or disease in the optic apparatus. Flashes of light, the appearance of shining stars, a glittering as if from the points of innumerable needles, or the sides of innumerable prisms may occur in choroiditis, or in the commencement of amaurosis. In some peculiar and distressing cases of ocular hyper-æsthesia the patient is annoyed by the sensation as if his eyes were directed towards globes of light swimming or revolving before him, or as if he were looking at a sea of molten gold.

Slight pressure on the retina may excite a luminous sensation; an excrescence on the inner surface of the eye-lid may produce a continued pressure on the eye-ball and excite the appearance of a luminous circle before the eyes; congestive pressure on the retina may do the same; flashes of light are often the precursors of convulsive attacks, such as epilepsy, &c.

Treatment.—Ignatia is indicated in nervous, spasmodic and hypochondrial cases, when white zig-zag vibrations appear out of the line of vision; or when there is a circle of white shining, flickening zig-zags outside of the line of vision, when reading, the letters at which one looks becoming invisible, while those to one side become more bright.

Borax, in dyscratic cases, when there are bright waves before the eyes moving from side to side, or upwards and downwards; or dancing before the eyes while writing, so that nothing can be seen distinctly.

Belladonna, in acute and severe, or nervous congestive cases, when there are large bright sparks before the eyes; or white stars of the size of a plate, with white silvery clouds passing over them.

Crocus, when there are sudden flashes before the eyes like electric sparks.

Digitalis, is one of the most homœopathic remedies in this disorder, when great nervous debility is present, attended with dazzling and sparks before the eyes, and appearance as if all objects were covered with snow.

Quinine, in congestive cases, when there is an intense light and sparks before the eyes.

Sepia, Phosph.-acid, Fluoric-acid and Graphite, may be used in obstinate and chronic cases.

CHRUPSIA.

(*Visus coloratus.* Seeing of colors.)

This symptom may depend either upon some derangement of the lenses of the eye, by which its achromatic power is disturbed, or on some irritation, or pressure upon the convex surface of the retina, or optic nerve.

In injuries of the cornea and prolapse of the iris, or after an attack of paralysis, all objects may appear of a greenish hue.

In scrofulous sclerotitis, brilliant blue, green and red colors may play over objects looked at, such as the face of a person, or a white handkerchief.

Nine persons poisoned with Hyosciamus, saw, say they, dimly on the first day, and on the second day every thing appeared as red as scarlet. Many other drugs produce similar appearances. One patient saw all white objects of a deep orange color, approaching to scarlet; a lady often saw white objects of a very bright blue color, &c.

The explanation of some of these appearances is easy: Thus, if we look at a window from the end of a long apartment, then promptly close the eyes, turn from the window, and cover them with the hands, we will perceive an accurate representation of the window, with the bars dark and the panes bright; but if we turn the *closed* eyes again to the window, the bars will appear bright and the panes dark. The explanation of this is, that the part of the retina which has received the luminous visage remains for a time in an occupied or excited state, while that which received the dark image from the bars is in an unoccupied or unexcited state, and hence capable of receiving the much more feeble influence of light when the closed eyes are turned again to the window and the hands removed.

If we look steadily for a considerable time at a red spot on a white or black ground, a green border will appear around it; then if we look at another white or black ground we will perceive a spot of green of the size and form of the red spot. The spectrum which is seen by fatiguing the eye with looking at a violet object, is yellow; that of green, red; that of yellow violet. Hence these are *opposite* or *complementary* colors.

Mackenzie says, to understand the meaning of the term *complementary* as applied to such colors, it is necessary to observe, that the color of the spectrum is always such as being added to the color of the object with which the retina has been fatigued, makes up the sum of the three primary colors, red, yellow and blue, which by their combination form white light; hence the name *complementary*, which has been given to the colors of ocular spectra. Green, then, which is composed of yellow and blue, is the complementary color to red; violet, a compound of red and blue, to yellow; and orange, a mixture of red and yellow, to blue. Two colors, which together yield a grey color, such as black and white, are also complementary.

The explanation of colored spectra from colored objects is as follows. White light contains all the primitive colors, viz, red, blue and yellow, as its elements. Then if the retina, when it has been long fixed on a red object, is rendered insensible to the red light, but is still susceptible of the impression of the other colored rays; if it be now directed towards a white surface, being no longer sensible to the red rays contained in the white light, it perceives only the remaining component rays of white light, viz., yellow and blue, which form green, which is hence the complementary color of red.

When the retina is in a state of intense excitement, colored spectra may appear from colored objects, although the eyes are in apparent total darkness. The green baizes or curtains in the darkened room, although almost invisible to the healthy eye, may excite red spectra in the morbidly sensitive eye; gilded frames, although they look black to the healthy eye, may excite violet colored spectra, or those formed by the combination of the red and blue rays which are the only ones then observed by the eye. A variety of colored objects, even in a darkened room may cause the most varied and intricate combinations and separations of color only visible to the morbidly sensitive eye.

Hence those drugs which cause objects to appear yellow, render the eyes insensible to blue and red rays; those which make objects appear red, have paralyzed the susceptibilities of the retina to the blue and yellow rays; those which cause greenish spectra, have left the eye susceptible to the blue and yellow rays, but not to the red; those which cause the appearance of blue colors have destroyed the susceptibility of the retina to the red and yellow rays. Variegated spectra are produced by drugs which cause derangement of the lenses of the eye, by which its achromatic power is disturbed.

It is probable that insensibility to certain colors, or color blindness may become a curable affection by aid of these hints.

Dr. Wilson of Edinburgh found that as many as one person in 55, confounded red with green; one in 60, brown with green; one in 46, blue with green.

Mackenzie says that persons affected with insensibility to certain colors are most apt to confound red with green, and pink with blue; in other words that red light, or colors in which red forms an ingredient, and its complementary color, i. e., green are not distinguishable from one another by those who labor under the defect in question. The only colors they can truly distinguish are yellow and blue. In some, blue may even be imperfectly distinguished from red. In all color-blind persons, the perception of yellow is the most perfect; by gas-light, or candle-light, or other yellow light, the distinction between red and green, which is so slight to them by ordinary day-light, becomes in many cases quite apparent. Yellow spectacles help some of these persons very much. Much attention has lately been drawn to this disorder by the discovery of Dr. Wilson, of Edinburgh, that several employees on railroads were unable to distinguish between red and green danger-signals.

Treatment.—When everything appears *yellow*, Sulphur, Digitalis, Galvanism, Hyosciamus, Kali-carb., Ammon.-mur., and Alumina are homœopathic.

When things appear *red*, Crocus, Conium, Digitalis, Hyosciamus, and Stramonium are indicated.

When they appear *green*: Digitalis, Merc., Nitric-acid, Kali-carb., Zincum, Strontian, and Phosph.

When *blue*: Galvanism, Kali-carb., Zincum.

When *variegated*: Euphorbium. Digitalis, when various colors appear before the eyes, red, green and yellow and a sort of twinkling light composed of these colors; Kali-nit., when there are colored wheels before the eyes; Zincum, when there are yellow, blue and green wheels before the eyes; Stramonium where objects appear of various colors.

SPECTRAL ILLUSIONS.

Certain spectral illusions it is well known attend delirium tremens; the patient supposes his chamber to be haunted by rats, cats, snakes and various other spectres, and often calls for assistance to drive them away. He imagines vermin to be crawling over his bed, and endeavors to pick them off; or frequently puts out his hand, as if to catch something floating before him in the air. In some cases of this sort, Mackenzie says, both sense and judgment are affected; but in other cases, sense only. In the latter case the patient is readily convinced that he is laboring under illusions; in the former, his delirium prevents this conviction. A somewhat similar state of things occurs in typhus and other fevers, and in poisoning with various narcotic drugs.

The explanation generally given is, that normal perception being in ordinary cases attended by some unknown motion or change in the brain, in the above diseases the brain is so altered and excited, that if the person happens but to think or dream of any past impression, the same change in the brain is repeated as in actual perception.

Spectres, or resemblances of natural objects often present themselves from similar causes. They seem to be dreams or imaginations reduced to sight.

These spectral illusions are infinitely various; sometimes bearing the aspect of a single person, or object; in others imitating the impression which might be produced by crowds of human beings moving before the spectator, or by scenes of endless diversity. (*See Treatise on Nervous Diseases and Mental Derangements by* Dr. PETERS, p. 50.)

Treatment.—Cocculus was the most important remedies, in a case where the patient saw a black figure before his eyes, walking in front of him, to and fro; when he turned the figure turned also, nevertheless the patient saw everything in a full light. Petroleum, when vibrations and black figures appear before the eyes; Camphor, when strange figures hover before the eyes; Digitalis, when all sorts of forms and visions appear before the eyes; Stramonium and Belladonna, when objects which do not exist are seen in the room; Argentum-nitricum, when grey spots and bodies in the shape of serpents move before the sight; Arsenicum, when he sees vermin crawling about his bed; Phosphor, when a horrid mask seems looking out of every corner; Lycopodium, when phantoms crowd upon one; Causticum, when one sees distorted human faces; Ambra and Argentum, distorted figures and faces; Stramonium and Belladonna, when one sees ghosts and insects; Stramonium and Opium, when one sees a number of persons and grasps at them, yet they are not present.

ILLUSIONS OF SIZE, AND DISTANCE.

Treatment.—Nux-vom., Carb.-an., Sulphur and Stramonium

are homœopathic when objects appear far off; Bovista, when they seem too near.

Stramonium and Platina, when every thing seems *small* and distant.

Niccolum, Hyosciamus, Oxalic-ac., Laurocerasus, Zincum, Staph., and Euphorbium, when objects appear larger.

Sulphur, when one imagines that he is growing thin and dwindling down to a skeleton.

MUSCÆ.

These are of two kinds, viz., *floating and fixed.*

1. FLOATING MUSCÆ.

These occasionally arise from a layer of mucus and moisture upon the cornea; occasionally from similar corpuscules floating in the aqueous humor, between the focal centre of the eye and the cornea.

But the larger proportion of floating muscæ are situated posterior to the focal centre of the eye. If one looks at the flame of a candle, two or three feet distant, or at the sky, through a hole made in a blackened card with the point of a fine needle, four sets of spectra will be seen:

a) The most remarkable set appears nearest the eye, and consists of twisted strings of minute pearly globules, hung across the field of view.

b) The second in point of remarkableness, is farthest of the four from the eye, and consists of watery-like threads destitute of any globular appearance, and depending chiefly from the upper part of the field of view.

Mackenzie calls the first the *pearly spectrum* and the latter, the *watery spectrum.*

Between these two layers of strings of pearly and watery threads, there float two distinct sets of globules, which are never aggregated into rows or threads, but which always remain isolated from each other.

c) The individual globules of the set farther from the eye are hazy and ill-defined, and are compared by Mackenzie to small grains of sago;

d) The globules of the set nearer to the eye are clear in

their centre, exteriorly to which they present a sharp black ring and still more exteriorly a lucid circumference.

These four sets of spectra never mingle with one another, so as to change the order in which they stand before the eye: *a*) the pearly spectrum or appearance of rows of pearls always appear the nearest; then the sharply-defined black ring-like isolated globules; then the obscurely-defined isolated sago-like globules; and farthest away, the watery threads.

An exaggeration of these appearances which can always be produced in the healthy eye, form what are called *muscæ volitantes*.

The muco-lachrymal substance on the surface of the cornea forms one variety; the corpuscules forming the rows of pearls or the pearly spectrum are situated close to the sentient layer of the retina; the watery spectra and the isolated globules, both sharp and ill-defined, occur in the middle spaces of the eye.

All muscæ volitantes are but exaggerations of these natural appearances.

Muscæ volitantes, produced by the watery spectrum.

The natural appearance of the watery spectrum as seen through the perforated card, is that of threads depending from the upper portion of the eye; each of the watery threads is bounded by two dark lines, within which there is a broad space, which is clear and destitute of anything like globules; their general direction is downwards and slightly tortuous; they often divide at their lower extremity into two or more branches, which seem to melt away insensibly; they have much the appearance which we might suppose streams of tears to have as they descend from the lachrymal ducts and flow over the cornea, but they are much deeper-seated; at first view they seem to slide down slowly from the upper to the middle part of the field of view; they are rarely seen in the lower part of the field of view, and must exist, therefore, chiefly in the lower portion of the entohyaloid space, as they are seen inverted.

When this natural state becomes exaggerated and forms a disease, it is most apt to be perceived on first going out in the morning; it is compared by some patients to the appearance of threads of spun-glass, laid across each other, or to that of a fine lock of wool. It appears a little above the centre of the field of vision, and of course seems greatly magnified by the distance of the surface against which it is viewed; it always retains the form of numerous watery threads, never containing globules, but these threads may be irregularly heaped together, and often assume zig-zag figures.

Treatment.—When there are threads, filaments, little feathers or hairs hanging before the eyes, Conium, Kreosote and Castoreum are the principal remedies; in very obstinate cases, Carbo.-an., Calcarea, and Alumina may be tried. When zig-zag appearances are present, Conium, Ignatia and Fluoric-acid are the principal remedies; Sepia, Graphite and Natrum may be required in obstinate cases.

Globular muscæ volitantes.—The ill-defined globules (*c*) which lie directly behind the watery spectrum, rarely give rise to muscæ volitantes; but the globules (*d*) which occupy the next plane, and whose edges are sharp and dark, frequently appear to the naked eye, either as simple black points or rings.

Treatment.—Carbo-vegetabilis and Pulsatilla are the principal remedies.

Muscæ-volitantes, produced by the pearly spectrum.

Almost every eye, even the most healthy, will detect these on looking towards a luminous field through a fine pin-hole.

At first only a few small pearly globules may be perceived; but soon numerous strings of them are discovered, generally twisted in different forms and presenting a variety of knots, loops and agglomerations; sometimes they are so numerous as to form an extensive shower or cloud; the pearly threads are of different lengths; the globules or pearls which form the strings of beads or rosaries are merely in apposition like the blood-globules.

When these appearances are exaggerated, they form by far the most common kind of muscæ-volitantes; one or more dark bodies may be seen dancing in the air, leading the patient to suppose that a bit of dust or soot is sticking to the eye-lashes, or that a small spider is before the eye; it is only on attempting to brush them away, that the mistake is discovered.

In other cases a thin cloud, somewhat like the wing of a fly, or spider-web may be seen, or like black lace. On moving the eye from side to side, the spectrum moves also with great swiftness. This state may last for months or years without progressing, or attracting much attention—sometimes the annular shape of the darkest portion of the muscæ may cause an appearance like that of black stars. At all times if the patient turns his eye to a clear sky, the clouds, cobwebs, or wings of insects resolve themselves into a great number of pearly globules or minute rings, moving as the eye moves and connected together by some invisible film.

Frequently there is a twisted tubular appearance, resembling that of a twisted snake, or a quill with the withered substance within its cavity. It is probable, that these appearances are much exaggerated in delirium tremens, and give rise to the appearance of snakes, beetles, rats, &c.

These pearly muscæ volitantes are rarely seen in the axis of vision, but some distance from it, either outwards or inwards, upwards or downwards, but most frequently outwards towards the temple. These muscæ never move unless set in motion by the movement of the eye-ball.

They are not the result of disease, nor do they indicate its approach, although they may arise from abuse of the eyes and intense application of the mind.

They are often supposed to be a sign of congestion in the head and eyes, and precursors of apoplexy.

Severe influenza is a common cause. Loss of sleep, disordered digestion, disturbed action of the heart, or nervousness may produce them; anxiety, distress and grief may cause them.

It is a very harmless disorder; even the greatest possible accumulation of them never can cause amaurosis, or cataract; but sometimes in reading a number of them may gather together, so as to render portions of the page before one temporarily obscure. They often remain stationary for ten or twenty years; but the eye may become more and more susceptible to the impression on the retina, which these objects cause, if they be searched for and examined too curiously.

Treatment.—When there is congestion to the head, Aconite and Quinine are the principal remedies.

When there is bilious derangement or torpor of the liver, and constipation, Nitric-acid, Nux, Merc., Sulphur and Petroleum.

When there is disturbance of the heart, Digitalis and Veratrum.

When there is derangement of the genital organs or kidneys; Phos., Thuja, Terebinth and Ruta.

When there is great nervousness, Moschus, Hyosciamus, Anacardium, Agaricus.

When there is great debility, Phos. and Ammon.-c.

Giving up the use of sugar has cured some cases; Merc., Iod.-pot., Ether and Valerian have cured others.

FIXED MUSCÆ.

These are much more serious in their import, as they generally point to some affection of the retina; they may be single or numerous; of different sizes and a great variety of forms; their color is generally black, or at least much darker than the floating mucæ; they are often so black, that a person's countenance, standing before the patient seems obliterated, or his head cut off, or the flame of a gas-light extinguished. They, however, appear of a greyish-white while the eye is closed, but instantly assume a black velvet color on opening the eye in the light.

White objects seem to have black, ill-defined blotches upon them; sometimes the patient sees black letters like a T or X in the air; at others he seems as if looking through a riddle, the interstices of which gradually become less and less, till the disease ends in total blindness.

A fixed musca in the centre of the field of vision, gradually expanding its circumference, generally ends in one of the most intractable varieties of amaurosis; although I have seen it disappear and return several times. It arises from a change of structure in the central spot of the retina.

The appearance of a spider with its legs stretched out generally is a floating musca.

Fixed muscæ may arise from distension of the blood-vessels of the retina and effusion of blood (apoplexia retinæ). Then Opium, Arnica and Kreosote are the principal remedies.

From aneurism of the artery, or varicose enlargement of the veins (Lycopodium.)

From partial paralysis of the retina; such muscæ disappear after a glass or two of wine, &c.; Nux-vomica, Strychnine, Ferrum, or Plumbum.

Small black points deposited on the concave surface of the retina (melanosis) and larger red bodies on its convex surface (neuromata) may give rise to fixed muscæ; they may be treated with Carbo-an., and Thuja.

Fixed muscæ are generally attended with photopsia or coruscations and haloes of sight; floating muscæ; morbid sensibility of the retina; the alternate appearance and disappearance of small objects; hemopia; partial or oblique vision; chrupsia; undulating clouds before the eyes through which small objects are seen by fits, and then obscured again; bright objects exhibit a tremulous or undulating light and shade; the edges of objects are ill-defined and shaggy, and as if fringed with hoar-frost; perpendicular lines may appear disfigured; printed letters broken or indented; circular objects deprived of their regular shape, &c.

CASE 226.—A gentleman had a fall on his right side about a year ago, after which he complained of the following symptoms; inability to see with the affected eye, without the aid of the other, considerable obscurity of vision, and many muscæ volitantes before the eyes, which prevented him from seeing distinctly.

Arnica was given without benefit, Merc.-sol. 12, however, cured him entirely.—*Pract. Beitr.* 3. 24. THORER.

CASE 227.—Cicuta in deceptive sight.

Symptoms.—Objects appeared double, letters seemed to move about, surrounded by all the colors of a rainbow; this also took place in looking at a lighted candle; while walking and looking at objects, the patient became dizzy; photophobia; at times burning pain in the eye, and agglutination in the morning; dilated pupils, blue circles around the eyes, headache over the eye.—*Caspari, Erfahrungen*, 176.

CASE 228.—A lady, aged 30, had been affected for nine months past, with impaired sight; it seemed as if a spiderweb was before her eyes, or as if she were looking through a veil; watering of the eyes; pupils somewhat dilated.

Bellad. 3, once in forty-eight hours, cured her in three weeks perfectly.—*All. H. Ztg.* 13. 51. LOBETHAL.

CASE 229.—A stout man, aged 30, of sanguinous temperament, formerly healthy, was suddenly seized without any apparent cause with the following condition of the right eye.

Dull appearance of the right eye; black spots before the eye; even on a clear day objects appeared as if enveloped in a fog; in the morning and evening he could not see with the right eye; pupil somewhat dilated; the patient was very timid.

Treatment.—May 12. Bell. 15, one drop.

May 22. Is able to distinguish objects in the morning and evening, and without straining the eye; during the day objects appear a little misty yet; and he saw stars dancing about the light of the candle. Pulsat. 12, one drop, cured him completely in a week.—*Arch.* 2. 66. GROSS.

CASE 230.—A lady, aged 30, in the fifth month of gestation, had been ailing for 1¼ years, after a cold bath which she had taken at that time.

Symptoms.—Very frequent muscæ volantes; whenever she used her eyes more than ordinarily, she experienced pain in the same; printed letters seemed to dance about in a dense fog; she was often obliged to rub her eyes; had dull pain over the eyes, and a sense of tightness about the head.

Treatment.—Arnica 3, five drops, in Alcoh. ℨj. every morning one drop in water. After two weeks, the headache had much diminished; and in four weeks she could read without any trouble.—*Hyg.* vi. 403. GRIESSELICH.

CASE 231.—A young man, aged 24, of slender build, and pale face, had been very anxious about his health, for the last two years, as he has had almost constant headache persistent obstruction in frontal sinus (chronic catarrh), burning in the eyes, and frequent diarrhœa.

Treatment.—From Aug. 21, to Nov. 25, he took Sulph., Bell., Nux-vom., Calc.-carb., Sulph., Petroleum.

On Dec. 3, he had violent pains in the eyes, burning, fleeting stitches, which were worse during the day; deceptive sight during the evening by candle-light; very great intolerance of light, with intolerable pains, lasting until very late at night, when they became most excruciating, with the sensation as if the ball of the eye would burst. Sclerotica pale red, more so towards the outer canthus; uncommon lustre of the eyes; great paleness of the face, and daily diarrhœa.

Spirit.-Phosph., gtt. xx. in Spirit.-vin.-rect. ℨj., six to eight drops every morning; this was followed by much improvement of the whole condition; in three weeks every thing, with the exception of some headache had disappeared.—*Allg. H. Ztg.* 22. 246. WEBER.

CASE 232.—An old maid, aged 52, of tranquil temperament, underwent the change of life, 2½ years ago; previous to that time her menses always had been regular; cessation of menstruation had been followed by gradual impairment of sight.

Symptoms.—Objects appear as if enveloped in a cloud, deceptive sight, variety of colors before the eye, stitches in the eyes, pupils sluggish in their action. Digestion good, but attended with occasional cramps in the stomach.

Treatment.—Sept. 25, Bell. 30, and on Oct. 2; again repeated on Oct. 9; she was then able to use her eyes as formerly.—*Annal.* 4. 167. H. HARTLAUB.

CASE 233.—Appearance of zig-zags vvv. before the left eye, at first hardly appreciable, colorless, gradually changing into variegated colors, and forms, and, not even disappearing on shutting the eye. Inclination to vomit; several hours later, violent sticking pain over the right eye, as if a nail had been driven into the head, increased on coughing, &c.; headache during the night, ceasing in the morning, but followed by confusion in the head; in the morning, appearance as if he could not see objects distinctly; he always felt pretty well before an attack came on.

Digitalis, Nux, and Ignatia were given without benefit; after the use of magnetism for some time, the whole disappeared.—*Allg. H. Ztg.* 22. 242. STRECKER, observed in his own person.

ASTHENOPIA. *Debility of the Eyes.*

By this disease is understood that state of vision in which the eyes are unable to sustain continued exercise upon near objects, although one can see them distinctly at first, and can employ his sight for any length of time upon distant objects; there is no external appearance of disease of the eyes.

Symptoms.—The patient is unable to continue for any considerable length of time to regard small or near objects, as in reading, sewing and the like; but is obliged, partly from the confusion and obscurity which seem to spread over the objects, partly from a feeling of fatigue in the eyes, to interrupt the exertion. With most patients the attack begins by a sensation of constraint in the eyes, which they sometimes try to get rid of by repeated winking. Others complain of a feeling of tension or weight in the eyes, heat, lachrymation, and double vision. If the patient persist in using the eyes, notwithstanding the feeling of lassitude, and the indistinctness of vision, the effort is followed with heaviness in the head, pain in the eye-balls, orbits, temples and forehead. The attack of asthenopia often comes on in a few minutes, or half, or one hour after commencing to use the eyes on small objects.

In the open air the patient can discern large distant objects clearly and without fatigue.

After the attack, a very short period of rest is in general sufficient to recruit the sight. Tailors and seamstresses affected with this disease sometimes manage to continue their employment during the first three or four working days in the week with comparative ease, but in the next two or three days they find their sight so weak that they can hold out with difficulty, or are actually forced to drop their work. The repose of Sunday restores strength to their eyes and enables them to resume their occupation on Monday. In some cases the attacks are so easily and repeatedly produced that the patient is not able to apply himself to any trade requiring the use of the eyes, and may even never be able to read. Hence it is an infirmity much more to be dreaded than many disorders of the eye which present a far more formidable appearance.

Diagnosis.—Asthenopia may very easily be confounded with morbid sensibility of the retina, photophobia, incipient near-sight and far-sight, night- or day-blindness, and commencing amaurosis.

Morbid sensibility of the retina and photophobia may be distinguished by the intolerance of bright light.

Near-sightedness can only be mistaken for asthenopia when it occurs suddenly in young persons after severely trying their eyes upon minute objects; the discerning of small objects is then attended with unusual effort, and they may be unable to distinguish objects on the other side of the street, which a few days before they saw perfectly. The application of concave glasses will disclose the true nature of the case.

Sudden far-sightedness in young persons may also be mistaken for debility of vision; in the latter affection a short period of rest renews the power of distinguishing near objects, while in far-sightedness rest has no effect. Both diseases are relieved by the use of convex glasses.

In incomplete amaurosis there is always an indistinctness of sight, extending to all objects both large and small; in asthenopia, vision only becomes obscure after being exerted on near objects. In commencing amaurosis the patient generally sees best after fixing his eyes, or *steadying* them, as he often terms it, for some time on some object; in asthenopia, it is only then that he begins to see badly.

But asthenopia may be complicated with all the above diseases, and with others, and it may require some care and skill to separate the symptoms of the different diseases one from the other.

Treatment.—Quinine and Iron have relieved many cases; also Sulphate of Zinc and Cod Liver Oil; Belladonna lessens the disposition to fatigue in the eyes in a very remarkable degree; Nux-vomica has been found useful.

In scrofulous cases, Hepar-Sulph. is useful, especially when looking at things produces a twinkling before the eyes and darkness, followed by great weakness of vision.

Menyanthes, when there is frequent obscuration of sight when reflecting or reading.

Quinine, when there is blackness before the eyes on exerting them.

Agaricus, when everything seems obscured as if by turbid water.

Zincum, when there is frequent vanishing of sight while writing; for a fortnight.

Mercurius, when there is complete vanishing of sight for five minutes, every half hour.

Spigelia, when there is vanishing of sight, when looking at anything attentively.

Bromine, when there is a vanishing of sight while reading, as if the thing looked at were blown away.

Stramonium, when the letters seem to move and become blurred while reading.

Iodine, when one is unable to do fine sewing on account of the stitches flitting from before the eyes.

Causticum, when on looking at a thing too long, the objects begin to waver before him, and become confused, followed by an aching in the eyes.

HEMERALOPIA. *Night-Blindness.*

According to Mackenzie the first attack of the disease generally excites great alarm. The patient is busy, perhaps at his occupation, or enjoying himself in the midst of his family, when suddenly he finds his sight fail, and as evening advances becomes almost completely blind. The medical attendant is immediately sent for, and is often as much amazed and little less alarmed than the patient. He probably finds the pupils dilated, but no vertigo, pain, or other sign indicative of any serious affection; he gives a very unfavorable opinion, but to the joy of all concerned, the patient wakes in the morning with his sight perfectly restored. But, again on the approach of evening, symptoms are perceived of returning blindness. Objects appear as if covered by a bluish or grey mist, and in the course of a few minutes the patient is obliged to grope his way like a blind man. Candles are brought; if he perceives that they are present, they appear as if glimmering through a fog, and scarcely ever enable him to see with distinctness.

Night after night the blindness returns, and becomes more and more complete. For a time the restoration to vision through the day appears to be tolerably perfect, but at length the sight is evidently weak by day as well as by night; intolerance of light occurs, and near-sightedness sets in; vision becomes more and more impaired, and if neglected and maltreated, the disease may finally end in incurable amaurosis.

Occasionally a tolerable degree of sight is restored by the use of candle-light.

The pupils are generally dilated during an attack, and do not contract on exposing the eyes to the light of a candle, or of the moon. In some the pupils continue contracted even during the day; in others they are contracted and evince a painful irritability on exposure to strong light. If the patient happens to look at the direct rays of the sun, or a strong glaring reflection of them, as from the sea, pain and temporary blindness are apt to be induced, and from which he recovers by closing his eyes for a time and retiring into the shade.

Causes.—Exposure to bright sun-light during part of the day, and living in darkened and damp rooms; sleeping in the moon-light. It occasionally occurs in an epidemic form.

Duration.—It generally lasts for two or three months; sometimes only one night; then again it may last from six to nine months, or for years, or for life.

Prognosis.—The majority of cases recover.

Treatment.—The Russian peasants are said to cure this disease in seven or fourteen days at the most, by drinking an infusion of the Centaurea-cyanus.

A cure has been effected by confining the patient to a darkened room for two or three days.

General Remarks.—In a treatise on hemeralopia, G. Marschall closes with the following remarks.—Among the homœopathic remedies for this disease, is Solan.-n.; not less useful are, Staphys. and Secale-cor.; next in consideration come Verat., Puls., Con., Anacard., Aconite, Digitalis, all of which may by administered in dilutions, or in tinctures. The remedies have to be frequently repeated.—*Allg. H. Ztg.* 16, 22.

CASE 234.—Tinct.-Pulsatilla was given in doses of one drop, on account of menstrual irregularities, and loss of sight towards night, attended with the sensation, as if the eyes were tied up by a handkerchief. Pulsatilla improved the sight very considerably, but was not continued.—*Annal.* IV., p. 395. BETHMANN.

CASE 235.—A boy, aged 10, with large head, prominent eyes, and much dilated pupils, had been suffering for some time with loss of vision at night, and for which Hyosc., Datur., Digit., had been given without benefit; he was then attacked with nocturnal diarrhœa, for which Verat. 9, was given with such success, that not only the diarrhœa was cured, but also the eye-complaint.

CASE 236.—A man, aged 57, of quick temper, had been affected for about two months with loss of vision at night; he was cured by Hyosc. 1, in a few days.—*Annal.* 4, 426. HAUPTMANN.

CASE 237.—Loss of vision at night (in four persons), otherwise healthy.

During the day, even if cloudy, and until sunset, they all could see perfectly; but after sunset they were totally blind, and by candle-light they saw the outlines of objects tinged with the colors of a rain-bow.

The *first*, a carpenter, aged 62, had blue eyes and very contracted pupils; he had been affected from nine to ten weeks. Pulsatilla was given, without result; also Belladonna 9; but after taking Bellad. 3, he recovered his sight perfectly the next day.

The *second*, 25 years old, with black hair, and dilated pupils, had been affected for six weeks. Bellad. 6, cured him in twenty-four hours.

The *third*, 17 years old, had been sick twenty-eight days, and was cured by Bellad. 9, in twenty-four hours.

The *fourth*, a brother of the above, aged 20, had been affected for six weeks; he was also quickly cured by Belladonna 6.—*Annal.* 4, 336. HAUPTMANN.

It is evident that Bellad., Stramon., and Hyosciamus are homœopathic to this temporary amaurosis; Plumbum and Quinine may be tried in obstinate and chronic cases.

DAY-BLINDNESS.

Cases of this occur very similar in their nature to the night-blindness just described. The patient may be totally blind during the day, but see nearly as well as formerly by moon- or star-light.

HEMIOPIA. *Half Vision.*

Hemiopia signifies a partial blindness obscuring about one half of the field of vision. Generally it is the right half, or the left half of all objects which appear dark, and that whether they are regarded with one eye only, or with both. In other cases only one eye is affected.

This disease is apt to be sudden in its attack, and to recur at considerable intervals of time. It is generally transient.

Treatment.—Stramonium is indicated when the patient sees things as if through coarse linen, viz., only fragments of them; and or as if they were cut through; of a face he only saw the nose.

Aurum, when there is half-sightedness, as if the upper half of the eye were covered with a dark body, so that he can only see the lower objects with the inferior half; the upper half of things remained invisible.

Muriatic-acid, when one half of objects seem to be cut off from the other half, in a perpendicular line.

Kali-carb., Calc., Natrum, Sepia and Lycopodium deserve attention.

DIPLOPIA. *Double Vision.*

This often arises from want of correspondence in the action of the muscles of the eye-ball.

At other times it arises from irregular refraction, when the surfaces of the cornea or crystalline lens are not perfectly regular.

Occasionally a straight black line drawn on a sheet of paper appears double when it is held vertically, but is seen single the instant it is turned in a horizontal direction.

Remedies.—Stramonium is the principal remedy. But Bellad., Secale, Cicuta-vir., Conium and Senega deserve attention in acute cases.

In obstinate and chronic examples, Iodine, Graphite, Nitric-acid, Ammon.-carb. and Petroleum, may be used.

Stramon., Bellad., Cicuta, Conium and Secale are most useful, when the muscles of the eye are affected.

Senega, Iodine, Ammon.-c., Petroleum, Graphite and Nitric-acid, when the cornea or crystalline lens are in fault.

MYOPIA. *Short-Sightedness.*

According to Mackenzie, there is a certain distance from the eye, called *the point of distinct-vision*, at which objects are perceived better than at any other distance. This point varies, however, in different individuals, or even in the two eyes of the same person. It averages from about fifteen to twenty inches, and the shortest distance at which objects can be seen with any ordinary degree of distinctness by common eyes, is about seven or eight inches. But some eyes can discern no object distinctly unless it be brought nearer than the ordinary distance for distinct vision, while others require the object to be removed farther than the average point of vision; the former are said to be *myopic*, or short-sighted, while the other are *presbyopic*, or long-sighted. In both cases, the eyes may be said to be out of focus.

In the myopic eye it is supposed that the rays of light must either be refracted too much, so that they converge into foci anterior to the retina, or that the axis of the eye must be longer than natural, so that the retina is too far back, and does not receive that perfect impression which is necessary for distinct vision. To remedy these defects the short-sighted person brings the object looked at nearer to his eye, in order that the image may be thrown so far back as to fall upon the retina.

The eyes of short-sighted persons are frequently prominent and the cornea preternaturally convex; there may also be an approach to the state of hydrophthalmia, the anterior chamber of the eye being more than commonly deep; the pupil is generally large and not very lively, the eyeball firm, the eyelids often tender.

Only a few of these defects can be remedied; the cornea cannot be rendered less convex, nor the anterior chamber less deep, but the pupil may be rendered more lively and contractile, and the lids less tender by the aid of Nux-vomica and Aconite.

As the myopic eye has its point of distinct vision as well as the perfect eye, those affected with the greatest degree of near-sightedness bring every object which they wish to see clearly to the distance of two or three inches, or even as close as one inch from the eye; a few are able to see clearly at the distance of six to nine inches, but the eye which perceives nothing distinctly beyond ten inches must be considered myopic.

Short-sighted persons see more distinctly and somewhat farther off by a strong light than a weak one, *on account of the contraction of the pupil* which is thereby produced, and which serves to exclude all but the more direct rays of light, and consequently to lessen the apparent confusion. On the same principle when they endeavor to see any distant object distinctly they almost close their eye-lids; objects also appear clearer and better defined through a pin-hole in a card than with the naked eye.

All these facts point to the benefit which might be derived in short-sightedness by the use of remedies which contract the pupil.

In an obscure light, short-sighted persons, owing to the largeness of their pupils, commonly see better than those whose sight is good. They also generally attribute to distant objects a greater magnitude than do those who have a good common sight.

If a short-sighted person looks at a candle placed a yard or two off, it appears dim and enlarged, and seems doubled, tripled or quadrupled. This multiplication by the myopic eye in viewing distant objects, must arise from each surface of the dioptric media forming an image in succession. Similar multiplied images may be seen by ordinary eyes, when they are forcibly adapted for shorter vision than is requisite to see the object looked at distinctly. This would lead us to suppose that some portion of short-sightedness is at times owing to a spasmodic compression of the eyes, which might be relieved by remedies, such as Conium or Opium.

The left eye is generally more short-sighted than the right.

Too great convexity of the cornea, according to Mackenzie, is by no means a constant, or even a very frequent attendant on short-sightedness. When it does occur, it is generally accompanied by an evident superabundance of aqueous humor, and occasionally by a degree of pressure backwards on the iris, so that this membrane, instead of being plane, becomes concave anteriorly. This might probably be removed by the use of Kali-hydriod., both internally, and to the eye.

Too great thickness of the cornea may undoubtedly produce short-sightedness; if any remedy will remove it, Kali-hydriod. will doubtless prove the most useful one.

Too great convexity of the crystalline lens will assuredly produce short-sightedness, whether the over-convexity be on one only, or on both sides of that body. Mackenzie says we must not merely admit the possibility of this cause, but the likelihood of its frequent existence. This of course cannot be removed by any remedial means, but can only be palliated by the use of concave glasses.

Unusual density of any or all of the transparent portions of the eye would infallibly produce short-sightedness. The eyes are then generally considerably firmer to the touch than natural. Plumbum might prove a homœopathic remedy.

Abnormal elongation of the eye-ball, so that the distance between the cornea and retina is increased, will of course occasion short-sightedness, and has even been regarded by some as the only admissible cause of this disorder. When congenital, it has been attributed to unnatural shortness of the recti-muscles; when acquired, to abnormal contraction of these muscles, and of the obliqui.

Plumbum and Nux-vomica are probably the most homœopathic remedies.

Over-activity of the power inherent in the eye, of accommodating itself to the vision of near objects may be regarded as a probable cause of short-sightedness. Olbus has calculated that if the distance of the crystalline lens from the retina could be varied to the extent of a line, we should be enabled to see objects with equal distinctness from a distance of four inches to the utmost extent of human vision. This effect would be still more obvious if the radius of the cornea could be varied two-fifths of a line.

Plumbum, Zincum, or Nux-vomica will also prove the most homœopathic remedies.

The large pupil which almost always accompanies myopia has been generally set down amongst the causes of the disease, whereas it may be an effect, for short-sighted persons being able to see near objects distinctly, there is no occasion for contraction of the pupil such as happens in far-sighted and ordinary sighted persons when they look at near objects intently; hence the pupil may remain in a permanent state of dilatation.

Young people seldom discover that they are remarkably near-sighted until about the age of puberty, and when they begin to use their eyes in earnest. Occasionally myopia occurs suddenly, and may then be mistaken for amaurosis, as the effort to see at the usual distance, or even to read, will cause pain and confusion of sight.

Generally, however, near-sightedness is gradual in its progress, manifesting itself about the period of puberty and increasing from that period up to twenty or twenty-five years of age. Still, many persons reach the age of thirty or forty years, who have no notion that they are near-sighted, until they happen accidentally to look through the concave glasses of some other persons, when they are surprized and delighted to find that they perceive remote objects with a clearness and sharpness of outline to which they had formerly been altogether strangers. When very young children are quite short-sighted, we should examine carefully for cataract; when adults suddenly become myopic we should suspect conical cornea, dropsy of the aqueous humor, or some affection of the retina.

It is a vulgar error, that short-sightedness is relieved as the patient grows older; it tends generally to increase rather than to diminish as age advances, and should a glaucomatous state of the lens be supperadded, the patient will be obliged to bring any object which he wishes to see distinctly, within a very short distance of the eye.

The most frequent cause of short-sightedness is using the

eyes too much in early youth on small and near objects. Children born with eyes which are capable of adjusting themselves to the most distant objects, gradually lose that power soon after they begin to read and write; those who are most addicted to study become near-sighted more rapidly. Hence, as myopia may to a certain extent be regarded as a habit, arising from too frequent adjustment of the eyes to near objects, an opposite exercise of the eyes should be instituted in a methodical and perservering manner.

Concave glasses will have to be used, but the shallowest or weakest that can be used will be the best; objects should simply appear clear through the glass that is chosen; if it makes them seem smaller than natural, or gives them a dazzling or glaring appearance, or if the eye feels strained or fatigued after looking through it for a short time, it is too concave, and a lower number should be selected.

It is a common error with those persons who begin to use concave glasses, to tire of those which they first employ, and soon to have recourse to deeper ones, in this way they often produce such a condition of the organs of vision as will render them unfit to engage in any ordinary pursuit. It should always be remembered that near-sightedness generally continues in nearly the same degree during the greater part of life. Therefore, the same glass will continue, for many years, to afford precisely the same assistance, and ought not to be heedlessly changed for one of deeper concavity.

When once a near-sighted person has experienced the pleasure of seeing remote objects with that distinctness and comparative brilliancy which the aid of concave glasses affords, it is not easy to persuade him to renounce their use. But it is highly advisable that near-sighted persons should not wear spectacles constantly, but only on occasions when they more particularly require such assistance. When they have been worn for a considerable time, the person does not at first see so well on leaving them off as he did before; but this is only temporary.

In point of fact, the experience of many short-sighted persons is similar to that of Dr. Kitchener. When he was about fifteen years old he discovered that he could not discern distant objects so distinctly as people commonly do. He then paid a visit to an optician, and purchased a concave glass, No. 2. After using this some little time he accidentally looked through a concave, No. 3, which appeared to afford his eye very much greater help. After using No. 3 for a few months he tried No. 4, and again found the same increase of sharpness which he had first experienced on using both Nos. 2 and 3. However, in a few months he could see no better with No. 4 than he had formerly done with the weaker glasses. Hence he inferred that he was weakening and injuring his eyes by means of too powerful glasses, and returned to the use of No. 2, which he then wore for 31 years, with nearly if not quite as much relief as when he first began to employ it.

In some few instances the operation for squinting has been found to relieve short-sightedness. In these cases Spigelia might have proved the homœopathic remedy.

Remedies.—In sudden attacks of short-sightedness, Gratiola, Hyosciamus, Pulsatilla, Anacardium, Agaricus and Euphorbium are the most homœopathic remedies.

In chronic cases, Phosphorus, Manganese, Phosphoric-acid, and Carbo-vegetabilis are the most suitable remedies.

Hyosciamus may be used when the patient is scarcely able to discern any thing at the distance of three steps; lasting for four days.

Anacardium, when he cannot distinguish any thing at a distance, while he distinctly sees every thing which is held near his eyes.

Agaricus, when there is short-sightedness and dim-sightedness of both eyes.

Gratiola, when there is short-sightedness with burning heat in the face.

When these remedies fail, *Pulsatilla* may enable one to see better at a distance than formerly.

Manganese is the principal remedy, when there is great short-sightedness for many days; *Phosphorus*, when the patient is short- and dim-sighted. *Carb.-veg.*, when he becomes short-sighted after using his eyes for a short time.

PRESBYOPIA. (*Far-sightedness.*)

This may occur suddenly, and at any period of life, yet, in by far the greater number of instances, it is merely part of the changes which the human system undergoes from advancing years.

As the individual advances beyond the prime of life, the refractive powers of the eyes become more feeble, or their axes shorter than natural, whence the rays of light are not converged sufficiently soon to be brought to focal points upon the retina. Hence the image cast upon the retina is diffused, and the perception of it indistinct; to remedy this, the patient moves the object or himself to some distance beyond the normal point of distinct vision, by this means counteracting the tendency of the rays of light to concentrate into foci behind the retina, instead of upon it.

In far-sighted eyes we generally find more or less diminution of the size of the eyeball, which is also more sunk in the orbit; also more or less flatness of the cornea, shortening of the axis of the anterior chamber, and smallness of the pupil.

According to Mackenzie, it is generally about the age of forty-five years that the eyes commence to be far-sighted, i. e. the patient begins to see near objects less perfectly, especially by candle-light, and hence are either obliged to illuminate them more, or to remove them farther from the eye than formerly. At the usual distance the person experiences difficulty in reading small print, threading a needle, &c.; in fact on attempting to examine any small object close at hand, its outline becomes obscure, as if it were seen through a mist; very minute objects, such as the letters in a small type are either not seen at all, or they seem obscure, running into one another, or double; and if the attempt to see such objects be persevered in, the eye soon feels fatigued, and the head begins to ache. Distant objects continue to be seen as well as before. Thus the person can read a distant sign, or tell the hour by a church clock, when he cannot read a common printed book, or see the figures or hands of a watch held in his hands.

This far-sightedness increases as the patient grows older, so that he is obliged to have recourse to convex glasses, or is forced to renounce all employments which require the use of close eye-sight. It also increases more rapidly in some persons than in others; some eyes at thirty years of age require the use of convex glasses, as much as others do at fifty, although this is rare.

The greatest mistake that is made in this affection, is the use of too strong glasses; a very few persons soon after commencing the use of spectacles, may be obliged to change them every few years for others of a shorter focus, but a very large majority commence with glasses which are altogether too strong, thus weaken their eyes, and are forced to resort to others still stronger, and finally bring on an excessive degree of exhaustion and debility of their eyes.

Flatness of the cornea from a diminution in the quantity of the aqueous and vitreous humors is supposed to be one of the most frequent causes of far-sightedness; this diminution of the fluids of the eye being supposed to depend on the impeded manner in which the function of secretion is performed in advanced life. Arsenicum may prove a useful remedy.

Flattening of the lens, from a certain degree of atrophy, or shrinking, is supposed by Mackenzie, to be a still more frequent cause of far-sightedness.

Treatment.—The use of convex glasses is absolutely necessary; this should be commenced neither too soon or too late in life; many injure their sight by adopting the use of magnifying-glasses too suddenly, and before they have any need of them; while others, equally stupid, refrain from using glasses long after the period when they, if judiciously selected, would not only have afforded valuable assistance, but have proved a means of saving sight.

Mackenzie truly says, that is may be laid down as a general rule, that whenever a person of forty-five years of age, or upwards, finds that in order to see small objects distinctly, he is obliged to carry them far from his eye; or, that he moves, as it were intuitively, nearer to the light when he wishes to read or work, or holds the book or other objects close to the light, in order see with facility; or that small objects, after he has looked at them earnestly for some time, appear confused; that his eyes, after slight exertion, become so much fatigued, that he is obliged to turn them to other objects in order to give them some relaxation; and that his sight on awaking in the morning is very weak, and does not recover its usual power and clearness for some hours; then he may begin to use convex glasses.

In selecting glasses, the lowest power, or those of the longest focus which answer the purpose of rendering clear without magnifying them should be preferred, and no others should be used.

As it is chiefly by candle-light, that the far-sighted person complains of his deficiency of sight, even after he has supplied himself with proper glasses, it is advisable that he should refrain as much as possible, from employing himself at night in occupations which require close and continued use of the eyes. The moment that the eyes begin to feel hot and fatigued, while reading or writing or the like, especially by candle-light, the patient should take the hint, and allow them a period of repose.

It may seem absurd to some to use internal remedies to relieve far- or near-sightedness; but these agents, if they do not cure or entirely remove the difficulty, may prevent its too rapid increase; and it is undeniable that there are always a few sudden attacks which may be entirely removed.

Thus Mackenzie says, it is undeniable that these diseases sometimes occur suddenly; far-sightedness may set in, even in children, after an attack of influenza, or inflammation ot the tonsils, when attended with considerable febrile excitement. Even in the dominant school, cures have been effected by the rude appliances of leeches to the temples, blisters behind the ears, and small doses of Calomel, followed by Quinine; or even by purgatives.

In acute cases, Belladonna, Drosera, Stramonium and Argentum-nitricum are the most homœopathic remedies.

In chronic cases, Calcarea deserves most attention.

In a very short-sighted person, Hyosciamus produced far-sightedness, accompanied with great clearness of sight; this improvement continued for several days, and then decreased gradually.

CASE 238.—A boy, aged 12, had a fall upon the arcus supra-orbitalis of the left side, about a year ago, since which time he has only been able to see one-half the distance with the left eye that he could with the right. After the use of Arnica, $\overline{21}$, one dose every fourth day, aided by the external application of diluted Arnica to the eye; he was cured in the course of four weeks.—*Pract. Beitr.* 3. 22, *Thorer.*

CASE 239.—Mrs. R., aged 36, of irritable temper, had formerly been affected for four months with syphilitic ophthalmia, after which her eyes remained weak, and far-sighted.

. *Symptoms.*—Sight very good at a distance, but she could not see her thread while sewing; vanishing of sight while reading; the letters run together, she feels badly, has to go out into the fresh air, after which she feels better, and can read again for some minutes. Fire and the light of the day dazzles her eyes. During menstruation she feels sleepy, with spasms in the eyelids, while looking into the fire. Eyes always dry; nose dry.

Treatment.—Drosera 27, one drop, followed by improvement until the tenth day; Hyosciamus 9, on the twelfth day; six days from that time she is able to read, and do fine sewing without trouble.—*Arch.* 3. 3. 69. *Caspari.*

STRABISMUS. (*Squinting.*)

Mackenzie says, one of the most frequent causes of squinting is weak-sightedness; the distorted eye being in almost every case, very considerably inferior in power of sight to the other. The impressions on the retina of the weak eye then being considerably less perfect than on the other, the defective eye is very liable to be neglected altogether, and instead of being fixed on the object before it, is left to wander from the true axis of vision.

Occasionally a spasm or paralysis of some one of the motor muscles of the eye will cause strabismus.

In two hundred cases, examined by Dr. Hall, the following causes were assigned by the patients themselves or their parents:

Convulsions during infancy, in nine cases, (Bellad.); falls on the head, in seven, (Arnica); difficult dentition, in three,

(Chamomilla, Borax); hooping cough, in two, (Bellad., Drosera, Cuprum); intestinal worms, in three, (Spigelia); epilepsy, in two, (Artimesia, Sedum-acre.); excessive fright, in two, (Acon., Opium); ophthalmia, without opacity (Euphrasia); opacity of the cornea, in eighteen, (Cannabis); a habit of looking at the sun or blazing light, in five; amaurosis in two, (Plumbum and Quinine); imitation of a squinting person, in thirty-nine cases; watching the motion of a shuttle; voluntarily trying to squint; a habit of looking at scars or pimples on the eyebrow, nose, check, &c.

In only four instances out of two hundred, was the squinting congenital.

The only remedies, which have been reported as having effected cures, are Bellad. and Stramonium.

The operation for strabismus will be found correctly detailed in either of the homœopathic books upon surgery; although Hill and Hunt are far more full in their directions and representation of instruments than Helmuth.

INDEX.

I.

L.

M.

N.

O.

Made in the USA
Monee, IL
20 October 2026

66035294R00174